W9-BCZ-155

GERMAN DEMOCRATIC REPUBLIC

Marxist Regimes Series

Series editor: Bogdan Szajkowski,
Department of Social Administration,
University College,
Cardiff

Further Titles

GERMAN DEMOCRATIC REPUBLIC

Politics, Economics and Society

Mike Dennis

 Pinter (Publishers)
London and New York

Wingate College Library

© Mike Dennis 1988

All rights reserved. No part of this publication may be reproduced, stored in a retrieval system, or transmitted by any means without the prior written permission of the copyright holder. Please direct all enquiries to the publishers.

First published in Great Britain in 1988 by
Pinter Publishers Limited
25 Floral Street, London WC2E 9DS

British Library Cataloguing in Publication Data

A CIP catalogue record for this book is available from the British Library.

ISBN 0-86187-412-9
ISBN 0-86187-413-7 (Pbk)

Library of Congress Cataloging-in-Publication Data

Dennis, Mike, 1940–
    German Democratic Republic.
    (Marxist regimes series)
    Bibliography: p.
    Includes index.
    1. Germany (East)—Politics and government.
2. Germany (East)—Social conditions.   3. Germany
(East)—Economic conditions.   I. Title.   II. Series.
DD283.D46   1988   943.1087   87-32889

ISBN 0-86187-412-9
ISBN 0-86187-413-7 (pbk.)

Typeset by Joshua Associates Limited, Oxford
Printed in Great Britain by SRP Ltd, Exeter

Editor's Preface

The German Democratic Republic, half of a divided German nation, is in many respects perhaps the most stable socialist state in Eastern Europe. Its economic achievements are formidable. After years of diplomatic isolation it has emerged as an equal partner of other members of the international community.

This book traces the development of a country—one which for many years was written off as a Soviet satrapy—from its foundation to the present. It is thus far the most comprehensive monograph on the German Democratic Republic, providing an expert analysis of its politics, economics and society. The study also contains an in-depth appraisal of the current complex inter-German relations as well as the GDR's place in the context of larger developments within Eastern Europe, which is rapidly responding to challenges of *glasnost* and *perestroika*.

The study of Marxist regimes has commonly been equated with the study of communist political systems. There were several historical and methodological reasons for this. For many years it was not difficult to distinguish the eight regimes in Eastern Europe and four in Asia which resoundingly claimed adherence to the tenets of Marxism and more particularly to their Soviet interpretation—Marxism–Leninism. These regimes, variously called 'People's Republic', 'People's Democratic Republic', or 'Democratic Republic', claimed to have derived their inspiration from the Soviet Union to which, indeed, in the overwhelming number of cases they owed their establishment.

To many scholars and analysts these regimes represented a multiplication of and geographical extension of the 'Soviet model' and consequently of the Soviet sphere of influence. Although there were clearly substantial similarities between the Soviet Union and the people's democracies, especially in the initial phases of their development, these were often overstressed at the expense of noticing the differences between these political systems.

It took a few years for scholars to realize that generalizing the particular, i.e., applying the Soviet experience to other states ruled by elites which claimed to be guided by 'scientific socialism', was not good enough. The relative simplicity of the assumption of a cohesive communist bloc was questioned after the expulsion of Yugoslavia from the Communist Information Bureau in 1948 and in particular after the workers' riots in Poznań in 1956 and the Hungarian revolution of the same year. By the mid-1960s, the totalitarian model of communist politics, which until then had been very much in force, began to crumble. As some of these regimes articulated demands for a distinctive path of socialist development, many specialists studying these systems began to notice that the cohesiveness of the communist bloc was less apparent than had been claimed before.

Also by the mid-1960s, in the newly independent African states 'democratic' multi-party states were turning into one-party states or military dictatorships, thus questioning the inherent superiority of liberal democracy, capitalism and the values that went with it. Scholars now began to ponder on the simple contrast between multi-party democracy and a one-party totalitarian rule that had satisfied an earlier generation.

More importantly, however, by the beginning of that decade Cuba had a revolution without Soviet help, a revolution which subsequently became to many political elites in the Third World not only an inspiration but a clear military, political and ideological example to follow. Apart from its romantic appeal, to many nationalist movements the Cuban revolution also demonstrated a novel way of conducting and winning a nationalist, anti-imperialist war and accepting Marxism as the state ideology without a vanguard communist party. The Cuban precedent was subsequently followed in one respect or another by scores of Third World regimes, which used the adoption of 'scientific socialism' tied to the tradition of Marxist thought as a form of mobilization, legitimation or association with the prestigious symbols and powerful high-status regimes such as the Soviet Union, China, Cuba and Vietnam.

Despite all these changes the study of Marxist regimes remains in its infancy and continues to be hampered by constant and not always pertinent comparison with the Soviet Union, thus somewhat blurring the important underlying common theme— the 'scientific theory' of the laws of development of human society and human history. This doctrine is claimed by the leadership of these regimes to consist of the discovery of objective causal relationships; it is used to analyse the contradictions which arise between goals and actuality in the pursuit of a common destiny. Thus the political elites of these countries have been and continue to be influenced in both their ideology and their political practice by Marxism more than any other current of social thought and political practice.

The growth in the number and global significance, as well as the ideological political and economic impact, of Marxist regimes has presented scholars and students with an increasing challenge. In meeting this challenge, social scientists on both sides of the political divide have put forward a dazzling profusion of terms, models, programmes and varieties of interpretation. It is against the background of this profusion that the present comprehensive series on Marxist regimes is offered.

This collection of monographs is envisaged as a series of multi-disciplinary textbooks on the governments, politics, economics and society of these countries. Each of the monographs was prepared by a specialist on the country concerned. Thus, over fifty scholars from all over the world have contributed monographs which were based on first-hand knowledge. The geographical diversity of the authors, combined with the fact that as a group they represent many disciplines of social science, gives their individual analyses and the series as a whole an additional dimension.

Each of the scholars who contributed to this series was asked to analyse such topics as the political culture, the governmental structure, the ruling party, other mass organizations, party-state relations, the policy process, the economy, domestic and foreign relations together with any features peculiar to the country under discussion.

This series does not aim at assigning authenticity or authority to any single one of the political systems included in it. It shows that, depending on a variety of historical, cultural, ethnic and political factors, the pursuit of goals derived from the tenets of Marxism has produced different political forms at different times and in different places. It also illustrates the rich diversity among these societies, where attempts to achieve a synthesis between goals derived from Marxism on the one hand, and national realities on the other, have often meant distinctive approaches and solutions to the problems of social, political and economic development.

University College   *Bogdan Szajkowski*
Cardiff

Contents

List of Illustrations and Tables

Preface and Acknowledgements

The American social scientist Lyman Letgers (1978, p. 4) once speculated on how a latter-day Rip Van Winkle would react to the fundamental changes in the political, social and economic system of the GDR upon emerging from a long hibernation. When he had fallen asleep in the mid-1950s, the GDR was widely regarded as an appendage of its totalitarian master in the Kremlin. The Soviet tanks which had helped disperse rioters and protesters from the streets of East Berlin in 1953 had reinforced this harsh Cold War image.

Our sleepy friend would have rubbed his eyes in amazement when he awoke in the mid-1980s. Although not as prosperous as its West German sibling, the GDR still enjoyed the highest living standards in COMECON and it had cast off its diplomatic shackles at the beginning of the 1970s. Furthermore, in 1984, an open dispute with the Kremlin over the GDR's determination to insulate the mini-German *détente* from the freeze in superpower relations was an indicator that the former Soviet zone of occupation had acquired a political mind of its own. And within the GDR small autonomous peace, ecological and women's groups and critical writers such as Christa Wolf, Volker Braun and Hanns Cibulka bear witness to the widening of the parameters of political discourse.

However, the 'barbed wire of prejudice' has not been completely dismantled. The mass circulation West German newspaper *Die Welt* has not removed the apostrophes of illegitimacy from the 'DDR'. And President Reagan continues to draw upon the ideological arsenal of the Cold War. The Berlin Wall, in Reagan's view, is a symbol of the total failure of totalitarian regimes and of the imprisonment of the creative spirit. In June 1987, in the shadow of the Brandenburg Gate, he denounced the 'totalitarian world' for producing backwardness 'because it does such violence to the spirit, thwarting the human impulse to create, to enjoy, to worship' (*The Guardian*, 13 June 1987, p. 36).

While the human cost of the Berlin Wall cannot and should not be denied, the simple dichotomy of totalitarian communism and free democracies glosses over the complexities of political life in both West and East. The GDR cannot be reduced to one simplistic ideological construct. It is the compound of a complex present and an even more problematic past. The German question, in its various manifestations, bedevils the regime's efforts to create a separate GDR national identity and elements of party-political authoritarianism and coercion are a regrettable legacy of the Stalinist era. These elements intermingle with the humanist impulses of Marxism and with the ecological and technological problems of an advanced industrial society.

The present book has the modest aim of providing a survey of the history of the GDR followed by a picture of the contemporary social, economic and political system. In portraying 'the state which would not die', I have drawn upon the invaluable contributions of investigative journalists such as John Dornberg and Jonathan Steele who sought to make the GDR *terra cognita* as it emerged from out of the diplomatic cold. As the 1960s turned into the 1970s academics, too, joined in this voyage of discovery: David Childs in Great Britain, Peter-Christian Ludz in West Germany and Arthur Hanhardt in the United States. The tradition of critical journalism has been continued by Wolfgang Büscher and Peter Wensierski. Anyone who studies the GDR must acknowledge a heavy debt to that *magnum opus*, the *DDR Handbuch*, edited by Hartmut Zimmermann.

I am grateful to Marion Ferguson of the Royal Holloway and Bedford New College for her valuable comments on the manuscript.

I could not have undertaken the study without the facilities provided by the Humboldt library in East Berlin, the DDR-Archiv of the Free University in West Berlin as well as by the library of Wolverhampton Polytechnic.

I am also indebted to various bodies whose financial assistance has enabled me to conduct research into the GDR. I am grateful in particular to the British Academy, the British Council, the Nuffield Foundation and the School of Humanities and Cultural Studies of Wolverhampton Polytechnic.

Mike Dennis
Wolverhampton, 1987

Basic Data

Official name	German Democratic Republic
Population	16,648,059 (1985)
Population density	154 per sq. km.
Population growth (% p.a.)	0.1 (1985)
Urban population (%)	75 (1985)
Total labour force	8,539 million (1985)
Life expectancy	
Men	69 (1985)
Women	75 (1985)
Infant death rate (per 1,000)	5.2 stillborn, 9.6 under 1 year (1985)
Capital	Berlin (East) (pop. 1,202.9 million) (1985)
Land area	108,333 sq. km., of which 58% arable and pasture, 27% forest, 15% built-up areas, road, rivers and lakes, and waste land
Official language	German
Other language	Sorb
Administrative division	15 regions (*Bezirke*), 191 rural and 36 districts (1985)
Membership of international organizations	UN since 1973, CMEA since 1950, Warsaw Treaty Organization since 1955
Foreign relations	Diplomatic and consular relations with 132 countries (1983)
Political structure	
Constitution	1968, amended 1974
Highest legislative body	People's Chamber of 500 deputies
Highest executive body	Council of Ministers
Prime Minister	Willy Stoph
Ruling party	Socialist Unity Party of Germany
Secretary General of the Party	Erich Honecker (since 1971)
Party membership	2,304, 121 full and candidate members (1986)—18.0% of the adult population

Growth indicators (% p.a.)	1981–85	1985 (prov.)
Produced national income	4.3	4.3
Industry	4.2	3.7
Construction	3.4	3.0
Crop production	10.4	11.7
Animal production for market	1.1	2.9
Retail trade	2.1	4.1
Foreign trade	9.4	0.1
Imports	6.6	4.3
Exports	12.2	−2.1

Trade and balance of payments
  Exports   93,490.3 million Marks (1985)
  Imports   86,701.0 million Marks (1985)
  Exports as % of GNP   37.0 (1983)
  Main exports (%)   Machinery, equipment and means of transport (46.6); fuels, mineral raw materials, metals (20.0); other raw materials and semi-manufactured goods for industrial purposes, raw materials and products of the foodstuffs industry (7.7); industrial consumer goods (14.1); chemical products, fertilizers, synthetic rubber, building materials and other goods (11.6) (1985)

  Main imports (%)   Machinery, equipment and means of transport (26.8); fuels, mineral raw materials, metals (42.5); other raw materials and semi-manufactured goods for industrial purposes, raw materials and products of the foodstuffs industry (16.1); industrial consumer goods (6.2); chemical products, fertilizers, synthetic rubber, building materials and other goods (8.4) (1985)

  Destination of exports (%) Socialist countries 66, non-socialist countries 34 (1985)

  Main trading partners   Soviet Union, Czechoslovakia, FRG, Poland, Hungary, Bulgaria, Romania, Austria (1985)

Foreign debt	Net hard currency debt US$5.5 billion. Cumulative trade deficit with FRG:US$ equivalent 1.6 billion. Cumulative trade deficit with USSR 3.6 transferable roubles (equivalent to US$4.7 billion) (June 1986)
Foreign aid	Net capital aid of 0.14% of GNP
Main natural resources	Brown coal, nickel, tin, copper, salt, natural gas, timber, potash, uranium
Food self-sufficiency	Shortage of grain especially for fodder but high level of self-sufficiency; imports of tropical fruits, coffee beans and edible pulses
Armed forces	Army of 123,000, navy of 16,000, and 40,000 in the air force; 49,000 border troops, 13,000 police alert units, and about 6,000 members of the Friedrich Dzierzynski guard regiment (1986)

Education and health

School system	Compulsory education 6–16
Primary school enrolment: Classes 1–4 ('000 1985)	807.6
Secondary school enrolment: Classes 5–10 ('000 1985)	1,135.4
Higher education	54 universities and colleges of higher education. 7.5% of workforce have a university degree and 13.4% are technical college graduates (1985)
Adult literacy (%)	100
Hospital beds per 10,000 population	102 (1985)
Medical doctors per 10,000 population	22.8 (1985)

Economy

GNP	US$120,948 (1980 World Bank estimate)
GNP per capita	US$7,180 (1980 World Bank estimate)
GDP by %	Agriculture 8.1; industry and construction 76.2; services 12.8; others 2.9 (1985)
State budget (expenditure)	234.4 billion Marks (1985)
Defence expenditure % of state budget	7.76 (official 1985)
Monetary unit	Mark of the German Democratic Republic
Main crops	Wheat, rye, barley, oats, potatoes, sugar beet, carrots, apples

Land tenure	Cooperative and state farms 95%; LPG members and workers on the cooperatives are allowed to work up to 0.5 hectares for private use
Main religions	Catholic (7.1% of the population), Evangelical (41.6) (1983)
Transport (1985)	
Rail network	14,054 km.
Road network	1,850 km. motorways, 11,261 km. trunk roads and 34,040 km. regional roads
Piplines	1,307 km.
Waterways	2,319 km.

Population Forecasting

The following data are projections produced by Poptran, University College Cardiff Population Centre, from United Nations Assessment Data published in 1980, and are reproduced here to provide some basis of comparison with other countries covered by the Marxist Regimes Series.

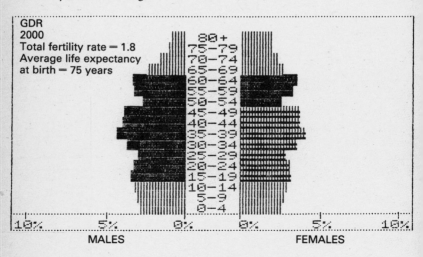

Projected Data for GDR 2000

Total population ('000)	16,915
Males ('000)	8,289
Females ('000)	8,626
Total fertility rate	1.77
Life expectancy (male)	72.9 years
Life expectancy (female)	76.8 years
Crude birth rate	11.2
Crude death rate	11.2
Annual growth rate	0.00%
Under 15s	17.53%
Over 65s	14.89%
Women aged 15–49	24.11%
Doubling time	—
Population density	156 per sq. km.
Urban population	83.2%

List of Abbreviations

APO	Abteilungsparteiorganisation (Departmental Party Organization)
BPO	Betriebsparteiorganisation (Enterprise Party Organization)
CAD	Computer-aided design
CAM	Computer-aided manufacturing
CDU	Christlich–Demokratische Union (Christian Democratic Union)
CPSU	Communist Party of the Soviet Union
DBD	Demokratische Bauernpartei Deutschlands (Democratic Farmers' Party of Germany)
DFD	Demokratischer Frauenbund Deutschlands (Democratic Women's Association of Germany)
DIW	Deutsches Institut für Wirtschaftsforschung (German Institute for Economic Research)
DNVP	Deutschnationale Volkspartei (German National People's Party)
DTSB	Deutscher Turn- und Sportbund der DDR (German Gymnastics and Sports Association)
EEC	European Economic Community
EOS	Erweiterte allgemeinbildende polytechnische Oberschule (Extended Secondary School)
FDGB	Freier Deutscher Gewerkschaftsbund (Confederation of Free German Trade Unions)
FDJ	Freie Deutsche Jugend (Free German Youth)
FRG	Federal Republic of Germany
GDR	German Democratic Republic
GO	Grundorganisation (Basic Organization)
GST	Gesellschaft für Sport und Technik (Society for Sport and Technology
KAP	Kooperative Abteilungen der Pflanzenproduktion (Cooperative Crop-producing Farms)
KB	Kulturbund der DDR (League of Culture of the GDR)
KOR	Kooperationsräte (Councils of Cooperations)
KPD	Kommunistische Partei Deutschlands (Communist Party of Germany)
KVP	Kasernierte Volkspolizei (Garrisoned People's Police)
LDPD	Liberal-Demokratische Partei Deutschlands (Liberal Democratic Party of Germany)

LPG	Landwirtschaftliche Produktionsgenossenschaft (Agricultural Cooperative)
MfS	Ministerium für Staatssicherheit (Ministry of State Security)
NATO	North Atlantic Treaty Organization
NES	National Economic System of Planning and Management
NDPD	Nationaldemokratische Partei Deutschlands (National Democratic Party of Germany)
NSDAP	Nationalsozialistische Deutsche Arbeiterpartei (National Socialist German Workers' Party)
NVA	Nationale Volksarmee (National People's Army)
OECD	Organization for Economic Cooperation and Development
R & D	Research and development
SAG	Sowjetische Aktiengesellschaft (Soviet Limited Company)
SED	Sozialistische Einheitspartei Deutschlands (Social Unity Party of Germany)
SMAD	Soviet Military Administration in Germany
SPD	Sozialdemokratische Partei Deutschlands (Social Democratic Party of Germany)
StJB	Statistisches Jahrbuch der Deutschen Demokratischen Republik (Statistical Yearbook of the German Democratic Republic)
StPB	Statistical Pocket Book of the German Democratic Republic
VdgB	Vereinigung der gegenseitigen Bauernhilfe (Farmers' Mutual Aid Association)
VE	Verrechnungseinheit (Unit of Account)
VEB	Volkseigener Betrieb (Nationalized Enterprise)
VEG	Volkseigenes Gut (Nationalized Estate)
VVB	Vereinigung volkseigener Betriebe (Association of Nationalized Enterprises)
WPO	Wohnparteiorganisation (Residential District Party Organization)

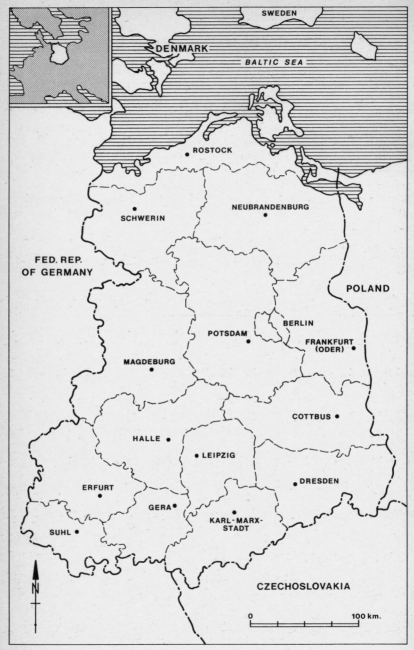

The German Democratic Republic

1 Historical Background

On 30 April 1945, one era gave way to another: the Chancellor of the thousand-year Reich committed suicide and Ulbricht, the 'founding father' of the GDR, returned to Germany after twelve years' exile in Paris, Prague and Moscow. Ulbricht and his nine communist colleagues were commissioned to assist the Soviet authorities in the reconstruction of the Berlin region in the Soviet zone of occupation. The activities of the Ulbricht group were paralleled by two other 'initiative' groups under the control of the Moscow *émigrés* Anton Ackerman, in Saxony, and Gustav Sobottka, in Mecklenburg-Pomerania.

The three groups were appalled at the scenes of desolation and human misery. The memoirs of Wolfgang Leonhard, the youngest member of the Ulbricht team, bears witness to the chaos:

> The scene was like a picture of hell—flaming ruins and starving people shambling about in tattered clothing; dazed German soldiers who seemed to have lost all idea of what was going on; Red Army soldiers singing exultantly, and often drunk; groups of women clearing the streets under the supervision of Red Army soldiers; long queues standing patiently waiting to get a bucketful of water from the pumps; and all of them looking terribly tired, hungry, tense and demoralised. [Leonhard, 1979, p. 298]

Anton Ackermann, too, recalled the feeling of hopelessness:

> What we met was a people in agony. That is the truth. They were paralysed by the poison of despair equally weighed down by the traumatic experience of nightly air raids and the other horrors of war, the carefully nurtured fear of bolshevism and the awareness of their shared responsibility for the fate that had befallen Germany. [quoted in Heitzer, 1981, p. 11]

Economic chaos prevailed. Industrial production in the zone was a mere 10 to 15 per cent of pre-war levels and about 40 per cent of industrial capacity had been destroyed as a result of war. Only about one-quarter of the housing stock had not been damaged during the war. Unemployment in December 1945 was running at 6.7 per cent of the male and 14.9 per cent of the female workforce. The situation was exacerbated by the exaction of reparations authorized by the Potsdam Agreement of August 1945. The Russians dismantled factories, railway track, mine installations and other equipment. In 1946, gross output amounted to about 43 per cent of the capacity of industry in 1936. Payment had also to be made out of current production (Autorenkollektiv Badstübner, 1981, pp. 28–30; Weber, 1985, p. 93). The heavy burden of reparations and the apparent arbitrariness of the dismantling process aroused widespread resentment against the Russians. Hostility was already deeply engrained as the Soviet Union, in its role of the occupying power, was blamed for Polish acquisition of German territories up to the Oder–Western Neiße river line, and tales were rife of looting and rape by the Red Army as it had swept across Germany.

From this inauspicious beginning there emerged four years later, in 1949, the German Democratic Republic, once described by Ernst Richert as 'a state that ought not to be'. Frequently disparaged as a state without popular mandate and the artificial creation of its Soviet big brother, the construction of the 'Berlin Wall of Shame' only served to cement this view of an illegitimate, totalitarian entity rejected by its own citizens and shunned by the West as a diplomatic leper. Yet as it approaches its fortieth anniversary, which means that it has already survived longer than the Weimar Republic and the Third Reich put together, the GDR enjoys a reputation as a model of its particular kind of socio-economic and political system. It has the highest living standard in Eastern Europe; on the surface there is little political unrest; its athletes enhance its reputation for proficiency; and it emerged from 'the diplomatic cold' in the early 1970s. The successful dismantling of the West German-inspired diplomatic barricade was capped by its entry into the United Nations in 1973. In short, the GDR can no longer be written off as a satrapy of Moscow; it is an increasingly more valued junior partner of its Soviet ally and its leaders exhibit greater confidence in their dealings with their West Germany counterparts. How did this change come about? Was the GDR essentially an artefact of the Cold War? Its sporting and economic achievements notwithstanding, does it still suffer a legitimacy deficit? In this chapter an attempt will be made to answer these basic questions.

The history of the GDR can be dated in a narrow sense either from the establishment of the Soviet zone in 1945 or since its foundation as a state in October 1949. However, its historical and cultural roots are firmly embedded in the 'unmastered' German past. The GDR's own understanding of its historical pedigree has long rested on the claim that it 'furthers the heritage of the best sons of the people, whilst at the same time it has radically broken with the reactionary past' (*The German Democratic Republic*, 1981, p. 33). Until the recent confrontation with some of the 'darker' chapters in German history, the progressive traditions were associated primarily with Thomas Müntzer, 'the most prominent leader of the insurgent peasants and the urban populace' in the Peasants' War of 1524–5; Marx and Engels, who 'put science and all the great achievements of human intellectual activity into the service of their liberation struggle'; and August Bebel (1840–1913) and Wilhelm Liebknecht (1826–1900) who helped create 'the first proletarian mass party that espoused Marxism as its ideological form' (*The German Democratic Republic*, 1981, pp. 30, 34–5). Their struggle was continued by Karl Liebknecht (1871–1919), Rosa Luxemburg (1870–1919) and the leader of the KPD's fight against fascism, Ernst Thälmann (1866–1944). The GDR therefore depicts itself as the culmination and embodiment of the long history of the German labour movement. This self-image did not preclude the gradual incorporation into the GDR's historical heritage of eminent Prussian military and political figures such as Clausewitz, Blücher, Lützow,

Gneisenau, Hardenburg, Scharnhorst and Stein, whose reforms in administration, agriculture and the military were deemed as paving the way for social progress in Prussia.

Arraigned against these progressive forces in German history which 'begat' the GDR are a collection of feudal aristocrats, religious reactionaries, monopoly capitalists and fascist mercenaries. For purposes of political legitimation the Federal Republic is cast as the heir to this reactionary tradition. The sixteenth-century reformer, Luther (1483–1546), despite a more lenient scholarly assessment in the late 1960s, was usually portrayed as the lackey of the princes and scourge of the rebellious peasants because he supported the princes against the masses in the Peasants' War. Equally abhorrent was Bismarck (1815–98) whose reunification of Germany in 1871 was decried as a 'Prussian-inspired revolution from above, rather than as the result of a democratic revolution' from below; the new polity was condemned for perpetuating 'the domination of Prussian militarism and reactionary junkers' (*The German Democratic Republic*, 1981, p. 38). Subsequently, according to the standard interpretation, capitalism developed rapidly and production became concentrated in the hands of large monopolists. In 1914, these monopolists and Prussian–German militarism launched an effort to seize colonies and material resources and to redistribute the world in their favour. Despite the failure of this expansionist policy and the creation of the bourgeois–democratic Weimar Republic in 1918, militarism and imperialism survived to establish a fascist dictatorship in 1933. It was the disunity of the working class movement and the world economic crisis in the early 1930s which persuaded several big industrialists, bankers and landowners to petition Hindenburg (1847–1934), the President of the Weimar Republic, to appoint Hitler as Chancellor. Hitler's assumption of power finally occurred on 30 January 1933. According to GDR accounts, national socialism is not an accident in German history but an intrinsic product of capitalism. The industrial and financial magnates determined the policies of the national socialist government and the socio-economic foundations of the Third Reich remained monopoly-capitalistic. As a final link in the continuity thesis, GDR historians insist that capitalism in the Federal Republic can still serve as an incubator of fascism; in contrast, the GDR has found the appropriate antidote: socialism.

This simplistic dichotomy between progressive and reactionary traditions, which survived until the mid-1970s, possessed at least one merit: it presented communism as one of the authentic precursors of the GDR. After all not only is the SED world-view shaped by the founding fathers of communism, Engels and Marx, but the KPD and its functionaries were among the main victims of Nazi terror. According to a major GDR study, about 60 per cent of the KPD's experienced cadres had been imprisoned or murdered by the summer of 1939 (Mammach, 1984, p. 297). Furthermore, acknowledgement should be made of the many KPD members, probably one in every two, who took part in some form of resistance activity in the period immediately after Hitler's accession to power (Peukert, in Bracher, Funke & Jacobsen, 1983, pp. 642–3). By 1935, these activities had declined appreciably because of terror and persecution, the collapse of hopes of overthrowing the fascist dictatorship, and the mobilization of unemployed communists into the labour force. To ignore or underestimate the scope and intensity of communist resistance would, in the words of one recent Western historian, 'distort one's understanding of the GDR [and] ... be blind to its historical roots and to present it as a mere rootless imposition of Soviet military occupation' (Merson, 1985, p. 311).

Many KPD officials, who later attained high office in the GDR, either sought refuge in Moscow, like Pieck and Ulbricht, or were imprisoned by the Nazis. The KPD leader Ernst Thälmann was imprisoned in 1933 and murdered eleven years later. The present SED General Secretary, Erich Honecker, spent most of the Third Reich in the Brandenburg-Görden penal institution. Horst Sindermann, the President of the People's Chamber since 1976, was incarcerated in the Sachsen-hausen and Mauthausen concentration camps; a similar fate befell Hermann Axen in Auschwitz and Buchenwald. Given their experience in the communist movement and the anti-fascist resistance, there is no reason to doubt the older generation's abhorrence of fascism and their wish to see it extirpated from Germany.

The polarization of the GDR's historical heritage, in which Müntzer, Marx and Thälmann were lined up against Luther, Bismarck, Krupp and Hitler, also served as an integral component of the SED's demarcation policy against the Federal Republic in the 1970s. This policy culminated in the thesis of two separate German nations—one capitalist, the other socialist—in opposition to Bonn's propagation of the existence of two German states in one German nation. The SED's promotion of the concept of a separate socialist nation in the GDR based on a socialist social formation, proletarian internationalism, a highly selective set of progressive traditions and, in the early 1970s, even a rejection of many elements of its 'Germanness' failed, as far as one can judge, to attract widespread popular support. Partly for this reason, a new campaign was launched in 1976, gathering momentum in the 1980s, to nurture a separate GDR national consciousness. This time a more differentiated and more realistic appraisal of the past was attempted. The GDR now emphasizes that its historical heritage is German history in its entirety, not limited by time or place; the 'grey areas', too, have been explored in the search for its progressive traditions. The 'early roots of progressive traditions' are located as far back in time as the successful opposition of German tribes to Roman subjugation and, territorially, they are said to extend beyond the present boundaries of the GDR, encompassing, for example, the foundation of the Mainz republic in 1793. However, the most striking development has been the excavation of progressive traditions among the reactionary seams; the best-known finds have been a refurbished Martin Luther and Prussian absolutism.

The 'Pope' of GDR historians, Professor Walter Schmidt, Director of the Academy of Sciences' Central Institute of History, has attributed this more open confrontation with the complexity of the historical heritage to the maturity of GDR society now that the issue of power has been resolved and socialism finally established. Each society, in Schmidt's opinion, reprocesses and poses new questions of the past in accordance with a specific stage in its development. Thus during the anti-fascist, democratic revolution of the second half of the 1940s the emphasis lay on exposing and overcoming the spiritual and historical legacy of German imperialism, fascism and reactionary Prussianism. Then, in the second stage of the GDR's development, from the late 1940s to the end of the 1960s, attention shifted to those progressive traditions which form part of the heritage of the GDR. Finally, in the third stage, which commenced in the early 1970s, a clear definition was required of the relationship of the GDR to the whole of German history, as part of the need to devise a new socialist national identity (Schmidt, 1986, especially pp. 196-8, 201, 205-8). The more differentiated picture of the past which is now emerging from the GDR is obviously intended to remedy some of the more glaring deficiencies in the polarization of German history between 'good' progressive and 'bad' reactionary traditions. However, the remarks of Schmidt, like those of other GDR historians, such as Badstübner, Bensing, Heitzer and Lozek, who have contributed to the 'heritage and tradition' debate, can also be construed as a reflection of the growing confidence of the SED leadership to explore controversial historical issues. This confidence, as will be argued later, is partly derived from the GDR's relative success in coping with the challenge of closer relations with the Federal Republic.

The major reinterpretations have affected three of the main representatives of the reactionary past: Luther, Frederick II (1740-86) and Bismarck. While it would be a gross misrepresentation of the achievements of GDR historical science to suggest that valuable research had not already been undertaken on these three figures and their societies, the recent historical reprocessing has brought to light their positive achievements, above all those of the great Protestant reformer. Luther, most of whose activity was centred on Saxony, was lauded by Gerhard Brendler of the Central Institute of History at the Academy of Sciences as 'a progressive agent in the process of the early bourgeois revolution' whose achievements 'enabled bourgeois politic to break away from feudalism' (1983, p. 105).

Perhaps even more surprising than the embellishment of Luther's historical image is the unveiling of the new progressive elements in Hohenzollern Prussia. The renaissance of Prussia from the late 1970s is important for the self-identity of the GDR since the former Prussian state coincides to a large extent with the present territory of the GDR and East Berlin contains many of the monuments and buildings of the traditional Prussian capital. Potsdam, the former stronghold of the Prussian monarchy, is situated only a few miles from Berlin. In a major contribution to the reinterpretation of Prussian history, three eminent GDR historians, Horst Barthel, Ingrid Mittenzwei and Walter Schmidt, writing in the SED journal *Einheit*, drew attention to both reactionary and progressive elements. The progressive side of Prussian history, they averred, was represented not only in the peasant uprisings of the late eighteenth century, the 1848 Revolution and the working class struggle against exploitation; it was also located among the nobility and monarchy. Prussian absolutism was now deemed to have a Janus-head: government policy benefited the *Junkers* and the forces of militarism, but Prussian rulers such as Frederick II contributed to social progress by stimulating industrial and agricultural development and by facilitating the transition from feudalism to capitalism. Frederick II, who in some earlier historical writings had already received qualified praise, was commended for his patronage of scholarship and culture, his policy of religious toleration and his reform of the legal system (Barthel, Mittenzwei & Schmidt, 1979, pp. 639–42). Despite their harsh criticisms of the Prussian monarchy's aggressive foreign policies and the militarization of society, the three historians had nevertheless broken a taboo: the Prussian ruling classes were no longer depicted as uniformly reactionary but as making a contribution to social progress. Other symbols of the renaissance of Prussia included the unexpected reappearance in 1980 of Daniel Rauch's statue of Frederick II on East Berlin's Unter den Linden and the opening of an exhibition of the work of Karl Friedrich Schinkel, the great nineteenth-century architect, whose classical buildings such as the Old Museum and the New Guardhouse are among the major showpieces of East Berlin. An important biography of Frederick the Great by Ingrid Mittenzwei appeared in the previous year.

The recognition by Barthel, Mittenzwei and Schmidt that the 'exploiting class' in Prussia did not constitute a homogenous unit but was subdivided into diverse groupings with varying orientations toward the fundamental issues of their age (1979, p. 640) paved the way for a partial rehabilitation of the Iron Chancellor. Bismarck had long been reviled as the author of the anti-socialist laws (1878–90), the founder of the militaristic, undemocratic Second Reich (1871–1918) and a key link in German history's 'chain of misery'. The traditional GDR condemnation of Bismarck owes more to the critique of Bebel and Wilhelm Liebknecht than to Marx and Engels who, though initially opposed to 'the revolution from above', came to accept it as a solution to the German problem (see Mitchell, 1983, p. 69). It was therefore a major landmark in GDR historiography when, in 1985, Ernst Engelberg's biography, *Bismarck: Urpreuße und Reichsgründer*, represented the creation of the Second Reich as significant historical progress on the grounds that by ending territorial fragmentation it enhanced the further development of capitalism. Germany would no longer be the plaything of foreign powers. Nor was this all. Engelberg did not dismiss the Second Reich at the time of its establishment in 1871 as inevitably retrograde: 'It was not yet determined whether the unified nation-state of 1871 could be complemented by a democratic transformation, and thereby be fulfilled with a new content' (Engelberg, 1985, p. 762).

The dismantling of the historical–ideological arsenal has not been restricted to Luther and Prussia. Saxony's absolutist rulers, too, are being reassessed. Augustus the Strong (1694–1733), elector of Saxony and King of Poland, usually depicted as the ruthless exploiter of his subjects, was recognized in a 1984 article in the teachers' newspaper *Deutsche Lehrerzeitung* as having furthered social progress through his foreign and domestic policies (Kuppe, 1985, p. 279). Representatives of the German feudal class in the Middle Ages have also been integrated into the progressive lineage. Henry I (919–36), for example, is credited with having created 'the first German state which accelerated the process of the various tribes growing together to become one German people' (*The German Democratic Republic*, 1986, p. 26).

The historians' search for a more differentiated picture of the whole of German history has, of course, long been complemented by the cultivation of the classics of the 'humanist cultural heritage', Bach, Goethe, Lessing and Schiller. But if the 'new' history offers a more realistic appraisal of the GDR's heritage and the ambivalence of its traditions, it should, on the other hand, be recognized that this partial re-Germanization contains a potential challenge to the SED's insistence that the German question is closed. The problem is clearly stated by Asmus:

> Will the average East German Bürger read biographies of Frederick II and Bismarck, or come away from the historical exhibitions being sponsored by the SED convinced that the 'socialist' nation in the GDR embodies all progressive German historical traditions ... or is he more likely to be reminded of the common historical ties that bond Germans in East and West and conclude that indeed theirs is only a single common German nation. [Asmus, 1986, p. 24]

Whilst a clear answer cannot be given to Asmus's question, occasional remarks reveal that all-German sentiments have not completely disappeared even among the SED's leaders. Honecker, in a letter to Chancellor Kohl in October 1983, called for a halt to the deployment of missiles in the name of 'the German people'. Even more explicit was his statement in February 1981:

> when the working class in the Federal Republic proceeds with the socialist transformation of the Federal Republic, then the question of the reunification of the two German states will appear in an entirely new light. And no one should have any doubts about how we will decide. [*Neues Deutschland*, 16 February 1981, quoted in Asmus, 1984b, p. 416]

The appropriation of the German past has even loosened the bonds of socialist internationalism. The Politburo member and Central Committee Secretary for ideology and culture, Kurt Hager, in an interview with the West German magazine *Stern*, sought to distance the GDR from Gorbachëv's domestic reform programme by emphasizing that all socialist countries, including the GDR, possess their own historical and cultural traditions which have to be respected. He reminded his interviewers that the GDR does not copy everything in the Soviet Union and that the manifesto of the KPD in June 1945 had made it clear that it would be wrong to impose the Soviet system on Germany (*Neues Deutschland*, 10 April 1987, p. 3). It needs to be stressed, however, that the GDR's renewed cultivation of its 'German-ness' has not altered its basic position on the existence of two separate nations and two divergent political orders in the FRG and the GDR. Nor, despite the elasticity of the definition of what constitutes progressive traditions, has the SED abandoned its claim to be the heir to all the revolutionary, progressive and humanistic traditions in German history; and it continues to unload the 'regressive' on to its capitalist neighbour. Nowhere can this be seen more clearly than in the interpretation of national socialism and communism before 1945. The blurring of the polarization of the two class lines in German history is not observable in a period which is crucial for the self-identity and historical legitimacy of the GDR.

The historians of the GDR still base their concept of national socialism on the 1935 Comintern definition of fascism as 'the open terroristic dictatorship of the most reactionary, most chauvinistic and most imperialistic elements of finance capital'. Marxist historians in this field are regarded as participants in the current class struggle, for through their research they make

> a contribution to combating the reactionary forces which are ever reappearing in new guise and, on the basis of their historical experience, proceed from the standpoint that the anti-fascist struggle can only be carried to victory through the complete removal from power and overcoming of monopoly capital. [Ruge, quoted in Kershaw, 1985, p. 11]

Fascism, it is stressed, though a major beneficiary of the world economic crisis from 1929 onward, is a product of the monopolistic stage in the development of capitalism; it is not the creation of the Führer of the National Socialist Party (Petzold, 1984, pp. 44–5). Although GDR historians now concede that the NSDAP attempted to win over large sections of the working class by propaganda and by means of the so-called 'leftist' Strasser-wing (see Gossweiler, in Eichholtz & Gossweiler, 1980, pp. 120–2) and that membership dues played a role in the ultimate success of the party, they insist that the vital contribution was made by its wealthy industrial and agrarian backers, notably Fritz Thyssen. Despite the divisions and contradictions within the various monopoly capitalistic groupings and despite the industrialists' suspicions of the 'socialism of the fascists', the collapse of the right wing and liberal parties, the combined electoral strength of the KPD and SPD in the November elections of 1932, and the realization that only the NSDAP was prepared to deal ruthlessly with the working class persuaded several industrialists, landowners and bankers—Schacht, von Schröder, von Papen, Thyssen—to intercede with President Hindenburg to appoint Hitler as head of government (Petzold, 1983, pp. 230–1). Once in power, the Nazis fulfilled their designated role as the brutal instruments of the monopolists. However, as a feature typical of state monopoly capitalism, competition and conflicts abounded between the various monopolist groupings such as those between the iron and steel sector and electro-chemicals and between their representatives in the party and state apparats of the Third Reich.

Whereas the major responsibility for the creation of a fascist dictatorship is attributed to the monopoly capitalists, GDR historians represent the KPD as the only political party to have defended the interests of the workers, resisted militarism and imperialism and to have waged the struggle against fascism with determination and from an early date. The KPD, founded in January 1919, attracted mass support in the 1930s: between 1928 and the end of 1932 paid-up membership rose from 130,000 to 252,000 and voters from 3.2 million to 6 million (Fowkes, 1984, p. 205). In his memoirs, Erich Honecker dismisses as 'a historical lie' the claim of some bourgeois authors that the communists did not appreciate the danger of Hitler fascism until the Comintern World Congress in 1935. In his support, he cites the KPD leader Ernst Thälmann as branding fascism, in the years before 1933, as 'the deadly enemy of the workers' movement and of the Soviet Union'. In short, he rejects the charge of 'bourgeois and social democratic historians' that the Weimar

Republic was wrecked by 'the terror from the left and from the right' (Honecker, 1981, pp. 58–9).

Although SED historians readily acknowledge that the KPD was not interested in the long-term survival of the Weimar Republic, which in the communist view exploited the working class in the interests of capital, they are keen to demonstrate how the KPD strove to mobilize the working class and other groups against the Nazis. Fundamental to their argument is the appeal in April 1932 by the KPD Central Committee for an Anti-Fascist Action with the SPD and the free trade unions. While the SPD leadership rejected the call, numerous anti-fascist action groups were formed in June and July in which communist and social democratic workers combined to protect party offices and the dwellings of well-known workers' functionaries (Petzold, 1984, pp. 63–4; *Geschichte der SED*, 1978, pp. 54–5). The struggle against von Papen's manoeuvres to remove the SPD government in Prussia from office in the summer of 1932 is advanced as another instance of the KPD's determination to frustrate the forces of reaction. Not only did the KPD support the Braun-Severing government in the Prussian parliament, but after Chancellor von Papen had deposed it by decree on 20 July 1932 the party appealed to the SPD and all workers to stage a general strike. Although GDR historians believe that the idea of a strike commanded considerable support among the workers, the SPD and trade union leaders opted for capitulation. This was also the fate of Walter Ulbricht's call on behalf of the Central Committee for a general strike against the appointment of Hitler as Chancellor on 30 January 1933. The pusillanimous SPD leaders, it is alleged, were opposed to extra-parliamentary action and wished to conduct the struggle by constitutional means. The weakness of the KPD among organized labour prevented the communists from launching a general strike on its own initiative. While SED leaders and historians admit that several tactical errors were committed by the KPD—for example, the social fascism line—they insist that 'reformism' bears a much greater share of the responsibility for the establishment of the fascist dictatorship. The right-wing leaders of the SPD and the free trade unions were too blinkered by a deep-rooted anti-communism and by their constitutional illusions to undertake joint action with the KPD against the fascist enemy (Petzold, 1984, pp. 74, 76, 78; *Geschichte der SED*, 1978, pp. 53–4, 56; Voßke, 1983, pp. 88–9).

This presentation of the role of the KPD in the twilight of the Weimar Republic is not wholly uncritical: GDR historians acknowledge that errors were committed, such as the propagation until 1935 of an undifferentiated social fascism concept and the KPD's participation in the August 1931 referendum on a dissolution of the Prussian Parliament initiated by the NSDAP and the right-wing DNVP and Stahlhelm. Moreover, they are quite justified in highlighting the SPD's failings, notably the stubborn adherence, as late as 1932–3, to the constitutional and legal path and the party's passive reaction to von Papen's *coup de main* in Prussia. On the other hand, GDR accounts are still insufficiently critical of the social fascism thesis adopted by the KPD after the Comintern Congress of 1928. The party's general line between 1929 and 1933 was determined by the ultra-left concept of the Soviet-controlled Comintern. At the 1928 Congress, the Comintern predicted an imminent general capitalist crisis and warned of the danger of an attack by the capitalist countries on the Soviet Union. The severe intensification of the crisis required, accordingly, the mobilization of the workers and a struggle against social democracy, which was supposedly communism's most dangerous enemy. The label 'social fascism' was pinned on to the social democrats, the main 'social prop' of the bourgeoisie and, thus, of the survival of capitalism. Given this thesis, it is not surprising that from 1929 onward SPD and KPD usually faced each other as bitter enemies. Even as late as May 1933 the KPD Central Committee was still denouncing the social democrats as the main social support of the capitalist dictatorship, despite the forcible suppression of the organizations and the press of the 'social fascists'.

KPD attacks on social democrats and their trade union allies and the party's misconceived fascism concept had serious consequences. First, it virtually doomed in advance a favourable reaction by a highly sceptical SPD leadership to the communists' temporary shift in 1932 toward a united front. It should, of course, be recognized that the previous history of bitter relations between the two parties, dating from the brutal overthrow of the Spartakist–KPD coup in January 1919 by the Freikorps in collaboration with the SPD Defence Minister, Noske, made cooperation unlikely in principle; on the other hand, the communists' revolutionary professions, their futile putchism in the early 1920s and then the subsequent tightening of Moscow's control over the party and its leader (since 1925), Ernst Thälmann, were hardly conducive to securing the cooperation of the SPD. Secondly, the KPD's persistent denunciations of reformism as the major foe contributed initially to a serious underestimation of the national socialist threat. This error was compounded by the KPD's application of the term 'fascist', not only to social democracy, but also to the Brüning, von Papen and von Schleicher governments of 1930–2, and reinforces the charge against the KPD of having contributed to the underestimation of the real dangers inherent in a national socialist dictatorship. This argument may be illustrated by Thälmann's apparent approval in 1932 of a statement contained in a KPD document to the effect that 'A Social Democratic coalition government faced with an incapable, divided, confused proletariat, would be a thousand times greater evil than an open fascist dictatorship, one that confronts the united masses of a class-conscious proletariat that is determined to fight' (quoted in Hamilton, 1982, p. 304). Thus, despite the communist's physical stuggles with the Nazis in the 'battle for the streets' and despite the culpability of the SPD and the other political parties, the SED's interpretation of the KPD's role in the collapse of Weimar and the accession of Hitler must still be viewed as an inadequate response to this aspect of the historical record. The historical legacy remains 'clearly ambiguous'.

That mistakes had been committed was recognized, however, by KPD leaders such as Wilhelm Pieck and Walter Ulbricht, possibly by the Autumn of 1934. Influenced by the new Comintern line, pronounced at its Seventh Congress in 1935, the KPD sought a *rapprochement* with the SPD, now no longer derided as 'social fascism'. It called for a Popular Front of all anti-fascist forces based on a united front of communist and socialist functionaries and members. A unity party of the working class, it was envisaged, would eventually emerge from this experience of cooperation. Little progress was made with the united front proposal: the SPD remained suspicious of communist motives, especially as the KPD continued to adhere to the goal of a proletarian dictatorship. The KPD adjusted its policy: for example, in 1936 and at the 'Berne' conference in 1939, it proposed a broad alliance with other anti-fascist groups culminating in a democratic people's republic. Although such proposals were premature, they would resurface in more propitious circumstances after the war and provide an element of legitimacy to the attempt to implement an anti-fascist democratic revolution (Krisch, 1974, pp. 10–20, *Geschichte der SED*, 1978, pp. 58–60, 63–5, 70–1).

Formation of the Present Regime, 1945-49

During the war the allies had discussed the future of a defeated Germany at a series of meetings and conferences, notably the heads-of-government meetings at Tehran in November–December 1943 and at Yalta in February 1945. The European Advisory Commission, based in London, was responsible for drafting the occupation statute. The Big Three conference at Potsdam between 17 July and 2 August 1945 confirmed earlier decisions to divide Germany within its 1937 borders into British, Soviet, American and French zones of occupation and the area of Greater Berlin into four sectors.

Agreement was soon reached at Potsdam on the dissolution of the NSDAP and the demilitarization of Germany. A Council of Foreign Ministers, including representatives of the Soviet Union, the United States, Great Britain, France and China, was entrusted with preparing a peace settlement for Germany 'to be accepted by the Government of Germany when a government adequate for the purpose is established'. In the meantime, the four military governors were to form an Allied Control Council, in which the principle of unanimity prevailed, to deal with questions relating to Germany as a whole. Furthermore, the Potsdam Agreements stipulated that 'so far as practicable' the population was to be dealt with uniformly throughout the country and Germany treated as an economic unit. The principle of treating Germany as a single unit clashed with the supremacy of each zone commander within his own domain. This conflict would emerge most sharply over reparations. Washington had no wish for the Soviets to take what they wanted in reparations from the industrial areas of Western Germany and refused Soviet requests for a commitment to a fixed sum. However, as the Western zones were more industrialized, the Soviets were granted 10 per cent of the industrial capital equipment of the Western zones which was considered unnecessary for the German peacetime economy and a further 15 per cent in exchange for foodstuffs and other goods from the Soviet zone. The question of exchange rapidly developed into a bone of contention between East and West.

Other matters discussed at Potsdam concerned the revival of political life, Germany's new borders and access to Berlin. Denazification and democratization were accepted as desirable principles, but as in so many other instances the

Conference failed to provide specific guidelines and the occupation regimes would prove to have different ideas on what constituted democracy. The Eastern border of the Soviet zone was fixed on the Oder–Western Neiße rivers. Former German territories east of this line were placed under Polish administration until the final peace settlement was concluded with a future German government. Poland was thereby compensated for land lost on its Eastern border to the Soviet Union. Arrangements for the Western sectors of Berlin represent the most glaring example of the failure of the allies to devise satisfactory formulae for the occupation regime. Even though American representatives on the European Advisory Commission had pressed their government to insist upon binding Soviet guarantees of access by land and water across their zone to Berlin, only three air corridors were formally approved, in November 1945. The Western sectors soon found themselves virtually marooned in the middle of the Soviet zone.

The failure at Potsdam to reach agreement on many fundamental issues reflected not only the contradictions between the occupying powers but also uncertainties within each country as to the most appropriate way of dealing with Germany. American policy had long fluctuated between the economic rehabilitation of Germany and a punitive settlement before finally opting for a prosperous Germany in order to enhance general economic recovery and to lighten the load on the American taxpayer. Stalin, at times, toyed with the idea of dismemberment, as in his meeting in December 1941 with the British Foreign Secretary Eden and at the Tehran Conference two years later. In fact, the Soviet Union undoubtedly preferred the option of an all-German framework for the achievement of its basic goals of security against a future German threat and the recovery of the Soviet economy. In 1945, these goals could most effectively be achieved through the joint occupation of Germany which would enable the Soviets to influence events in the Western zones and to exact reparations from their own zone as well as from the Western industrial areas. They were particularly anxious to obtain reparations from the Ruhr.

If the most desirable solution from the point of view of the Soviet Union was the installation of a socialist system on the Soviet model, this represented, in 1945, little more than a long-term goal, dependent upon a series of complex variables, one of which was German attitudes toward communism. If, as Stalin told the leader of the London-based Polish exile government, Mikolajzyk, in 1944, 'communism fitted Germany as a saddle fitted a cow', then the Soviet leader did not appear to have entertained high hopes of transplanting Soviet-type communism on to the whole of Germany.

Another possible option was the eventual creation of a united, neutral Germany unattached to any bloc. An undesirable alternative, at least in the circumstances prevailing after the war, was a divided Germany with a Western state closely linked to the United States and hostile to Soviet aspirations. Developments in Germany would obviously depend very much on American willingness to remain in Europe. In the meantime, the Soviets were determined to consolidate their own power and that of their German communist assistants in their own zone (on Soviet policy, see

Fischer, in Kolloquium, 1980, pp. 15–19, and McCauley, in Childs, 1985, pp. 149–50).

What kind of system would best serve Soviet interests in its own sphere? The response of a leading GDR historian, Rolf Badstübner (1978, pp. 51, 65–6), that in 1945 the Soviet Union did not wish to impose its own system on the zone nor to export revolution is a defensible position, as is his identification of a desire in the Western and Eastern zones for fundamental social and political changes. The strong authoritarian tradition in German political culture, too, might have been conducive to the anti-fascism from above favoured by SMAD and the SED (see Staritz, in Gerber, 1986, pp. 38–9. Opinion surveys conducted in the immediate post-war years, albeit in the American zone, indicate that authoritarian attitudes were probably still widespread throughout Germany). A policy of change directed from above meant, however, that the anti-fascist democratic revolution of the late 1940s would not be based on a lasting cooperation between the authorities and the anti-fascist groups, committees and grass-roots organizations which had sprung up spontaneously in many towns and villages throughout Germany to cope with local needs immediately before and after the collapse of the Third Reich. These groups were mainly composed of communists and social democrats, together with some middle-class activists. Günter Benser (1978, pp. 785–9) has identified about 500 such groups throughout Germany, although subsequent research is expected to unearth more, especially in smaller communities.

These popular initiatives by socialists, communists, trade unionists and other activists have been interpreted by some Western historians as offering Germany, both East and West, the opportunity of a radical new beginning. Yet, as Dietrich Staritz has observed (1984, p. 97), not enough is known about the political goals of these committees in the Soviet zone to judge whether they might have formed the basis for a new departure. In any case, though initially a welcome supplement to the efforts of the Soviet authorities and the KPD to restore conditions in the zone, the 'Antifa' committees soon came to be regarded as counterproductive. Experienced communist cadres were needed and expected to work within the framework of the KPD, not in the loosely organized 'Antifa' committees. Ulbricht, accordingly, ordered his associates in Berlin to bring about their dissolution. Most of them were suppressed in Berlin during May; others lingered on in less accessible areas until August. Wolfgang Leonhard, one of Ulbricht's colleagues involved in this process, later observed:

> The dissolution of the Anti-Fascist Committees was ... nothing other than a disruption of the first emergence of what might prove to be a powerful independent anti-Fascist and Socialist movement. It was the first victory of the apparat over the independent stirrings of the anti-Fascist, left-inclined strata of Germany. [Leonhard, 1979, pp. 325–6]

Anti-fascist democratic reconstruction was the order of the day but along lines approved of by the Soviet Military Administration in Germany (SMAD) and in conjunction with experienced communist cadres such as Ulbricht. Not only did they wish to encourage the revival of political life in the zone but also to remove the socio-economic preconditions of militarism and fascism. A comprehensive de-nazification process was launched. It was a challenging task: approximately 72 per cent of teachers and 80 per cent of judges had belonged to the NSDAP. By August 1947, denazification commissions had investigated 828,000 former Nazi Party members and 520,000 had lost their posts, especially public servants. The members of the old educational and propertied elites tended to be replaced by representatives from underprivileged social strata, many of them from the KPD or the later SED (Staritz, 1984, pp. 100, 102; Weber, 1985, p. 108); they therefore acquired a stake in the new system.

Another decisive step along the self-styled, anti-fascist democratic road was SMAD's unexpected authorization of free trade unions and political parties in June 1945. The surprisingly early recognition of political parties, before their authoriza-tion in the Western zones, was determined by SMAD's wish to influence the development of political parties throughout the whole of Germany and to persuade the German population in its own zone to assist in the work of reconstruction. In addition to the two workers' parties, the KPD and the SPD, SMAD permitted the establishment of the Christian Democratic Union (CDU) and the Liberal Democratic Party (LDP). The four parties agreed in July to form a bloc of anti-fascist democratic parties; a committee composed of five members constituted the main policy coordinating body. The bloc system was operated by SMAD and the SED as one of the main levers for transforming the political and social system of the zone.

The programme of the KPD, issued on 11 June 1945, is indicative of the carefully designed strategy initially pursued by its leadership and SMAD. The manifesto, which was targeted at all parts of Germany, proclaimed:

> We believe it would be wrong to force the Soviet system on Germany, because it bears no relation to Germany's present stage of development. We believe the overriding interests of the German people at present prescribe a different road – the establishment of an anti-fascist, democratic regime, a parliamentary, democratic republic, with all democratic rights and liberties for the people. [quoted in Stern, 1965, p. 104]

Moreover, whilst the KPD advocated the expropriation of the Nazi bosses and war criminals and public ownership of public utilities, it pledged its support for the development of trade and private enterprise on the basis of private property. Although the absence of any reference to the building of socialism and the creation of the dictatorship of the proletariat caused consternation among many old communists, the KPD's appeal for an anti-fascist bloc of democratic parties could be justified as appropriate to the immediate post-war situation. Its determination to root out the preconditions of fascism and to punish the Nazi bosses was shared by the other parties. It could claim to be linked to proposals in the 1930s for a broad alliance of anti-fascist groups. And the avoidance of the term 'communism' was tailored to the needs of a cooperative effort. The publication, in February 1946, of

Anton Ackermann's article 'Is there a Special German Road to Socialism?', with its emphasis on a non-Soviet, peaceful transition to socialism along national lines, was clearly designed to make *rapprochement* more palatable to broad sections of the population.

Ackermann's thesis was also intended as a contribution to a merger between the KPD and the SPD. Initially, in June 1945, Ulbricht had rejected the SPD's leaders' proposals for a united party on the grounds that 'organizational unification must be preceded by a process of ideological clarification' (quoted in Leonhard, 1979, p. 350). The initial willingness of SPD leaders such as Grotewohl, Dahrendorf, Fechner and Gniffke to form a united party was based on their awareness of their party's numerical superiority and on the political lessons drawn from their experience of the collapse of the Weimar Republic and the Nazi dictatorship. Indeed, the SPD programme of 11 June was in many points more socialist and more radical than that of the KPD. The KPD leadership changed tack sometime in late September to early October 1945 and pressed the SPD's Berlin Central Committee for a merger. Events outside Germany may have influenced SMAD and the KPD: the setbacks suffered by the communists in the November elections in Austria and Hungary probably strengthened their resolve to seek a union in Germany. Of greater significance, however, was the situation within Germany itself. The KPD, indebted in part to the intervention of SMAD, had achieved parity of numbers (about 375,000 members) in the Soviet zone by the end of 1945. Furthermore, the communists were able to take advantage of growing divisions within the ranks of the social democrats and the increasingly isolated position of the zonal SPD. The emergence in the autumn of 1945 of the strongly anti-communist Kurt Schumacher as the leader of the SPD in the Western zones weakened the authority of the Berlin Central Committee and its leader Otto Grotewohl, who found it increasingly difficult to steer a course between Schumacher's inflexible opposition to any cooperation with the communists and the KPD's pressure for unification.

The interpretation of the merger of the KPD and SPD as a shotgun marriage is regarded by GDR historians as a legend concocted by 'right-wing social democrats', and subsequently propagated by bourgeois historians (Badstübner, 1978, pp. 75–80; Heitzer, 1981, pp. 37–8). However, SPD leaders like Dahrendorf and Klingelhöfer were justifiably aggrieved at SMAD's preferential treatment of the KPD. SMAD openly favoured the KPD in the printing and distribution of its literature and in placing communists in key administrative and economic positions. And it can hardly be denied that the heavy Soviet pressure on reluctant SPD leader and members, which sometimes involved imprisonment, was not also instrumental in the eventual fusion of the two parties as the Socialist Unity Party of Germany (Staritz, 1984, p. 122; Weber, 1985, p. 124).

Yet, despite the obvious discrimination against the SPD, the principle of cooperation continued to attract some support among the rank and file. Local groups sometimes took the initiative in merging and the desire for union was particularly strong in the factories. An important test of public opinion is also available: in March 1946, a plebiscite of SPD members was conducted in the

Western sectors of Berlin by opponents of amalgamation (a similar plebiscite was banned in the Soviet sector). Out of a total membership of 33,247, the vote cast was 23,775: 2,940 voted for and 19,529 against the question, 'Are you for the immediate merger of both workers' parties?'. On the other hand, this apparent rejection of merger was qualified by a high level of support for the notion of cooperation: 14,763 members expressed themselves in favour and 5,559 against the question, 'Are you for the alliance that would guarantee co-operative effort and exclude fratricidal support?' (Krisch, 1974, p. 184). Both sides have subsequently been able to derive some comfort from these figures.

The Socialist Unity Party (SED) was easily the largest party in the zone. At the time of the merger in April 1946 it comprised 600,000 communists and 680,000 social democrats. By mid-1948, membership had risen to almost 2 million. Offices and functions in the new party were divided equally between communists and social democrats. Grotewohl of the ex-SPD and Pieck of the ex-KPD were elected joint chairmen. The popularity of the SED was put to the test in the provincial elections (*Landtagswahlen*)of October 1946. It fought its campaign on the basis of the anti-fascist democratic revolution. The SED emerged as the largest party with 4.7 million out of the 9.9 million votes cast; nevertheless, it did not achieve 50 per cent of the vote in a single province and its 249 seats in the provincial parliaments were slightly less than the combined total of the CDU (133) and the LDP (121). In Greater Berlin, where the SED and the SPD campaigned separately, the SED (19.8 per cent) ran a poor third behind the SPD (48.7 per cent) and the CDU (22.2 per cent). It recorded 29.7 per cent in the Soviet sector as against 13.7 per cent in the three Western sectors (Autorenkollektiv Badstübner, 1981, pp. 70–1; Weber, 1985, pp. 142–3). Jonathan Steele, formerly *The Guardian's* correspondent in Eastern Europe, denies that the party's poor performance can be attributed to anti-communist propaganda in the Western media; its own policies and its close identification with the Soviet Union had cost it dearly (Steele, 1977, p. 59).

The other two political parties in the zone, boosted by this electoral support and a growing membership, proved to be troublesome associates of the dominant party within the bloc. In 1948, membership peaked at 231,000 for the CDU and 197,000 for the LPD. Both parties vigorously resisted the SED offensive in 1947 to increase its authority within the bloc and the CDU chairman, Jakob Kaiser, boldly proclaimed his party to be the 'breakwater of dogmatic Marxism and its totalitarian tendencies' (Staritz, 1984, p. 144). Furthermore, the CDU refused to accept the SED proposal for a National Congress designed to support the Soviet negotiating position at the Foreign Ministers' Conference in November 1947: the party had no wish for its appeal to suffer in the Western zones by appearing to be a pliant instrument of the SED. SMAD's response to CDU obduracy was to dismiss two of its leaders, Kaiser and Lemmer, in December 1947. The position of the CDU and LDP was decisively undermined in 1948 with the formation of two additional bourgeois parties, the National Democratic Party of Germany (NDPD) and the Democratic Farmers' Party of Germany (DBD), and their entry, together with the FDGB, into the bloc. The new parties were amenable to SED policy and acted as a counterattraction among the urban middle class and farmers to the CDU and LDP. The SED's control over the multi-party bloc system was sealed by the creation of the National Front in the following year.

Meanwhile, the SED itself was undergoing a fundamental change. In the aftermath of Stalin's dispute with Tito in June 1948 and Yugoslavia's expulsion from Cominform, the concept of a special road to socialism was abandoned. Communist parties throughout Eastern Europe were obliged to bring their party system into line with that of the CPSU and to recognize the Soviet Union as their model. In the Soviet zone Anton Ackermann was compelled to retract his thesis of a special German road to socialism, and the transformation of the SED into a party of a new type commenced in July 1948. The adoption of the Bolshevik model was the direct result of the Soviet–Yugoslav conflict, but it was also influenced by the widespread view that control over the fundamental political and economic change in the zone could best be accomplished by a highly centralized and tightly organized party. The official history of the SED justifies the transformation to a cadre party, albeit within a mass party, as an objective necessity in order to promote socialism and to defend and strengthen the democratic and anti-imperialistic achievements against the intrigues of the Western occupying powers and their German bourgeois and right-wing social democratic allies. Within the zone a considerable section of the populace, it is admitted, was still susceptible to Western propaganda: 'petty bourgeois views' within the working class and strong anti-communism and anti-Soviet feelings were prevalent among employees in the private sectors (*Geschichte der SED*, 1978, pp. 176–9).

By the end of January 1949, the SED's Central Secretariat had been replaced by a nine-man Politburo, the parity of status between former communists and former social democrats had been abolished to the detriment of the latter, and a small secretariat under Walter Ulbricht had been created to assist the Politburo in its day-to-day business and in its decision-making. Democratic centralism was recognized as the basic organizational principle and, as a newly constituted Marxist-Leninist party, the SED proclaimed itself as the conscious and organized vanguard of the working class. Ulbricht's emergence as the leading political figure in the zone was confirmed by his election as General Secretary in 1950 (for further details, see Staritz, 1984, pp. 151–9; Steele, 1977, pp. 67–8; Weber, 1985, pp. 173–85; Stern, 1965, pp. 110–12). The drastic organizational and ideological transformation was accompanied by a series of purges, launched in July 1948 and continuing until 1953. The purges created a disciplined party more in tune with the Bolshevik model than the original fusion of social democracy and communism. The Central Party control Commission under Hermann Matern supervised the expulsion from the party of, in particular, former social democrats, alleged agents of the Western SPD's Eastern Buro and former communists suspected of opposition views. In the first half of 1951 alone, 150,696 members were expelled, and between 1948 and 1952 party membership fell from 2 million to 1.2 million as a result of expulsions and the more exacting entry requirements.

Social and Economic Change, 1945–46

The Soviet authorities and the German communists were determined to erase what they regarded as the socio-economic preconditions of fascism. Among the earliest radical measures were the land and educational reforms (1945), the nationalization of industrial property belonging to former Nazis and war criminals (1945–6), and the restructuring of the judiciary and the police (1945–6). The widespread popularity of such measures and their absence in the Western zones lend some weight to the claim that an anti-fascist democratic order, though not yet a full-scale socialist revolution, was being implemented in the zone.

The expropriation of the large landowners was supported by all four political parties in the Soviet zone, although some of the CDU leaders, notably Hermes and Schreiber, had reservations about the lack of compensation for those dispossessed owners who were untainted by Nazism. SPD Chairman Otto Grotewohl defended expropriation on the grounds that the *Junkers* had been the backbone of reaction in Germany. In the land reform of September 1945, all landowners with holdings exceeding 100 hectares, former Nazi activists and war criminals were expropriated without compensation. Over 3.3 million hectares, about one-third of useful agricultural land, were affected. Approximately 2.2 million hectares were redistributed among over half a million landless peasants, agricultural labourers, smallholders and others. The major beneficiaries were former manual workers and salaried employees who constituted 32.7 per cent of the total number of recipients; however, the average size of their plots was a meagre 0.6 hectares (Heitzer, 1981, pp. 28–30; Autorenkollektiv Badstübner, 1981, pp. 50–1; Weber, 1985, pp. 110–12).

In October 1945, SMAD authorized the confiscation of the property of the German state, the armed forces and national socialists. Part of this property, mainly heavy industrial concerns, was partly converted into Soviet Joint Stock Companies; the other part was put at the disposal of the German administrative organs in March 1946. Although opposed by influential bourgeois politicians, such as Kaiser and Lemmer of the CDU, it was decided to hold a referendum on the question of nationalization in June 1946 in Saxony, where about two-fifths of the zone's industrial potential was located: 77.6 per cent expressed their approval of a law expropriating without compensation the enterprises owned by former national socialists and war criminals. Legitimized by the Saxon precedent, the other regional authorities proceeded to enact similar expropriation laws. By the spring of 1948, firms accounting for about 40 per cent of total industrial production had been expropriated by the state or municipal authorities (Weber, 1985, pp. 114–15; Autorenkollektiv Badstübner, 1981, pp. 65–9).

The Division of Germany

While the socio-economic and political restructuring of the zone was drawing it closer to the Soviet model, the deterioration in relations between the Western powers and the Soviet Union was rapidly reducing the likelihood of a reunited

Germany. A major quarrel occurred over reparations. Indignant at the Soviets' refusal to supply food and other commodities to the Western zones and at their insistence on the delivery of an additional 10 per cent of reparations in the form of industrial capital equipment from the West, General Lucius Clay unilaterally suspended dismantling operations and reparations deliveries from the American zone in May 1946. For their part, the Russians were angered by Washington's failure to accommodate the Soviet request for a loan to assist economic reconstruction, by American disengagement from various commitments entered into at Yalta and by attempts to circumscribe Soviet power in Eastern Europe. In fact, the United States and the Soviet Union were both seeking to take advantage of the opportunities and ambiguities of the wartime agreements and to readjust their policies to the containment of each other's power rather than continue a cooperative approach to post-war reconstruction. The shift in American policy toward Germany was signalled by the Secretary of State's proposal, in July 1946, to unify the economy of the American zone with that of any of the other zones. On 1 January 1947, the British and American zones were formally merged into Bizonia. In effect, Byrnes's proposal was an expression of his government's commitment to the economic recovery of Germany, a policy which conflicted with Soviet insistence on the priority of reparations from current production over the German standard of living.

The crumbling of allied unity in Germany doomed to failure the deliberations on a peace treaty for Germany at the conference of the foreign ministers of the four powers in Moscow in March 1947. Soon after the commencement of the conference President Truman enunciated his 'Doctrine' in which he promised American support to the 'free peoples' of the world and vilified the communist way of life as one 'based upon the will of a minority forcibly imposed upon the majority'. The economic prop of the Truman Doctrine, the European Recovery Programme or Marshall Plan, was announced in June 1946. The Western zones were targeted as the main beneficiaries of Marshall Aid to Germany; the United States never seriously intended to include the Soviet zone or the People's Democracies. However, much to the chagrin of SMAD, Jakob Kaiser of the CDU advocated the inclusion of the Soviet zone in the Marshall Plan. Many private entrepreneurs, too, would have welcomed such a move.

In order to spur economic recovery in their zones, the Western powers finally decided to replace the worthless Reichmark with the new Deutschmark on 18 June 1948. In the deteriorating political climate the Soviet representative had withdrawn from the Allied Control Council, three months earlier, thus removing a major obstacle to a reform of the currency. The Western allies pressed ahead at the same time with plans for the creation of a separate West German state: the six-nation London conference agreed on 7 June 1948 that the West Germans could draft a constitution for a separate state. The Western powers, rather than Stalin, were taking the initiative in cutting Germany into two.

The Soviet reaction to the London conference and the Western currency reform was to sever all road, rail and canal links to the Western sectors of Berlin on 24 June 1948. After some discussion of the proposal of the American military governor,

Lucius Clay, to call the Russians' bluff by sending an armed convoy to Berlin, Washington decided to relieve West Berlin's population of over 2 million by means of the famous airlift. The Soviet blockade was eventually called off in May 1949.

Why had Stalin, confronted by an American monopoly on nuclear weaponry, run the risk of provoking a Western attempt to break the blockade by force? Western scholarship has still not resolved whether he regarded Berlin as a lever or the prize, or both. As a lever, Berlin might be used as a final effort to force the Western powers to abandon their plan for a separate West German state or to obtain economic concessions, for example, over the Ruhr. On the other hand, Berlin alone might have been a sufficient prize, especially if the Soviets were planning to answer the *fait accompli* of a West German state by setting up an East German counterpart (for a review of the debates, see Adomeit, 1982, pp. 71–3).

In contrast, GDR historians propagate the view of a self-imposed Western blockade. By rejecting Soviet offers of food supplies to the Western sectors, the Western powers deliberately triggered off a crisis and imposed a counter-blockade on trade with the Soviet zone. The hysteria surrounding the Soviet 'blockade' and the myth of a Soviet threat were manipulated by the Western powers to consolidate plans for a West German state (Keiderling, 1982, pp. 101–3, 411). The Soviet Union was therefore obliged to take countermeasures, such as the restrictions on traffic, against Western attempts to integrate the whole of Berlin, or at least the three Western sectors, into the West German state and against their transforming Berlin into a bastion of counter-revolution within the Soviet zone and into an instrument for rolling back the new democratic order. Furthermore, it was necessary to protect the population and economy of the Soviet zone against the new currency and to thwart attempts to use the magnet of an economically prosperous West Germany to undermine the Soviet zone in such a way that it would eventually be incorporated into the imperialist sphere of influence (Keiderling, 1982, pp. 37, 44, 96, 411). GDR authors conclude that by planning a separate West German state and by introducing the new currency into Berlin, the Western powers had violated the Yalta and Potsdam agreements and had forfeited their occupation rights in Berlin (Adomeit, 1982, p. 69; Keiderling, 1982, pp. 98, 411; Autorenkollektiv Badstübner, 1981, pp. 93–5; *Geschichte der SED*, 1978, pp. 170–4).

In fact, the Soviet action was essentially reactive, though it entailed considerable risks. What were the choices still available? In view of the transparent unpopularity of communism in the Western zones and the setbacks suffered by the SED in elections within the Soviet zone in 1946, it is highly improbable that the Soviet Union seriously entertained the increasingly obsolete option of establishing a communist regime and socialist system in the whole of Germany. Secondly, the quadripartite administration of Germany was on the verge of collapse. A third possibility, a neutralized, unified German state, still had much to commend it in 1948 but this solution entailed the abandonment of a Soviet-type system in the Soviet zone and the risk of a Germany with a stronger orientation toward the West. Yet the solution which was becoming increasingly likely, that is, a Germany divided into two separate states, also had serious disadvantages: the loss of Soviet interests in the economic exploitation of the Western zones; the resilience of German nationalism; and the problem of the viability of the Soviet zone. The uncertainties surrounding the fundamental objectives of Soviet policy during the first Berlin crisis may therefore be accounted for by Soviet hesitancy between a neutral and a divided Germany and its apparent lack of a clear conception as to how to resolve the German problem (Adomeit, 1982, pp. 121–33). Finally, it should be noted that Western perceptions of the aggressive side of Soviet behaviour in the Berlin crisis hastened the final establishment of a West German state. A constitution—the Basic Law—came into force in May 1949, the first elections for the Federal Parliament took place on 14 August, and a government was constituted in the following month.

The groundwork for the possible formation of a separate East German state had already been laid by the People's Congress Movement created in late 1947. The People's Congress, which numbered about 2,000 representatives, included 464 West German members. The movement performed a dual role: it professed commitment to national unity but in the event of the failure of its all-German aspirations it was expected to create the institutional framework for an East German state. Thus not only did the movement maintain the appearance of keeping options open, but it could be utilized in any attempt to absolve the Soviet Union and the SED from responsibility for the division of Germany.

The key decisions were taken at the Third Congress in May 1949. In the elections to this body, voters were asked whether they were in favour of German unity and a just German peace treaty. A vote in favour was interpreted as a vote for the single-list of bloc candidates. People could only vote 'yes' or 'no'. From the authorities' viewpoint a relatively disappointing 66.1 per cent voted in favour. The 2,016 delegates, including 616 from West Germany, then elected a People's Council of 330 members, which agreed upon a draft constitution for the German Democratic Republic on 30 May 1949. The People's Council proclaimed the foundation of the GDR on 7 October. It set itself up as a provisional People's Chamber (*Volkskammer*) and approved the constitution. Otto Grotewohl was entrusted with the formation of a government and Wilhelm Pieck was elected provisional President of the new republic. Elections of delegates to the People's Chamber were finally held in 1950. The device of a single-list of candidates was utilized once more and the allocation of seats was determined in advance (Staritz, 1984, pp. 165–9; Krisch, 1985, pp. 9–10).

The History of the Present Regime

The Construction of Socialism and Recurrent Crises, 1949–61

Although greeted by Stalin as a turning-point in the history of Europe, the young republic's survival prospects were unpropitious: it did not enjoy full sovereign rights; the Federal Republic was a powerful counterattraction for East Germans; and only the Soviet Union, the People's Democracies of Eastern Europe, China and North Korea entered into diplomatic relations with the new state in 1949. Furthermore, it had been severed from its natural hinterland, onerous reparations had been rendered to the Soviet Union, and the emphasis on the development of heavy industry hit the consumer hard. Numerous citizens decided to try their luck in the West: 129,245 in 1949 and 197,788 in 1950 (Zimmermann, 1985, p. 419). What is more, the all-German policy goals of the SED appeared, at least outwardly, to envisage the ultimate withering away of the GDR as a separate state. Wilhelm Pieck had registered with satisfaction 'the fact that the struggle of the national front of all Germans for German unity and a just peace treaty has entered a new phase with the foundation of the German Democratic Republic' (quoted in Steele, 1977, p. 71). And Stalin's congratulatory telegram had described the newly created state as the 'foundation-stone for a united, democratic and peace-loving Germany' (quoted in Staritz, 1985, p. 66).

The famous Stalin note of 10 March 1952 also raised the possibility of the dismantling of the GDR. In his note to the three Western powers, Stalin proposed negotiations on German reunification and the signing of a peace treaty with an all-German government. Free elections would be permitted and a neutral Germany would be allowed armed forces in relation to her defence requirements. Stalin's initiative was obviously designed to forestall the rearmament of the Federal Republic and its entry into the European Defence Community then under discussion. But as Stalin's note was not pursued by the Western powers, the sincerity of the offer to negotiate was not put to the test. Whatever the intentions of Stalin, the episode does at least indicate that he was not averse to consideration of measures which amounted to a termination of SED rule if it was compatible with the Soviet Union's military and security interests (Staritz, 1985, pp. 70–3; Moreton, 1978, pp. 14–16; Weber, 1985, pp. 224–6). The SED as well as the GDR still appeared expendable.

However, the decision at the SED Party Conference in July 1952 to proceed with the construction of socialism, thereby reinforcing the divergence in social development of the two republics, reduced the likelihood of eventual reunification. The foundations of the socialist order were laid by the socialization of small and medium-sized industrial enterprises, the start of collectivation in agriculture and crafts, and the replacement of the old provincial administration (*Länder*) by new regional units (*Bezirke*). The churches came under greater pressure. The struggle reached a climax in the spring: about fifty ministers, deacons and lay-helpers were arrested and about 300 pupils who belonged to the *Junge Gemeinde* were expelled from school. This attack by the SED on the old order and the party's open commitment to the construction of a Soviet-type socialism was a risky experiment in view of the open border in Berlin and the counterattraction of the Federal Republic, even though a five-kilometre-wide prohibited area between the two states had been created in May 1952.

The June Uprising, 1953

The regime's ambitious goals imposed a heavy strain on extremely scarce resources. In order to achieve savings elsewhere, the industrial ministries were forbidden to increase salaries and wages in excess of plan targets and in the spring of 1953 higher prices were introduced for a variety of foodstuffs and clothes. Dissatisfaction was rife. The churches protested against the arbitrary treatment of Christians. From the late autumn of 1952, symptoms of worker unrest and opposition manifested themselves in the factories and on the construction sites (Staritz, 1985, pp. 79–81; Fricke, in Spittmann & Fricke, 1982, p. 7). Surveys of the mood of the population initiated by the SED revealed 'a general indifference to the work of the SED, open hostility among the workers toward the measures taken by the party, the government and the mass organizations and hopelessness and apathy among the functionaries of the factory and district branches' (Lippman, 1973, p. 153). Emigration to the West rose rapidly from about 22,000 in December 1952 to over 58,000 in March 1953, the highest monthly rate until the final closing of the frontier in 1961.

The internal crisis was compounded by the death of Stalin in March 1953. The new Soviet leadership rejected, in April, the GDR request for financial and material assistance and demanded the revision of the SED's hard line. The SED Central Committee's countermove was the announcement on 14 May of an increase in work norms by at least 10 per cent, without a corresponding raise in pay, in order to alleviate the country's pressing economic difficulties. Although the new work norms were still set at a relatively low level, they encountered fierce opposition as the overfulfilment of norms enabled workers to supplement their wages by work performance bonuses which were a vital contribution to coping with the high cost of living (Staritz, 1985, pp. 82, 84; Fricke, in Fricke & Spittmann, 1982, p. 9; Zentralkomitee, 1954, pp. 411–12). In spite of the internal and external pressures, the Council of Ministers, on 28 May, not only confirmed the Central Committee decision, but also announced a reassessment of all norms in the near future.

It was only a virtual diktat from Moscow, conveyed by Vladimir Semyonov, the Soviet High Commissioner, which finally pushed the Politburo into making concessions. The New Course was announced in the party newspaper *Neues Deutschland* on 11 June. The Politburo now confessed that mistakes had been committed by the SED and the government. The errors included the placing of abandoned farms under trusteeship, the emergency measures for the collection of taxes, and the neglect of the interests of sections of the population such as farmers, independent tradesmen, craftsmen and intelligentsia. For these and other reasons the Politburo decided to withdraw the price increases of April and to restore the intelligentsia's ration cards. It promised that people who had fled the GDR would not be disadvantaged if they returned to the republic and that young Christians would not suffer discrimination at school or university. Finally, assurances were given of a shift of emphasis from heavy industry to the needs of the workers, farmers, the intelligentsia, craftsmen and other members of the middle class (Zentralkomitee, 1954, pp. 428–31). The work norms of the industrial workers were not rescinded, however; this was undoubtedly a serious error in view of the disaffection in industry and construction. On 16 June, a demonstration against the work norms by construction workers on the prestigious Stalinallee building project in East Berlin triggered off strikes and demonstrations elsewhere in the republic on the following day. State and party functionaries were taken aback. Their reaction is described by Heinz Brandt, then Secretary for Agitation and Propaganda on the SED regional staff in East Berlin:

> The party and state officials were caught unawares and progressively paralysed. Something incomprehensible was taking place before their eyes: the workers were rising in revolt against the 'Workers and Peasants State'. Victims of their own mass deception, they had taken the fiction for reality. [Brandt, 1970, p. 208]

Apart from East Berlin, the centres of the uprising were the industrial areas of the GDR: Bitterfeld, Dresden, Halle, Merseburg, Leipzig, Magdeburg and Gera. GDR sources estimate that strikes occurred in 272 towns affecting about 300,000 workers, that is, 5.5 per cent of the total labour force. Western estimates are slightly higher: 274 towns, 370,000 workers and 6.8 per cent of the workforce (Baring, 1972, p. 52). The vast majority of the middle class and the intelligentsia, the main beneficiaries of the New Course, abstained; the uprising was essentially the revolt of the industrial workers.

The demands of the demonstrators, though mainly concerned with increases in wages and the lowering of the work norms, extended to calls for the release of political prisoners, the dismissal of Ulbricht ('The Goatee must go!'), free and secret elections and no victimization of the strikers. The GDR government calculated that twenty-one civilians and four policemen were killed, and that 187 civilians and 191 members of the security force were injured during the uprising. West German sources estimate that 1,386 demonstrators were sentenced to long-term imprisonment (Fricke, in Spittman & Fricke, 1982, p. 15; Zimmermann, 1985, p. 695).

The imposition of martial law and the introduction of Soviet tank patrols on 17 June soon quelled the disorders on the streets. However, in his authoritative study, Arnulf Baring contends that the rising had lost its momentum even before the deployment of Soviet troops: the demonstrators lacked decisive leadership; liaison between the various strike centres was inadequate; and Western forces failed to assist the insurgents (Baring, 1972, pp. 76–8). Despite the collapse of the revolt on the streets, it is now known that the struggle continued within the factories for several weeks. For example, strikes and protests were organized against the imprisonment of colleagues involved in the uprising. Demands were made for improvements in working conditions, work organization and housing. And strong protests were levelled at the lack of democracy at the workplace and the arbitrary methods of trade union officials. Two West German researchers, Ewers and Quest, claim that more workers were involved in these forms of resistance than in the mass unrest on 16 and 17 June (in Spitmann & Fricke, 1982, pp. 36–42).

Although many participants in the uprising were brought to trial, the authorities were careful to appease the workers by granting them a number of concessions. The work norms had been rescinded on 16 June; subsequently, minimum wages and pensions were increased and more dwellings were promised. In the interest of the consumer the SED reduced the price of staple foodstuffs and sought to increase the production of consumer goods at the expense of investment in heavy industry (Zentralkomitee, 1954, pp. 443, 458–9; Fricke, in Spittmann & Fricke, 1982, p. 17).

While the industrial workers had been in open revolt, the reviled General Secretary had been fighting for his political life behind closed doors. Ulbricht, not wishing to abandon 'the construction of socialism', had originally defied the Soviet leaders' demands in April and May for a relaxation of the SED's hard line; and he had complied with the New Course only with great reluctance. The most vigorous advocate of the implementation of the New Course appears to have been the Soviet Minister of the Interior, Beria, who had the support within the SED Politburo of the editor of *Neues Deutschland*, Herrnstadt, and the Minister of State Security, Zaisser. Although the precise details of their programme were not divulged, Herrnstadt and Zaisser seem to have favoured a slackening of the pace of the construction of socialism, greater concessions to the middle class and a reform of the 'degenerated' SED apparat. Herrnstadt, it was planned, should replace Ulbricht as General Secretary and Zaisser take over as Minister of the Interior. Within the Politburo they may have been able to count on the support of Ackermann, Rau and Eli Schmidt. Ulbricht had the backing of Matern and, after some hesitation, Honecker (Staritz, 1985, pp. 82–3; Stern, 1965, pp. 142–3).

The June uprising saved Ulbricht, whose dismissal, ironically, was high on the workers' list of demands. The Soviet leadership, however, preferred not to lose face by bowing to popular demand and opted to ride out the storm with the experienced General Secretary rather than risk exacerbating the situation by appointing a new leaadership group. Ulbricht was obliged to accept the New Course and to confess to the Central Committee: 'I would like to say openly before the highest forum of the Party that among Party leaders I bear the greatest responsibility for . . . the errors that have been committed' (quoted in Stern, 1965, p. 150). Another vital factor in Ulbricht's survival was the fall of Beria. He was arrested on 9 July 1953 and sentenced to death in December. One of the accusations levelled against Beria was his willingness to sacrifice the GDR for a reunited, neutral Germany with a Western orientation. However, the evidence that he and Malenkov were prepared to do a deal with the West is highly circumstantial (Brandt, 1970, pp. 187–9, 197; Wettig, in Spittman & Fricke, 1982, pp. 62–6). Ulbricht reasserted himself: Herrnstadt and Zaisser were ejected from their positions in the SED leadership in July 1953, and expelled from the party in January 1954.

Once it had recovered from the initial shock, the SED devised its own interpretation of the events. Major responsibility for the uprising and the violence was assigned to fascist *agents provacateurs* and to the roll-back policy of the Western powers. The plans of Eisenhower and Dulles to 'free' the peoples of Eastern Europe, it was claimed, had the support in the Federal Republic of politicians such as Chancellor Adenauer and the Minister of All-German Affairs and the former Chairman of the CDU in the Soviet zone, Jakob Kaiser. The Advisory Council on Questions Relating to the Unification of Germany was held to be directly responsible for working out plans for the restoration of capitalism in the GDR, a policy which had the backing of many West German businessmen. The official legend claims, on the flimsiest of evidence, that plans were laid for a counter-revolutionary coup which would take place on D-Day. On that day—17 June—armed fascist bands from the West sought to manufacture a general strike, incite the workers and overthrow the GDR government by force (Zentralkomitee, 1954, pp. 451–3; Heitzer, 1981, p. 96).

It is undeniable that many West Berliners joined in the demonstrations in East Berlin and that West German organizations were engaged in undercover activities in the GDR. In addition, RIAS, the American radio station in the American sector, contributed to the spread of the strikes by disseminating news of the events. However, the fundamental determinant of the uprising was not Western machinations, but the essentially spontaneous reaction of the industrial workers to the policies of the SED leadership, whose own internal divisions had paralysed the apparatus of rule. In fact, in their initial response to the uprising, that is before they had had time to concoct the legend of D-Day, the SED leaders had admitted their responsibility. The Fourteenth Central Committee meeting on 21 June 1953 had declared: 'If the masses of workers do not understand the party, then the party is guilty, not the workers'. And three days later, Otto Grotewohl confessed: 'We are guilty of the conditions which had led up to it' (both quotations appear in Spittmann, 1984, p. 204).

GDR historians now concede that the SED and the government did commit mistakes which led to dissatisfaction among the workers: the neglect of the consumer goods industry in favour of heavy industry provoked discontent among employees as it adversely affected their standard of living (Heitzer, 1981, p. 97; Autorenkollektiv Badstübner, 1981, p. 157). The introduction of higher work norms is admitted as another major error: by disturbing the SED's relations with the working class it was easier for the enemy to sow confusion and to launch its counter-revolutionary coup (*Geschichte der SED*, 1978, p. 293). While this modified version of the legend of a fascist coup still seriously underplays the depth of worker disaffection, the fact that workers' demands focused on economic conditions and work organization, not on questions of socialization and reprivatization, suggests, according to one West German authority, that the reforms of the legal and educational system, the redistribution of land (though not the collectivization measures), and the greater opportunities for women commanded widespread support among the industrial workforce (Spittmann, 1984, pp. 220–1). The intelligentsia and the middle classes, who had mainly stood on the sidelines in 1953, entered the fray in the wake of Khrushchev's denunciation of Stalin at the Twentieth Congress of the Communist Party of the Soviet Union in February 1956.

De-Stalinization and Revisionism

The animated debates on the reform of the economic and political system of the GDR in the aftermath of Khrushchev's attack on Stalin were anticipated, though in muted form, by the discussions following the pronouncement of the New Course in 1953: the censorship of the arts was attacked by prominent figures such as Bertolt

Brecht; and economists criticized the overcentralization of the economy. However, the decisive impetus for fundamental and widespread debates on reform was provided by Khrushchev's denunciation of the personality cult and the terroristic methods of the dead Soviet dictator. Ulbricht, who had once lauded Stalin as 'one of the greatest living theoreticians of scientific socialism' (Stern, 1965, p. 154), reluctantly joined in the polemics, asserting that the personality cult had stifled creative thinking and initiative. On the other hand, the SED leader had no intention of unleashing open and widespread discussions on the democratization of the party, changes in the rigidity of economic planning and the liberalization of intellectual life. By denying that Stalinism had existed in the GDR, he sought, in vain, to stem the tide of revisionism both within and outside the party hierarchy.

The overcentralization of the economy was a regular target of critical economists. Fritz Behrens denounced as Prussian and non-socialist the idea 'that the state can do everything and that every little concern, even the most private one, must be controlled and directed by the state ...' (quoted in Steele, 1977, p. 108). His colleague, Arne Benary, argued that socialism required workers' self-management of industry; Gunter Kohlmey proposed a more flexible price system; and Kurt Vieweg advocated the gradual collectivization of agriculture on sound economic principles. Eminent historians and philosophers, notably Kuczysnki, Streisand, Bloch and Harich, expressed revisionist ideas, too.

Wolfgang Harich and his group of supporters, among them Heinz Zöger and Manfred Hertwig, emerged as the most important representatives of the anti-Stalinist opposition. The Harich group, influenced by revisionist ideas then circulating in Hungary and Poland, devised a reform programme deliberately intended to provoke a critical discussion in the GDR. It aspired to abolish the state security system, to restore freedom of thought, to terminate the forced collectivization of agriculture, and to replace the dominance of the party bureaucracy by a democratic, socialist party organization. The programme was anathema to many members of the SED apparat. In March 1957, Harich was sentenced to ten years' imprisonment; he was accused of establishing a conspiratorial group which aimed to subvert the socialist order by threat or force. Several colleagues also received heavy sentences. The trial of the Harich group signified the end of the intellectual thaw and the onset, in autumn 1957, of a vigorous campaign against revisionists, including some members of the Politburo and Central Committee.

The chief advocates of de-Stalinization in the highest organs of the SED and the government were Karl Schirdewann, a member of the Politburo and the secretary of the cadre division of the Central Committee; Ernst Wollweber, the Minister of State Security; and Gerhart Ziller, the Central Committee Secretary for economic affairs. They wanted to slow down the pace of socialist construction, to liberalize political conditions by restricting the power of the Security Service and the party organizations, and to improve relations between the two German republics. Among their sympathizers were Fred Oelssner, a Politburo member, and Fritz Selbmann, the deputy chairman of the Council of Ministers, both of whom were highly critical of Ulbricht's economic policy. Criticism of the economic and political system also circulated among functionaries in the SED's regional and district organizations in Dresden, East Berlin, Gera, Halle, Potsdam and elsewhere (Lippmann, 1973, pp. 176–9; Brandt, 1970, pp. 292–3).

Ulbricht's position as party leader was once more under threat. There are indications that Khrushchev favoured Schirdewann's promotion to First Secretary on condition that Ulbricht's ouster did not precipitate a crisis in the GDR (Brandt, 1970, p. 292). Events outside the GDR, in particular the Hungarian uprising in October–November 1956, decided the fate of Schirdewann, the 'German Gomulka'. Khrushchev, now more wary of the consequences of the liberalization process in the Soviet bloc, did not wish to risk destabilizing the GDR; Ulbricht was therefore able to launch a counteroffensive. At the Central Committee session of February 1958, Schirdewann and Wollweber were expelled from the Central Committee and Oelssner from the Politburo. Ziller committed suicide in December. Between March and June 1958, opposition functionaries were removed by new elections, and approximately one-third of the full-time functionaries of the regional party executives were replaced (Weber, 1985, pp. 292–5; Staritz, 1985, pp. 116–18; Brandt, 1970, p. 293). Ulbricht owed his survival to the Soviet Union's fear of the unrest in Hungary and Poland spreading to the GDR and to the opposition's failure to mobilize widespread support for their proposals. The industrial workers remained relatively quiescent, a consequence of the harsh punishment meted out to the leaders of the 1953 uprising, but also of the SED leadership's more adroit policy in the next crisis: in June 1956, prices were lowered for industrial consumer goods and the workers were promised greater participation rights through the establishment of workers' committees.

The Second Berlin Crisis, 1958–61

When Ulbricht addressed the Fifth SED Congress in July 1958 he had cause for satisfaction. His position as party supremo had been secured. The intellectual opposition had been contained and the 'faction' of Schirdewann and Wollweber, like that of Herrnstadt and Zaisser five years earlier, had failed to unseat the conservative members of the party and government elite. Although outside events had favoured Ulbricht, his survival owed much to his own skills. His careful attention to detail and to cadre policy had enabled him to retain control of the party bureaucracy. He had also shown coolness and firmness of purpose in steering a difficult course between his revisionist critics and the fluctuations in the Soviet leadership's de-Stalinization policy. When Wilhelm Pieck, the President of the republic, died in September 1960, Ulbricht, as Chairman of the recently created Council of State, became *de facto* head of state.

Signs of internal consolidation in the late 1950s were another comfort for Ulbricht. Emigration was falling: the 143,917 *émigrés* in 1959 represented the lowest annual figure since 1949. Even among the groups leaving for the West by no means all refugees rejected the GDR's social order. West German in-depth interviews of young workers from the GDR revealed that only 42 per cent supported the reprivatization of public enterprises (Staritz, 1985, pp. 122–3).

Industrial production was rising: growth rates of 12 per cent were registered in the first half of 1958 and in 1959. Although the Five Year Economic Plan had to be terminated prematurely in 1959, its replacement, the Seven Year Plan for the period 1959–65, aimed to overcome the existing economic problems and to establish the basis for the final transition from capitalism to socialism. Not only would socialism be achieved, but the First Secretary, unwisely, set a highly ambitious target as the main economic task: the working people's per capita consumption of all foodstuffs and consumer goods would overtake that of the whole West German population by 1961. This would, it was contended, demonstrate the superiority of the socialist system.

The completion of the transition to socialism in the countryside received top priority. In the twelve months from the end of December 1957 the area of agricultural land belonging to collective LPGs (agricultural producers' cooperatives) rose from 25.2 per cent to 37 per cent. The process was accelerated in 1960: the proportion of agricultural land farmed by the LPGs increased from 45.1 per cent at the beginning of the year to 84.2 per cent by the close. The craft sector, too, was affected by the socialization process: the number of production cooperatives doubled between 1958 and 1960; and whereas 93 per cent of the total output of the craft sector was in private hands in 1958, it had fallen to 65 per cent by 1961.

The collectivization campaign in the countryside was spearheaded by brigades sent by the SED to persuade private farmers to join LPGs. GDR sources admit that doubts and reservations were widespread, notably among farmers with large and medium-sized holdings (Heitzer, 1981, p. 119; Autorenkollektiv Badstübner, 1981, pp. 211–12). The evidence advanced by Western historians that threats, bribery, blackmail and coercion had to be applied and that some farmers were imprisoned in November and December 1959 is rejected by GDR historians as part of an attempt to create a 'legend' of a forced collectivization (Prokop, 1986, p. 204). GDR historians prefer to emphasize what they regard as the positive aspects: the socio-economic preconditions of the restoration of capitalism in the countryside had been abolished and the basis had been laid for the gradual elimination of the fundamental differences between town and country. It is undeniable, however, that the confusion and disruption caused agricultural productivity to plummet and induced many farmers to leave for the West: about 15,000 emigrated in 1960 (Staritz, 1985, p. 135). This outflow heralded a new and serious test for the GDR in the second Berlin crisis of 1958–61.

The Berlin Wall

In the years immediately preceding the new Berlin crisis the GDR's standing within the Soviet bloc had undergone a significant improvement. After the failure of the Foreign Ministers' Conference in 1954 to find a solution to the problem of German reunification, the Soviet Union, in its note of 25 March, granted the GDR rights of sovereignty over its internal and external affairs. The inclusion of the FRG in NATO and the granting of sovereignty in May 1955 were soon followed, in September, by the Soviet Union's affirmation by treaty of the GDR's sovereignty and the assumption of full diplomatic relations between the two states. The GDR was one of the founder members of the Warsaw Pact (May 1955), although its formal entry did not take place until January 1956. The integration of the GDR into the Soviet bloc indicated the Soviet leadership's recognition of the division of Germany. Khrushchev's unveiling of his two-states' theory at a mass meeting in East Berlin in July 1955 underlined the Kremlin's new policy. German reunification, Khrushchev assured his audience, would not take place to the detriment of the socialist achievements of the GDR (quoted in Deuerlein, 1971, p. 168).

Nevertheless, the improvement in the GDR's international position was still a highly qualified one: the Federal Republic refused to accept the GDR as a sovereign state and devised the Hallstein Doctrine, whereby Bonn sought, with considerable success, to confine its socialist neighbour to diplomatic purdah, with the exception of the Soviet bloc and a few Third World states. The West German government refused to enter into diplomatic relations with any state, except the USSR, which recognized the GDR. Furthermore, even the Soviets were not prepared unreservedly to support the GDR's position that Berlin as a whole lay under GDR sovereignty. West Berlin was perceived by the GDR as a front-line city in the Cold War, an offence to its sovereignty and as a powerful cultural magnet for its citizens.

In November 1958, Berlin became the centre of another major international crisis when Khrushchev delivered his famous ultimatum to the Western allies: West Berlin should become a free, demilitarized city, possibly under the auspices of the United Nations, and any powers requiring access to the city would have to negotiate with the GDR. If the Western powers failed to comply with this demand within six months the USSR would carry out the planned measures by means of an agreement with the GDR. In February 1959, the Soviet Union widened the issue: if a peace treaty were not finally concluded with the two German states, the Soviet Union would sign a separate peace treaty with the GDR.

What were Khrushchev's objectives? The Soviet leader, emboldened by his country's impressive technological achievements, notably the Sputnik, was taking a calculated risk. By putting pressure on the presence of the Western allies in their West Berlin outpost, he was hoping to secure Western recognition of the existence of the GDR. Secondly, the neutral status of West Berlin, if it could be achieved, would remove a centre of subversive activity against Eastern Europe. Finally, Khrushchev may have envisaged Berlin as a lever for forestalling NATO plans to deploy nuclear missiles in the FRG (Adomeit, 1982, pp. 183–94; Moreton, 1978, p. 25; McAdams, 1985, pp. 17–21). The GDR leaders, though well pleased with the Soviet line, may have been disturbed by one aspect of the strategy: the Soviets still did not support the GDR's claims to full sovereignty over the whole city. Ulbricht must have been further disappointed when Khrushchev failed to implement his ultimatum. The Berlin question continued to smoulder for the next two years, however.

Khrushchev resumed the initiative in June 1961 by reiterating the Soviet Union's intention to sign a separate peace treaty with the GDR unless agreement was reached by the end of the year on West Berlin and a German peace treaty. However, the bargaining power of the Soviet Union was weaker than in 1958–9 as the GDR's internal situation was deteriorating rapidly. The nature of the social and economic crisis is well depicted by Hannes Adomeit:

> Inadequate labour supply, shortage of capital in industry and agriculture, high growth rates for heavy industry at the expense of consumption, collectivization, and bad harvests—all of these factors interacted forcefully, reducing supplies to the population of necessary foodstuffs, swelling the stream of people moving west, exacerbating the labour shortages still further and completing a vicious circle which, somehow, had to be broken. [1982, p. 235]

Twenty years later, Erich Honecker, who was encharged with the preparation and implementation of the closure of the border, presented, in his autobiography, the SED's interpretation of the crisis:

> Could we afford to look on passively while the open border was exploited to bleed our republic to death by means of an unprecedented economic war? Could we afford to remain inactive when a situation had arisen in the heart of Europe which with its hardly hidden mobilisations and intensified war hysteria on the Western side resembled that of the eve of the Second World War? Could we afford to twiddle our thumbs while Berlin–West was built up into a 'bridgehead' of the Cold War and exercised its 'nuisance function' more and more uninhibitedly? [Honecker, 1981, p. 209]

The refugee figures represented the most dramatic aspect of the crisis: 199,188 in 1960 and 155,402 between 1 January and 13 August 1961. Younger people, skilled industrial workers and members of the intelligentsia comprised a disproportionately high number of *émigrés*. GDR historians stress the role in the growing crisis played by the West German government's interruption of inter-German trade in the autumn of 1960. Although the action was called off in December, problems had arisen for the GDR economy which relied on vital supplies from the Federal Republic. The efforts to make the economy less dependent on the FRG (*Störfreimachung*) led to a stagnation of investments as well as a fall in the rate of increase in labour productivity and industrial development from 1960 to 1962 (Prokop, 1986, pp. 76–8, 145, 297–8). However, the impact of the GDR's policy on economic relations with the Federal Republic should not be exaggerated: Western data indicate that inter-German trade for the whole of 1961 (872.9 million units of account) totalled only about 86 million units less than in 1960 (Adomeit, 1982, p. 236). This is not to deny, of course, that the GDR suffered economically from the loss of trained workers and the cost of replacing them. The official history of the SED estimates that over 16 billion Marks had to be invested in higher and technical education and vocational training to replace the *émigrés* (*Geschichte der SED*, 1978, p. 424. However, the shortage of labour meant that not all the gaps could be filled). Emergency measures were required. On 13 August 1961, barbed–wire fencing and wooden barriers severed the sectoral border between East and West Berlin. The prefabricated concrete blocks followed soon afterwards. The final decision to erect a barrier was taken at a Warsaw Pact meeting from 3 to 5 August 1961. Ulbricht had probably urged this course of action at an earlier conclave in Moscow in late March 1961, but had been opposed by Khrushchev, Kadar and Gheorgiu-Dej (Adomeit, 1982, pp. 206–7, 273; Rühle, in Rühle & Holzweißig, 1981, p. 15). However, the vulnerability of the GDR required a drastic solution, despite the massive loss of prestige and the risk, though limited, of a Western military riposte and popular unrest. The Western powers, though denouncing the violation of the four-power status of Berlin, took no forcible counteraction for, as President Kennedy informed his appointments secretary Kenneth O'Donnell: 'It's not a very nice solution . . . but a hell of a lot better than a war' (quoted in Gelb, 1986, p. 201).

For its part, the GDR has attempted, unconvincingly, to justify the Wall as a security measure against the strategy of West German imperialism 'to annex the GDR by means of a "frontal attack"' (Heitzer, 1981, p. 127). A second argument, which has the benefit of hindsight, is that by securing the GDR's borders and by curtailing West Berlin's role as a front-line city, the protective measures afforded new opportunities for *détente* and peaceful coexistence (Autorenkollektiv Bad-stübner, 1981, pp. 228–9). Finally, the GDR historian Siegfried Prokop has argued that better objective conditions had been created for combating and repulsing the economic war pursued by imperialism during the era of the open border (1986, p. 146).

In private, the Soviet and GDR leaders adopted a less positive tone. Ulbricht is said to have expressed regret at having suffered such a resounding propaganda blow (Ardagh, 1987, pp. 324–5). And Khrushchev acknowledged, according to Hans Kroll, the West German Ambassador in Moscow, that the Wall was an 'ugly' thing but necessary for preventing the collapse of the East German economy (Rühle, in Rühle & Holzweißig, 1981, pp. 16–17). The then Governing Mayor of West Berlin Willy Brandt concurred, calling the Wall 'loathsome'; but he later acknowledged that, cosmetic inanities such as the 'Peace Wall' aside,

> The Russians may have regarded the Wall as a rearguard position from which to defend the GDR and an important item of Soviet property—in other words, a brutally extorted chance to consolidate the East German communist state, which had to be safeguarded against the loss of its major capital: large numbers of able-bodied workers. [Brandt, 1978, p. 24]

It was, of course, Ulbricht's responsibility to convince a highly sceptical population of the legitimacy of the GDR and of the SED's brand of socialism behind what Honecker has called 'the antifascist defence wall' (1981, p. 212).

Consolidation and Rapprochement, 1961–71

In the months immediately after the construction of the Wall many potential and actual opponents, who could no longer leave the GDR, were arrested or subjected to ideological and even physical pressure (Weber, 1985, pp. 329–31). This campaign began to lose its momentum before the end of the year. The regime preferred a *rapprochêment* with the populace which, while deeply resentful of the events of 13 August, would have to come to terms with the *fait accompli* of a closed border and, as in June 1953, with what many regarded as abandonment by the West.

Following the renewal of de-Stalinization in the Soviet Union, the SED, in late 1961, denounced the personality cult of the dictator and began to remove its outward manifestations, such as the Stalin monument in East Berlin. A significant change in the Stalinist heritage took place in the economic system. At the Sixth SED Congress in January 1963, Ulbricht unveiled the New Economic System as an integral part of the comprehensive construction of socialism. NES, the first serious attempt at economic reform in the Soviet bloc, was based on the ideas of the Soviet economist Professor Liberman and had affinities with the revisionist proposals of Behrens and Benary in the late 1950s. Ironically it now fell to Ulbricht to condemn the bureaucratization and overcentralization of the economic sytem. Instead, enterprises were to be allocated a limited degree of decision-making responsibility and profit was identified as a key economic lever (see Chapter 4). Economic experts such as Erich Apel and Günter Mittag were entrusted with the management of the new system and both entered the Politburo as candidate members in 1963. Party functionaries were required to undergo intensive retraining; technical and professional skills were upgraded; political affiliation ceased to be the decisive criterion of promotion; and science was discovered as a key productive force.

The New Economic System was accompanied by an improvement in living standards and a growth in production. Although living standards lagged behind those of the Federal Republic, between 1960 and 1970 the proportion of GDR households with a television set rose from 17 per cent to 69 per cent, those who possessed a refrigerator from 6 per cent to 56 per cent and those owning a washing machine from 6 per cent to 54 per cent. In 1970, 16 per cent of families had a car (Staritz, 1985, p. 166).

The less inflexible methods of governing and the efforts to woo the various groups in society were exemplified by the Family Code (1965), the Politburo Youth Communiqué (1963) and the Law on the Integrated Socialist System of Education (1965). Western visitors to the GDR, interviewed by INFRATEST in the late 1960s, provided information on the attitudes of GDR citizens, which were indicative of a gradual, though uneasy *rapproachment* between party and populace.

The economic achievements of the GDR, rising living standards and indications of an emerging GDR state consciousness encouraged Ulbricht, from 1967 onward, to propagate a *Modell DDR*. The GDR, it was contended, demonstrated the relevance and validity of Marxism–Leninism to a highly developed industrial society. Non-antagonistic social relations, a true human community (*Menschenge-meinschaft*) and the economic and social benefits of the scientific–technical revolution were presented by Ulbricht as the fundamental characteristics of the model. The Economic System of Socialism, a modified version of NES and unveiled at the Seventh Party Congress in 1967, envisaged that cybernetics, systems theory and computer science would improve the quality of economic planning, raise production and productivity levels, benefit the consumer and maintain the GDR's position as the leading socialist industrial power.

GDR-style socialism was officially described as the developed societal system of socialism and a relatively autonomous socio-economic formation in the transition from capitalism to communism, not a short-term transitional phase. This construct denoted Ulbricht's modification of the more sharply defined Soviet differentiation between communism and socialism. It also signified Ulbricht's growing self-confidence and his pride in the achievements of the GDR. It did not, however, entail a fundamental rejection of Soviet authority and it most certainly did not embrace the economic and political experiments in neighbouring Czechoslovakia. Anxious lest the reformist ideas of the Prague Spring disturb the still vulnerable social and political order of the GDR, the SED leadership allowed GDR troops to participate in the Warsaw Pact's suppression of the Czech reform movement in August 1968.

Satisfaction with the restoration of orthodoxy in Czechoslovakia was soon tempered by a new threat to the GDR's domestic consensus and its self-identity: the Ostpolitik of the socialist–liberal coalition government of Willy Brandt and the Soviet search for a European settlement on the post-war status quo. In his speech to the Bundestag in October 1969, Chancellor Brandt offered to respect the boundaries of 1945, to seek an accord with the GDR, to accept the plan for a Conference on Security and Cooperation in Europe, and to negotiate renunciation of force agreements with all the states of Eastern Europe. He formally announced the willingness of his government to accept the formula of two states in one German nation and with respect to Berlin he expressed his support for four-power negotiations, though not at the expense of the viability of West Berlin.

The abandonment of Bonn's traditional concept of exclusive responsibility for German interests and the promise of *de facto* recognition of the GDR, while not unwelcome to the SED leaders, gave rise to new anxieties: improvements in inter-German relations and more frequent contacts between citizens of the two states might jeopardize the GDR's stability and its claim to represent the progressive elements and traditions in German history. The enthusiastic welcome accorded Willy Brandt by Erfurters on the occasion of his meeting with Willy Stoph in their city in March 1970 could only have exacerbated SED fears.

The favourable reception of Bonn's overtures among the GDR's Eastern partners also gave cause for concern. Bonn concluded an accord with the Soviet Union in August 1970 and with Poland three months later. Four-power negotiations on Berlin commenced in May 1970. Brandt made it clear that a settlement on the Berlin issue was necessary to ensure sufficient support in the Bundestag for the ratification of the Moscow and Warsaw treaties. Ulbricht's strategy was to make acceptance of the GDR's full sovereignty a precondition for entering into formal negotiations with Bonn. From Ulbricht's point of view the question of Berlin's status and the GDR claim to the exclusive right to control the access routes to West Berlin were intimately concerned with his country's sovereignty. West Berlin should be treated as an autonomous political entity on 'GDR sufferance', not on any four-power status.

In pursuit of these fundamental goals—full recognition (*de jure*) of the GDR and acceptance of the autonomous status of West Berlin—Ulbricht was hoping for the backing of his Warsaw Pact allies. However, the Soviet Union and Poland completed negotiations on their treaties with Bonn without insisting on the prior recognition of the GDR. Ulbricht was also worried about the Soviet Union's concession in the course of the Four-Power negotiations on Berlin in 1970 that certain economic and political ties existed between West Berlin and the FRG. At the Twenty-Fourth CPSU Congress in March 1971, Brezhnev decoupled agreement on the status of Berlin from the issue of the acceptance of the GDR's full sovereign rights. Ulbricht's determined opposition to Four-Power responsibility for West Berlin and his obduracy on the transit routes threatened not only a speedy settlement to the negotiations on Berlin but, because of Bonn's coupling of a Berlin agreement with the ratification of the Moscow and Warsaw treaties and the calling of a European Security Conference, also jeopardized Brezhnev's policy on *détente*. When, on 3 May 1971, Ulbricht announced his retirement as First Secretary of the SED, most observers assumed that the Soviet Union had been instrumental in his removal.

For all the GDR's considerable strides, both economically and socially, as well as its internal political consolidation, Ulbricht's ouster underlined his country's junior status in its alliance with the Soviet Union. Ulbricht's stubborn insistence on what he regarded as the GDR's vital interests clashed with the broader interests of the Soviet Union as a global power. A GDR veto over Soviet approaches to the West could not be countenanced by the Soviet leadership. Not only did the enforced resignation of Ulbricht therefore remove an awkward obstacle to the realization of Moscow's goals, but it also relieved Brezhnev and his colleagues of the irritation of Ulbricht's lectures on the virtues of his socialist GDR model. Yet there is reason to believe that the decision to remove Ulbricht was not imposed on an unwilling SED Politburo. Growing irritation with Ulbricht's personal rule, his obduracy on the Berlin issue and his technocratic conception of socialism may have convinced key SED leaders such as Honecker and Verner of the need for his removal (see Moreton, 1978, pp. 182-7).

The worsening economic situation in 1970 may also have been instrumental in the replacement of Ulbricht by his *Kronprinz*, Honecker. Ulbricht's GDR biographer refers delicately to the ageing leader's inability to summon up sufficient energy to rectify these problems (Voßke, 1983, p. 376). Although production rates had been rising appreciably in petro-chemicals, electrical engineering and agricultural machinery, many key targets had not been achieved, especially in energy output, the manufacture of finished goods and the supply industry. As a result of what Heitzer calls 'this complicated situation', difficulties emerged in consumer supply and 'acted as a brake on the activities of the working people' (1981, p. 179). In December 1970, the Central Committee finally disbanded the reform concept, with which Ulbricht had been so closely associated, and reintroduced the system of centralized planning.

The Comprehensive Building of Socialism: the Honecker Era

The new SED leader, Erich Honecker, was born in 1912 in the market town of Neunkirchen in the Saarland. The son of a politically active communist and miner, Honecker joined the KPD in 1929 and later became the secretary of the Young Communist League in the Saarland. He was eventually arrested in 1935 and sentenced in 1937 to ten years' imprisonment. His climb to the post of First Secretary was negotiated via the chairmanship of the Free German Youth Movement between 1946 and 1955, candidate membership of the Politburo in 1950 and then full membership and the post of Central Committee Secretary for security in 1958. The latter required him to play a leading role in the building of the Berlin Wall. Before his accession to power in 1971 many observers regarded him as a drab junior Ulbricht, devoid of imagination, absolutely loyal to the Soviet Union and unsympathetic to liberal trends in culture. His more positive qualities became apparent after assuming high office. More genial than the austere Ulbricht, he is able to set people at ease. His political style, except when indulging in party gobbledegook, is less bombastic, more down-to-earth than that of his predecessor. During the 1980s, he has emerged as a statesman of some international standing, sufficiently confident to pursue the GDR's interests at the risk of annoying his Soviet ally. With Honecker as *Landesvater*, the GDR has not only come out of the diplomatic cold, it has come of age.

The main characteristics of Honecker's first quinquennium can be summed up as: a retreat from Ulbricht's modest ideological innovation; a closer relationship with the USSR; a re-emphasis on the primacy of the SED in political life; the elaboration of a policy of demarcation (*Abgrenzung*) from the FRG; a more relaxed attitude to writers and intellectuals; the assignment of an improvement in material and cultural living standards to a central place in party policy; and the gradual tightening of Honecker's hold over the party. Ulbricht, though occupying the nominal position of chairman of the party and remaining as Chairman of the Council of State, rapidly became a non-person.

Honecker carefully consolidated his own authority within the SED. Willy Stoph, a potential rival, was demoted from Chairman of the Council of Ministers to Chairman of the Council of State on Ulbricht's death in 1973. Between 1971 and 1973, Honecker promoted into the Politburo several of his former associates in the FDJ. Whereas only minor changes were made in the Politburo membership in 1971, turnover was much greater in 1973. At the Central Committee Plenum in October 1973, several functionaries who had all held important posts in the FDJ—Werner Felfe, Joachim Herrmann, Inge Lange and Konrad Naumann—were promoted to candidate membership of the Politburo. Erich Mielke, the Minister of State Security, appointed a candidate member in 1971, and Heinz Hoffmann, the Minister of National Defence, a full member since 1973, had both known Honecker for many years. Altogether, about one-third of the members and candidates of the reconstructed Politburo of 1973 were personally linked to the new First Secretary (McCauley, 1979, pp. 185–8; Ludz, 1980, pp. 150–2). Honecker was firmly in control and talk of a duumvirate with Stoph ceased; he not only held the top party office (retitled General Secretary in 1976) but also the chairmanship of the National Defence Council (since 1971) and of the Council of State (replacing Stoph in 1976). His style of rule tends, however, to be based on establishing a consensus within the Politburo rather than enforcing his will in the autocratic manner of his former mentor.

Ulbricht's ideological formulae were abandoned soon after his replacement by Honecker. The notion of a socialist human community was rejected as invalid on the grounds that it blurred significant differences between the social classes and strata. The developed societal system of socialism was replaced by a less pretentious concept, the developed socialist society; and the interpretation of socialism as a relatively autonomous social formation was laid to rest by one of its erstwhile supporters, Kurt Hager, the party's ideological spokesman. The ideological assimilation with the Soviet Union was capped by the renewal of the Treaty of Friendship in 1975. GDR–Soviet relations remained free, at least until 1984, of the tensions of Ulbricht's later years.

Between 1971 and 1973, a series of agreements were concluded which radically changed the GDR's political environment. A Four-Power Agreement on Berlin was signed in September 1971, a transit accord between the FRG and the GDR followed in December 1971, and the first general treaty between the two German republics, the Basic Treaty, was finalized in December 1972. Both German states became members of the United Nations in September 1973. And whereas nineteen countries had recognized the GDR between 1969 and 1972, sixty-eight states did so in the year following the signing of the Basic Treaty. Diplomatic relations were established with the United States in April 1974.

The GDR could derive much satisfaction from these developments: it had finally breached the diplomatic *cordon sanitaire* which Bonn had devised; the Federal Republic was committed by the Basic Treaty to the 'inviolability of borders and respect for the territorial integrity and sovereignty of all states in Europe', presumably including the GDR; and West Berlin had been denied the status of a constituent part of the Federal Republic (McAdams, 1985, pp. 118, 124). On the other hand, the GDR had failed to sever West Berlin from the FRG, for, according to the Berlin Agreement, ties between the two might 'be maintained and developed'. And the Soviet Union, not the GDR, guaranteed the free flow of traffic between West Berlin and West Germany. Another source of annoyance was the failure of the GDR to gain full diplomatic recognition in the Basic Treaty: permanent representatives were established instead of ambassadors; and Bonn's view of the 'special' nature of relations was underscored by the insertion of a reference in the preamble to the two states' different views of the national question, that is, the survival of a single German nation. Finally, the various treaties eased contacts between West and East Germans. Whereas 2.6 million people from the FRG and West Berlin had visited the GDR and East Berlin in 1970, the figure soared to about 8 million in 1973 (Staritz, 1985, p. 210). Telephone calls from West to East rose from 1.8 million in 1971 to 11.3 million in 1976 (*Die Berlin Regelung*, 1980, p. 19). Bearing in mind that the GDR was already heavily penetrated by the Western media (most GDR citizens outside the Dresden region and parts of north-east Mecklenburg are able to watch West German television), the SED leadership decided that the GDR needed to be protected from the potentially destabilizing effect of the dramatic increase in personal contacts.

Delimitation or demarcation (*Abgrenzung*) between the two German states was invoked as the formula for meeting the new challenge. Key groups of people, including party and state functionaries and conscripts, were forbidden contact with foreign visitors. A 'visitors' book' was introduced in which the names of 'foreign' visitors had to be registered (Wettig, in von Beyme & Zimmermann, 1984, p. 284). The major ideological innovation was announced by Honecker at the 1971 Party Congress: two separate nations were developing, the socialist nation in the GDR and the capitalist nation in the FRG (Asmus, 1984b, pp. 407–9. In fact, early warnings of this shift can be traced back to Ulbricht's later years). Historians and party ideologues were mobilized to refute Bonn's thesis of the continuity of the German nation based on a feeling of belonging together and a common history. Steps were taken to remove references to the apparently offensive term 'German'. In the 1974 Constitution, the GDR was defined as a socialist state of workers and peasants, not, as in 1968, a socialist state of the German nation. The national hymn, penned by Johannes Becher while in Soviet exile in 1943, could no longer be sung as it contained the words: 'Arisen out of the ruin and headed for the future, let us serve Germany, our united fatherland' (quoted in Asmus, 1984b, p. 409).

Yet the past cannot be erased so easily by the censor's pen or party diktat. The party newspaper's title remained *Neues Deutschland* and in 1974 Honecker informed a perplexed population that in filling out forms they should write: citizenship—GDR; nationality—German. And, as we have seen, from about 1976 onward, the SED has deliberately attempted to incorporate the GDR into the whole of German history.

The national problem notwithstanding, when Honecker addressed the Ninth SED Congress in May 1976 in the gleaming new Palace of the Republic overlooking the River Spree, he could look back with considerable satisfaction on his first five years as party leader. His personal authority had been secured without any major internal disruption and the country's political fabric had withstood the shock of closer contacts with the Federal Republic. The GDR, now recognized by 121 states, could be deemed an 'important' political actor in the international arena. At the signing of the Final Act of the Helsinki Conference on Security and Cooperation in 1975, Honecker had sat between Chancellor Schmidt and President Ford. At home, produced national income had risen by 30.1 per cent between 1970 and 1975 and industrial commodity production from 172 billion Marks to 235.4 billion Marks. And the housing programme, the centrepiece of the SED's social policy, had, according to Honecker, made considerable progress toward the 'solution' of the housing question as a social problem: in the preceding five years, 400,000 new homes and 209,000 modernized dwellings had been constructed (*Protokoll*, vol. I, 1976, pp. 51, 55).

However, economic and political storm clouds were gathering. The SED's enforced expatriation of the satirical balladeer Wolf Biermann, in November 1976, aroused the ire of members of the country's cultural elite and brought to a bitter end the mild cultural thaw of the first half of the decade. The explosion in the world market price of oil and other raw materials in 1973-4 and, even more seriously for the GDR, in 1979, and the higher prices for oil and natural gas charged by the Soviet Union from 1975 onward caused a serious deterioration in the terms of trade of the GDR, a country heavily dependent on imports of raw materials. Recession in the West compounded the GDR's trade problems. Net indebtedness to the West grew at a rate of more than 20 per cent per annum (Cornelsen, 1986a, p. 3). From 1975 onward, a trade deficit was recorded with the Soviet Union, the GDR's main supplier of raw materials. In 1981, net indebtedness to the West reached as staggering $11.66 billion. Then in the wake of the failure of Poland and Romania to honour their obligations, the GDR, too, from the middle of 1982, was unable to rely on acquiring new credits from Western banks. Furthermore, the Soviet Union cut back supplies of oil from 19 million tonnes in 1981 to 17.7 million tonnes in the following year. In 1982, the year when the crisis was at its most acute, the GDR consumer was also affected by the deteriorating economic situation: retail trade turnover, which was planned to increase by 3.7 per cent during the 1981-5 planning period, grew by only 1 per cent and that of industrial consumer goods actually fell by 0.1 per cent (Cornelsen, 1985, p. 67).

By a mixture of adroit economic and political management and an element of good fortune the GDR managed to overcome the crisis by 1984. The problems were tackled by a combination of short-term and long-term measures: a more intensive export drive with the West was launched in 1982; the production of domestic raw materials and fuels, especially lignite, was stepped up; a reduction in energy consumption relative to net material production was achieved; and the structure of industry was overhauled from 1979-80 onward by substituting large combines for the Associations of Nationalized Enterprises (VVBs). A more rapid diffusion of new technologies, such as industrial robots and microelectronics, was defined as a major goal by Honecker at the 1981 Party Congress; the SED aspired to link the 'advantages of socialism' to the scientific-technical revolution. In the short term, however, the West German connection proved far more vital than new technologies in finally overcoming the immediate crisis: one major benefit derived by the GDR from the link was the provision in 1983 and 1984 of two large credits of DM1 billion and DM950 million, both backed by the West German government. It is generally acknowledged that trading relations with the West were restored to normal during 1984. By the end of that year, the Western credit markets were once more open to the GDR and the net debt to the OECD countries, excluding the FRG, stood at $5.5 billion.

Turbulence in international relations from the late 1970s imposed yet another strain on internal stability and threatened to tear apart the delicate fabric of inter-German *détente*. The NATO decision in December 1979 to deploy Pershing II and Cruise missiles in Western Europe in response to the Soviet Union's installation of medium-range nuclear missiles in the Western part of the Soviet Union was followed two weeks later by the Soviet invasion of Afghanistan; these events marked the advent of a new ice age in East–West relations. The unrest in Poland and the emergence of Solidarity in the summer of 1980 further deepened the rift between the two superpowers. Within the GDR, a grass-roots peace movement protested at the creeping militarization of life and at the danger of a nuclear holocaust. Inter-German relations were inevitably affected by the international tension. In October 1980, the GDR suddenly raised the amount of currency that Western visitors were obliged to change into GDR Marks when visiting the GDR. Within a matter of months, the number of visits from the Federal Republic fell by one-third and from West Berlin by about a half (Martin, 1986, p. 9). In his hard-hitting speech at Gera, also in October, Honecker, with one eye on the troubles in Poland, raised four demands; they included West German recognition of a separate GDR citizenship and the upgrading of the permanent representatives to the status of ambassadors, and so virtually amounted to preconditions for the continuation of good neighbourly relations.

Yet it soon transpired that both German states had too many vested interests in their mini-*détente* not to attempt a salvage operation. Bonn appreciated that the accords of the early 1970s had, by increasing telephone, postal and personal contacts, given substance to its claim regarding the survival of the German nation. For its part, the SED leadership could derive satisfaction and confidence from having coped successfully with the influx of Western visitors, and it continued to obtain many economic advantages from the *rapprochement*, even after Kohl replaced Schmidt as West German Chancellor in 1982. The relationship appeared to be cemented when Kohl, whilst attending Andropov's funeral in February 1984, invited Honecker to undertake his postponed visit to the Federal Republic.

The visit, eventually scheduled for September 1984, would have been the first by a leader of the SED to the 'other' German state and a significant personal triumph for Honecker. The subsequent history of the visit highlights the dilemmas of GDR foreign policy-makers in the 1980s as they seek to increase the GDR's room for manoeuvre and to defend its interests between the countervailing pressures exerted by their socialist comrade and their German 'sibling'. The eventual postponement of Honecker's visit, in September 1984, was justified by GDR officials on the grounds of provocation by right-wing groups within the CDU; in fact, the visit primarily fell victim to the prevailing East–West tension and Soviet pressure.

Honecker must have ultimately decided that the balance of the GDR's interests required him to accede to Soviet wishes. He had been engaged since late April–early May in an open quarrel with his Soviet ally over the GDR's continuing dialogue with the FRG. Whereas Honecker advocated peaceful coexistence between states of divergent social orders, the Soviet Union launched attacks on West German revanchism and Bonn's use of economic aid as a lever to interfere in the internal affairs of the GDR (McAdams, 1985, p. 196). From the Soviet perspective, the German island of *détente* was incongruent with the new Cold War and with the Bundestag's decision in November 1983 to proceed with the deployment of

American medium-range missiles in the FRG. Moscow's retort was the installation of missiles in the GDR and Czechoslovakia. Although Honecker made a tactical retreat by postponing his visit to West Germany, what is more significant is that his overall strategy of damage limitation remained intact and was ultimately justified by his visit to Bonn, Munich and his home town of Wiebelskirchen in September 1987. Not only was Honecker received by Chancellor Kohl and President Richard von Weizsäcker but he was accorded a guard of honour and a band played the GDR national anthem upon his arrival. The capstone had been set on Honecker's career and the GDR's international standing received an invaluable boost.

In short, while the protracted affair illustrated at one level the continuing external restraints on GDR policy-making, the SED leaders had displayed considerable adroitness and sureness in successfully defending what they conceived to be the GDR's priorities. The GDR can no longer be written off as the 'sick man' of modern Europe (McAdams, 1985, p. 198), nor as Moscow's subservient satellite. The country's international status is encapsulated in the response of a GDR official to persistent questioning by a Western journalist: 'In some places we have been seen as a tame seal who jumps through the trainer's hoop. So we are not. Is that news?' (quoted in Asmus, 1985, p. 773).

2 Social Structure

Introduction

In the course of the GDR's short history the social structure has undergone a fundamental transformation. Even before the foundation of the republic in 1949, the
'anti-fascist and democratic revolution' has swept away the *Junkers* and big landowners and large-scale enterprises had been nationalized. Despite these radical
changes, agriculture and artisan enterprises were still predominantly in private
hands at the time of the launching of the construction of socialism in 1952. Furthermore, private concerns were responsible for about 20 per cent of industrial production. The 1950s witnessed the transition to cooperative production in agriculture,
the nationalization of small and medium-sized firms and the formation of artisan
cooperatives. This transformation of the ownership of the means of production
caused widespread dissatisfaction and fuelled the mass emigration to the West.

The Berlin Wall cut off this escape route, though it did provide the necessary
socio-economic stability for the introduction of the economic reforms of the NES
and for the regime's attempt to establish a *rapprochement* with the populace. In the
late 1960s, Ulbricht devised the notion of the 'socialist human community' which
embodied the harmonious integration of the divergent interests of the social classes
and strata. Interpersonal relations were supposedly characterized by friendly cooperation, mutual help and generosity. The ethical basis for this 'new' community had
already been laid in the 'ten commandments of socialist morality' proclaimed by
Ulbricht in 1958. Furthermore, Ulbricht envisaged that the scientific–technical
revolution, comprising automatic, electronic data processing, cybernetics and so
forth, would have a positive influence on social relations. Arduous physical labour
would no longer be required, the difference between mental and physical labour
would be narrowed and work would become a more enriching experience.

Ulbricht's vision of a harmonious socialist community proved to be a chimera
and the scientific–technical revolution an ambivalent process. With the advent to
power of Erich Honecker, the harmonious socialist community construct was abandoned along with the claim that the 'developed societal system of socialism' constituted a relatively autonomous social formation in the history of the transition from
socialism to communism. Ulbricht's notion of a socialist community, the SED now
decided, had blurred the differences between the social classes and overestimated the
degree of social convergence. The new SED programme of 1976, accordingly, conceded that the convergence process and the achievement of a classless, communist
society would be protracted and complicated. And the programme was more explicit
than its 1963 forerunner in acknowledging the existence of different interests, ideas,
talents and aspirations among the populace.

The 'main task' in the moulding of a 'developed socialist society', announced by Honecker at his first party congress as SED leader and later incorporated into the party programme, was defined as 'the further enhancement of the material and cultural standards of living of the people on the basis of a high rate of development of socialist production, greater efficiency, scientific–technical progress and the growth of labour productivity' (*Programm*, 1976, p. 26).

The disappearance of the term 'scientific–technical revolution' signified a more sober evaluation of the possibilities of science, which under Ulbricht had been raised to the status of a main production force. This greater pragmatism of the Honecker era is also reflected in the slogan of the 'unity of economic and social policy' which gives higher priority to present needs than earlier slogans like 'As we work today, we shall live tomorrow'. The upgrading of social policy is a further indication of the SED's aim to strengthen the social compact with the citizenry. The party was obviously anxious to avoid the kind of disturbances which had occurred in Poland in December 1970. Key aspects of social policy will be examined later in this chapter.

However, as the 1976 party programme admitted, the development of socialism is not without contradictions and strains. The deterioration in the economic situation in the late 1970s and the early 1980s exacerbated the contradictions; after all, the 'main task' requires a rapid acceleration of production as a precondition for improvements in living and working conditions. In its search for solutions to its foreign trade difficulties and to the vexing problems of overmanning and the slow diffusion of basic research, the SED has returned, in the 1980s, to the scientific revolution. Microelectronics, robots, CAD/CAM and flexible automation are the key technologies that will enhance productivity, innovative capacity and, so it is claimed, establish the material–technical basis for communism. However, the SED is less bombastic in its pronouncements and less utopian in its aspirations than in the late 1960s. The modernization push, nevertheless, has significant implications for the social structure.

Population Trends

On the eve of the Second World War the population of the present territory of the GDR was 16,745,385. The influx of refugees from the former Eastern territories and the return of prisoners of war inflated the figure to over 19.1 million inhabitants in 1947. By the time the regime finally shut the Berlin escape-hatch the population had declined to just over 17 million. The slight but uncertain recovery between 1962 and 1967 was not maintained and the population fell in each subsequent year, reaching a nadir of 16,640,059 in 1985 (see Table 2.1).

The explanation of the long-term downward trend includes the effect of the decline in the birth-rate during the economic depression of the 1930s, the heavy loss of life during the Second World War and, subsequently, the high rate of emigration to the West and the strikingly low birth-rate in the post-war period. Exact figures for

Table 2.1 Resident population, 1939–85 ('000)

Year	Total	Men	Women
1939	16,745	8,191	8,555
1940	18,488	7,860	10,629
1947	19,102	8,263	10,838
1949	18,793	8,344	10,450
1955	17,832	7,969	9,864
1960	17,188	7,745	9,443
1961	17,079	7,704	9,374
1965	17,040	7,780	9,260
1970	17,068	7,865	9,203
1975	16,820	7,817	9,003
1980	16,740	7,857	8,883
1985	16,640	7,878	8,762

Source: *StJB*, 1986, p. 1.

emigration to the Western zones are unavailable for the period before the foundation of the two republics (it may have been 438,700), but official Western registra-
tion records show that between 1949 and 1961 2,686,942 people left the GDR.
Departure to the West was closely related to political events and socio-economic
changes. Emigration rose sharply after the announcement at the 1952 SED Party
Congress of the construction of socialism and the subsequent acceleration of the
nationalization of private business and the collectivization of agriculture. In March
1953, it reached 58,605. Rumours of the impending closure of the border were a
major factor in the decision of 47,433 people to emigrate to the West in August
1961. Since the building of the Wall about 38,000 have risked life and limb to cross
the border (Zimmermann, 1985, p. 419). In recent years the normal flow from East
to West has been in the region of between 15,000 and 18,000 per annum. In 1984,
the number increased dramatically to over 42,000 with the permission of the GDR
authorities (Pratsch & Ronge, 1985, p. 716).

Among the major determinants of the population decline are the fall in the birth-
rate and the high war-time mortality rate. In the post-war period live births per
1,000 inhabitants reached a peak of 17.6 in 1961–3 but then fell to a trough of 10.6 in
1973–4, one of the lowest birth-rates in the world. The explanation for this trend
lies in changing attitudes to the value of a large family, the increasing use of contra-
ceptives, a high rate of female employment, and the legalization of abortion in 1972.
In fact, the GDR population failed to reproduce itself throughout most of the 1970s.
In 1969, for the first time in the country's history, the mortality rate exceeded the
birth-rate. Not until 1979 was this trend reversed, partly as a result of a series of

social welfare measures such as the baby year (see below). Furthermore, the fertility rate (the number of live births per 1,000 women of childbearing age, 15–45 years), which had fallen from 88.7 in 1963 to a low of 51.9 in 1974, increased rapidly to 67.4 in 1980. The overwhelming majority of live births are first- and second-born children (51.4 per cent and 36.6 per cent respectively in 1983). The balance between first-born and second-born children is relatively equal for married women (46.0 per cent and 42.6 per cent in 1983) but an increasing number of children, especially the first-born, are born to unmarried mothers. When Honecker came to power in 1971, 35,879 children were born out of wedlock; thirteen years later the number had risen to 77,003. Children born to married mothers showed a decline during the same period: 201,327 to 152,368 (*StJB*, 1986, p. 376).

Marriage continues to be a relatively popular institution, at least judged by the number of first marriages and by the rise in the annual re-marriage rate (the number of re-marriages per 100 marriages) of divorced men from 18.7 to 22.7 between 1979 and 1984 and of divorced women from 17.7 to 21.7 over the same period (*StJB*, 1986, p. 371). However, the upward trend in the divorce rate (from 18.1 in 1971 to 30.8 per 10,000 population in 1984) confirms that marriages come under great strain in the GDR as elsewhere (*StJB*, 1986, p. 373). Finally, one new development since the early 1980s, has been the tendency for people, whether single or divorced, to marry at a slightly later age. The average age of marriage for men and women in 1985 was 27.9 and 25.2 respectively (*StJB*, 1986, p. 373).

The age and sex structure was for many decades lop-sided. Mainly as a result of the heavy male casualties suffered during the war women outnumbered men: in 1950, the proportion of women to men stood at 125 to 100. As the age group most affected by the war (25–44 age group) has been gradually superseded by younger groups, the ratio now stands at 111 to 100 (*StJB*, 1986, p. 350). A similar and much-needed improvement is discernible in the country's age structure. Whereas the dependent population (inhabitants under 15 and people of retirement age) varied from 38.7 per cent in 1960 to 42.2 per cent in 1969, by 1985 it had dropped to 35.2 per cent, still high but the lowest proportion in the history of the GDR (*StJB*, 1986, p. 348).

Although the population density, 154 people per square kilometre in 1985, is low, densities are higher in the southern urban–industrial centres such as the Karl-Marx-Stadt region (313 in 1985) than in the northern regions. The Neubrandenburg region has the lowest density: 56 inhabitants per square kilometre. The capital city, with its concentration of industry and administration, dominates the other cities: its population in 1985 was 1,215,586 and its average density 3,016 persons per square kilometre (*StJB*, 1986, p. 1).

Internal migration occurred on a large scale in the late 1940s and early 1950s: many refugees settled in the northern areas and new industrial centres were created in Eisenhüttenstadt, Hoyerswerda and Schwedt. Mobility slackened after the completion of the major projects such as the Schwarze Pumpe lignite combine at Hoyerswerda and the petro-chemical combine at Schwedt. The annual movement across district (*Kreis*) boundaries tumbled from 47 per 1,000 persons in 1953 to 17 in 1980.

Mobility tends to take place within rather than across districts, essentially from rural areas and small urban centres to medium and larger cities.

The pattern of internal migration has created certain imbalances or 'disproportions' in the territorial structure. Migration to the large and medium-sized cities has resulted in population losses in rural settlements and small towns (121,874 and 37,606 respectively between 1977 and 1979). The movement from rural areas has reached a worrying level. Population fell by 11 per cent in the countryside, whereas it increased by 1.3 per cent in the towns between 1971 and 1980. This uneven development is above all the result of emigration rather than of natural factors such as birth- and death-rates (Belwe, 1987, pp. 519–20). The rural labour force has been so diminished that GDR experts believe that farming is not conducted as efficiently as desirable. Moreover, in the small towns some industrial enterprises, especially the smaller and medium-sized units, experience a labour shortage. On the other hand, existing deficiencies in the urban social and technical infrastructure are compounded by the migration to the large cities. Schools, kindergartens, crèches, stores and so forth must be built and suitable transporation provided to enable workers in the new residential areas to reach their workplace without undue loss of time. An additional problem arises from the age structure of the migrants: between 1977 and 1979 50 per cent of migrants came from the 20–30-year-old age group and children under 10; these age groups represent about 25 per cent of the country's total population. Rural settlements suffer a disproportionately high loss of younger people aged 15–25. The departure of younger people and a high proportion of women of child-bearing age from rural areas and small towns lowers the birth-rate and produces a surplus of deaths over births (Schmidt, 1983, pp. 36–8). The achievement of a balance between gains and losses on migration from the villages and small towns will require considerable expenditure on improvements in living and working conditions. An improvement in the quality of housing will undoubtedly help in stemming the flow of population from the land. However, such measures can only be beneficial in the distant future as the extent of the previous losses has been so great (Grundmann, 1985, p. 10).

Demographic projections for the period 1985–2000 anticipate little fundamental change in the overall population structure: the size of the population will remain fairly stable; the urban districts will continue to expand and the rural districts to contract; and the sex structure will become more balanced. The population under 15 will begin to fall after 1990, in particular after 1995, but it will maintain a 19 per cent share of the total population. In contrast, the number of senior citizens will decline only beginning to rise once more from 1995 onward; the proportion of this group in the total population will stay at around 16 per cent during the entire period. The working population is expected to show a slight increase in the urban districts but decline in rural communities; it will represent about 64–65 per cent of the overall population (Speigner, in *Jahrbuch für Soziologie und Sozialpolitik*, 1985, pp. 252–3). These developments in the population structure have important implications for the availability of labour, occupational mobility, the territorial structure and the distribution of resources for education, the health service and housing.

Social Stratification and Differentiation

Official ideologists depict the GDR as a 'kind of class society', despite the virtual elimination of private property. This official view of GDR society usually refers to the simple model of two classes associated with different types of socialist property—the working class with state property and the collective farm peasantry with collective property—plus the stratum of the intelligentsia and a variety of small strata and groups. The latter embrace private craftsmen, private wholesale and retail traders, private farmers, commission dealers and self-employed professional people. This basically tripartite model is a regurgitation of the earlier Stalinist image of Soviet society. Indeed, leading GDR sociologists have taken as their starting-point the assertion of the Soviet sociologist Glezermann that

> Socialism can no longer be regarded as a class society because the main attributes of class society—its division into antagonistic classes and the exploitation of man by man—have been abolished. But it also cannot be regarded as a classless society because class distinctions have not yet disappeared. [quoted by Lötsch, in Lötsch & Meyer, 1974, p. 33]

The retention of the class-like model of society and the emphasis on the working class, the largest class, as the leading social and political force provide an ideological justification for the leadership role of the SED, the party of the working class. This leadership role is certainly one major reason why GDR authorities and sociologists have been so sensitive to 'bourgeois' claims of convergence between industrial societies, whether socialist or capitalist, and to the alleged elitist predominance of the intelligentsia. It has also meant, bearing in mind the intense rivalry with the Federal Republic, that sociologists in the GDR have usually been less receptive than their Hungarian and Polish counterparts to concepts and models of society developed and utilized in the West. Empirical research in the social sciences was for a long time severely handicapped by the guardians of the purity of Marxism–Leninism.

Other socialist countries, notably Poland and Hungary but also the Soviet Union, were quicker to deploy characterizations of their society such as social stratification in which a multiplicity of social strata cut across—without necessarily superseding— the class system. Thus in addition to a society divided into classes in relation to the means of production, sociologists trace differences emerging from the division of labour, for example, along a manual–non-manual continuum. This reflects more accurately the complexity of society than does the simplistic tripartite division; it also facilitates a more effective social planning.

Although the discipline of sociology received the SED stamp of approval in 1963–4, partly because of a growing appreciation of the potential usefulness of sociological research for the planning and development of the economy during the NES period, ideological and political obstacles hindered empirical research and the elaboration of new concepts and models. Kurt Braunreuther's work in the late 1960s on a stratification model for the social structure of the GDR did not progress beyond the preliminary stage. The harmonious conception of a socialist community of people typical of Ulbricht's last years in power was hardly conducive to such a venture. However soon after Honecker's appointment as First Secretary several sociologists began to produce more highly differentiated characterizations of their society or its subsec- tors. One example is the 'Social Structural Investigation 1973' into the working and living conditions of employees in industrial enterprises (Laatz, 1984, pp. 20–4). And more recently, sociologists have been in the forefront of the debate on the promo- tion of certain types of social differences. Both Rudi Weidig and Manfred Lötsch advocate that incentives to performance—for example, income differentials—should be promoted in order to stimulate and reward outstanding achievements. This con- forms to the SED goal, in the 1980s, to encourage the rapid diffusion of new ideas in the interest of economic growth (see below).

Workers and Salaried Employees

The working class, which according to official terminology incorporates manual workers and non-manual employees, is regarded as the leading political and social force as well as the motor behind social progress. The standard justification for its pre-eminence is that: it comprises the absolute majority of working people; it has the most direct involvement with the social ownership of the means of production and produces the bulk of society's wealth; and it is the most highly organized and most politically conscious class, drawing guidance from a Marxist–Leninist party. The size of the 'working class' is correspondingly large: 78.4 per cent of employed persons in 1955 and 89.0 per cent in 1985 (see Table 2.2).

Table 2.2 Socio-economic structure of employed persons, 1955–85, including apprentices (per cent)

	1955	1985
Working class	78.4	89.0
Collective farmers	2.3	6.8
Craftsmen in cooperatives	0.0	1.8
Commission dealers, etc.	0.0	0.3
Independants	19.3	1.7

Source: *StJB*, 1986, p. 110.

Until 1963 GDR statistics on the occupational structure were more helpful as they separated workers from non-manual salaried employees. In 1950, for example, salaried employees accounted for 21.3 per cent and workers 52.1 per cent of all working people. Since this differentiation ceased, it is difficult to obtain precise data for evaluating the rate of social mobility and social equality. Although the production workers in large enterprises are officially esteemed as the 'core' of the working class, the usual lumping together of production workers, employees in the service sector and public administration and members of the intelligentsia produces an imprecise and unsatisfactory global category. However, the intelligentsia is sometimes differentiated from the workers and employees on the basis of its members' higher qualifications and their creative and/or management activity. The 1981 national census tacitly recognized the need for a less global category than 'working class'; it differentiated between four groups: production workers, workers in other occupations, management and administrative personnel, and intellectual workers. The data have not yet been published (P. C. Ludz & U. Ludz, in Zimmermann, 1985, p. 1222).

The vast majority of workers and salaried employees are located in the socialist sector of the economy; this sector has experienced a long-term expansion as a result of the decline in the private sector (see Table 2.3). The distribution of workers and salaried employees according to economic sector reveals a stagnation since 1960 in the proportion employed in industry (43.9 per cent in 1970 and 43.1 per cent in 1984) but a steady rise in the service sector (19.7 per cent and 22.3 per cent respectively). The so-called 'core' of the working class, the production workers, has shrunk in relative terms from 72.4 per cent of all workers and salaried employees in 1955 to 62.4 per cent in 1984.

Table 2.3 Workers and salaried employees (not including apprentices) according to the nature of ownership of enterprises, 1950–85 ('000)

Year	Total	Socialist	Commission dealers or state involvement	Private
1950	5,950.5	4,440.4	—	1,510.0
1975	6,963.4	6,669.7	28.2 (447.9 in 1970)	265.5
1985	7,557.2	7,286.3	24.0	246.9

Source: StJB, 1986, p. 113.

The complex mechanization and automation of work tasks has created a situation where many production workers are reduced to performing monotonous supervisory and monitoring functions with few opportunities for creative activity. Exacting mental demands such as setting up a conventional lathe and controlling its operation are being transferred to computerized systems. Discrepancies exist, among skilled workers in particular, between their relatively high level of qualification and job demands. Plant operatives in the chemical industry, for example, are often restricted to monitoring from a central control-room key variables in an automated production process; their alertness is impaired by long periods of inactivity. Participation in the innovators' movement and the various forms of socialist competition is insufficient compensation for the degradation of human labour.

Wolfgang Schirmer, professor of physical chemistry at the Academy of Sciences of the GDR, has concluded from conditions such as these that the GDR has not yet succeeded in 'completely abolishing alienation in certain parts or forms of work tasks' (Rundtischgespräch, 1983, p. 323). This is a serious charge as socialist relations of production are supposed to eliminate alienation and antagonistic contradictions.

On the other hand, routinization and the loss of job autonomy has not been the fate of those skilled workers whom Katherina Belwe and Fred Klinger (in Spittmann-Rühle and Helwig, 1986, pp. 77–8) have dubbed 'rationalization elites'. They work closely with technicians and managers in designing new work systems and are far more removed in terms of prestige, skills and job demands from the semi- and unskilled labourers. The stratification of the occupational groups by skill, status, education and income has resulted in social scientists devising complex models which encompass social differences according to the division of labour and qualifications. The ownership–class axis has been substantially modified.

The Cooperative Farmer

The cooperative farmers constitute the second 'main class' in GDR society and about two-thirds of all useful agricultural workers. They work about 87 per cent of useful agricultural land and own about 89 per cent of livestock. The collectivization of the land was completed during the 'socialist spring in the countryside' in 1960, the most far-reaching event in the history of German agriculture. Many farmers, annoyed and shocked by the methods and nature of the collectivization programme, sought refuge in the West.

The reduction in the traditional differences between town and country is a programmatic goal of the SED, although their elimination will have to await the stage of full communism. Improvements in working and living conditions, educational opportunities and wages are integral to the drawing together of peasant and worker. In fact, the educational standard of workers in agriculture, including the cooperative farmers, has improved considerably since the early 1960s: the proportion of agricultural workers successfully completing a vocational training rose from 18.1 per cent in 1963 to about 90 per cent in 1982, about 13 per cent above the national average. Most of these workers obtain a skilled worker's certificate (83.3 per cent in 1982); 2.5 per cent have acquired a degree. The net average monthly income of LPG members increased during the 1970s to a level on a par with that of workers and salaried employees in the socialist economy: 1,066 Marks in 1982 (Zimmermann, 1985, p. 515). The question of the quality of life in the village has assumed a greater urgency in the 1980s as the SED is seeking to stem part of the migration flow from small communities into the towns. In the 1960s and 1970s, the smaller settlements, in particular those in rural rather than in industrial areas, experienced the highest population losses. Improvements in housing, leisure opportunities, working conditions, shopping facilities, transport and health care and higher wages will be required to maintain the rural population (Autorenkollektiv Krambach, 1985, pp. 78–107).

The Intelligentsia

The intelligentsia, whilst not identified as a separate group in the GDR's main statistical source, the *Statistical Yearbook*, is normally referred to as a stratum or intermediate stratum. This group usually encompasses all those who have acquired a college or university degree and whose job is predominantly intellectual: natural and social scientists, engineers, teachers, physicians, artists and writers. The intelligentsia represents the most rapidly expanding social group: whereas only 5.8 per cent of working people (362,500) possessed a college or university degree in 1961, 13.7 per cent (1,019,200) did so in 1975 (Erbe, in Erbe, 1979, p. 409). Professor Rudi Weidig forecast, in 1980, that the intelligentsia would account for more than 22 per cent of all GDR workers by the end of the century (in Wittich & Taubert, 1981, p. 31). There is, however, no general agreement on the boundaries of the intelligentsia: Manfred Lötsch has discovered sixty definitions of the term (in Autorenkollektiv, 1980, p. 93).

In the period of reconstruction after the war the SED had to draw upon the old intelligentsia whose training and traditions were embedded in the former capitalist system, as the new educational system was not able to produce sufficient politically reliable and well-trained cadres. Although special privileges as regards income and housing were granted to members of the intelligentsia, at least 5,000 left the GDR for the West each year between 1949 and 1961 (Erbe, in Erbe, 1979, p. 406). The SED, however, was gradually able to replace the old intelligentsia by recruiting and training persons of working-class and peasant origins as well as individuals in whom political reliability was combined with practical experience. By 1964, about 80 per cent of college and university graduates had completed their training after 1951.

The drawing together (*Annäherung*) of the intelligentsia and the other social classes has long been regarded as one of the two fundamental developments of mature socialism. SED ideologists and functionaries firmly reject the view that the growing significance of science and technology undermines the revolutionary *élan*, the political predominance and the numerical strength of the working class, and they deny that it enhances the authority of the intelligentsia. Any admission of the emergence of the intelligentsia as a new elite would cast doubt on the SED's role as the vanguard of the working class and as the leading force in the development of socialist society.

The process of convergence, which is expected to be both long and complex, will occur, according to the SED's 1976 programme, on the basis of the perfecting of the productive forces, the higher development of the productive forces in town and country, the raising of the level of education, the perfecting of socialist democracy, and the further improvement of working and living conditions. In support of the thesis of a drawing-together of the intelligentsia and workers, GDR sociologists stress the opportunities for cooperation in the work process, such as the innovators' movement, and for joint participation in various political bodies, including the commissions of the National Front, the People's Chamber and the regional assemblies. Finally, the removal of distinctions between physical and mental work for a part of the scientific–technical intelligentsia and a section of production workers as a result of changes in the work process and the rapid expansion in the number of skilled production workers reinforces the general trend. Yet there exists clear evidence of countertendencies: the self-reproduction of the intelligentsia and the promotion of a privileged group of members of the scientific–technical intelligentsia as part of the SED's campaign to stimulate outstanding performances in science, technology and the economy (see below).

The Reassessment of the Tripartite Class Model

Conscious of the inadequacies of the Stalinist tripartite model and of the need to devise new models for empirical investigation of the complex structures and processes of their society, GDR social scientists have begun to make greater use of the concept of 'social differentiations'. It is contended, however, that social differentiation is determined by class and stratum and that social differentiation and the convergence of classes and strata (that is, social equality) stand in a dialectical relationship with each other. By incorporating the concept of social differentiation into the Marxist–Leninist framework and by retaining the official goal of social equality, this line of argument helps to legitimize the application of the concept. In many instances, however, sociologists now pay lip-service to orthodox formulations while they analyse secondary indices such as the degrees to which jobs are skilled or automated, enriching or monotonous and the level of income derived from them.

Various types of social differentiation are recognized by GDR social scientists, including those forms that survive from the preceding social formation, capitalism, and those that arise from socialist society itself. Several existing social differences are regarded as unavoidable: the current division of labour; different forms of social ownership of the means of production; the impact of the principle of distribution according to performance; the qualification and educational structures; differences in material living conditions; the division between town and country; socio-demographic differences; and the proportional development and the regional distribution of the productive forces (P. C. Ludz & U. Ludz, in Zimmermann, 1985, p. 1221; Hahn & Niederländer, 1982, p. 767).

Since the beginning of the 1980s the question of promoting certain social differences as driving forces of economic growth has triggered off a lively debate among social scientists. The main advocate of the creation of a privileged group of talented scientists and engineers has been Professor Manfred Lötsch of the Institute for Marxist–Leninist Sociology of the Central Committee's Academy of Social Sciences. He has been supported by other leading sociologists, notably Professor Rudi Weidig and Artur Meier. Their proposals for the more effective utilization of the skills and knowledge of the scientific-technical intelligentsia dovetail with the SED's strategy for intensifying the factors of economic growth. The heavy investment in the education and training of the intelligentsia, especially in basic and applied research, must, so they argue, be translated into outstanding results and products which can be sold on the world markets and earn the GDR hard currency (I. Lötsch & M. Lötsch, in *Jahrbuch für Soziologie und Sozialpolitik*, 1985, p. 159; Weidig, in Weidig, Wittich & Taubert, 1986, p. 23).

In this debate about the selective development of talented individuals GDR sociologists have modified, though not overturned, the official goals of the convergence of the social classes and strata and the further reduction of social differences. The whole issue has, according to Lötsch, aroused much heated controversy among sociologists on the grounds that this particular road to economic growth might relegate the goal of further social equality into second place or cause it to be delayed (I. Lötsch & M. Lötsch in *Jahrbuch für Soziologie und Sozialpolitik*, 1985, pp. 161-2). Lötsch and his colleagues seek to defend themselves by reaffirming their commitment to the erosion of fundamental inequalities in living conditions, income and the mental demands of work whilst simultaneously justifying the special treatment of a section of the intelligentsia on the grounds that top achievements in research and development are crucial for the realization of the 'main task' (Weidig, in Weidig, Wittich & Taubert, 1986, pp. 24-5, 33). Favourable conditions for the eventual transition to communism and the attainment of social equality will be created, argues Lötsch, if a higher development of the productive forces is promoted through the application of the remuneration principle and a greater differentiation within the intelligentsia. A measure of inequality is therefore both desirable and legitimate.

Lötsch proposes a comprehensive programme for the creation and furtherance of a 'creative core' or 'leadership group' among the intelligentsia: gifted individuals are to be developed systematically from childhood onward; creativity and initiative should not be shackled by routine tasks, that is, 'levelling downward'; special cultural interests should be catered for; and top international achievements by the scientific-technical intelligentsia should be rewarded by high financial payments (Lötsch, 1984, p. 11; Lötsch, in Wittich & Taubert, 1981, pp. 86-7). Such a programme undoubtedly entails a tendency toward the self-reproduction of the intelligentsia as children from intelligentsia families already enjoy certain inherent social advantages in the acquisition of the requisite skills and knowledge. That the self-reproduction of the intelligentsia is on the increase can be gauged from a 1977 investigation conducted by the Institute for Marxist-Leninist Sociology of the Central Committee's Academy of Social Sciences: 73 per cent of the fathers of the members of the intelligentsia aged 35-54 were either farmers or workers as against 54 per cent of those under 35 (Lötsch & Freitag, in *Jahrbuch für Soziologie und Sozialpolitik*, 1981, p. 98). However, full details have yet to be revealed as to how the SED will promote the development of a privileged group within the intelligentsia and how it will reconcile a degree of elitism with the legitimizing goal of social equality.

Income Differentials

In the debate about the role of the scientific-technical intelligentsia income differences are defended on the grounds that they are essential to reward and stimulate achievement and innovation and to ensure the allocation of the various positions in society to the most suitable persons. Scorn is poured on crude egalitarianism and the equalization of incomes:

> The proficiency principle has a deep moral character in that it elevates diligent, creative work to be one of the most important criterion of personality development. Thus, a striving for high levels of proficiency is a qualitative factor of work and life in socialist society . . . Any trend towards egalitarianism and levelling out, and putting in doubt the proficiency principle is thoroughly opposed in the GDR. [*Questions and Answers*, 1981, p. 71]

Published GDR statistics on levels of earned income are unfortunately far from comprehensive. The statistical handbooks provide a guide to average wages according to socio-economic groups and households but supplementary data on specific jobs and gender differentials are fragmentary or, in the case of the political elite's privileged access to special goods and scarce goods, virtually non-existent.

Despite these data problems, Western analysts agree that the range of average incomes, though quite wide, is considerably less than in Western countries. Two former GDR sociologists, Frank Grätz and Dieter Voigt, have collected data from a variety of sources to provide a rough indication of top earners in the GDR, notably physicians, engineers, natural scientists and leading political figures (see Table 2.4). They estimated, in 1976, that no more than 10,000 persons earned over 2,500 Marks per month (Vortmann, 1985, p. 88). In 1970, the gap between the lowest and highest earners in large industrial enterprises ranged from the 340 Marks per month gross of a messenger to the 3,000 Marks gross of the general director (Vortmann, 1985, p. 87).

The distribution of household income represents another indicator of the degree of income inequality in the GDR. Household income is determined by total wages and the number of employed persons. A comparison undertaken by the West Berlin German Institute for Economic Research shows that income distribution seems to be more equalized in the GDR than in the Federal Republic (see Table 2.5).

The GDR data on the incomes of broad socio-economic groups are of limited value as they have not differentiated between blue- and white-collar workers since 1960. The cooperative farmers and self-employed category enjoys the highest average monthly incomes per recipient (1,545 Marks in 1981), pensioners the lowest (398 Marks). If the incomes of cooperative members and self-employed were separated, it is certain that the incomes of the latter group would occupy first place. Perceptible income differentials exist between economic sectors. Earnings in the distributive trades remain well below those in the productive sectors. Within industry, earnings are highest in metallurgy and energy and lowest in food-processing, light industry and textiles (see Table 2.6).

Table 2.4 Gross income of top earners, *c.* 1975

	Marks per month
Head physician with income from private patients	6,000–10,000
Engineers and natural scientists with special contracts, above all in R & D	3,000–15,000
Politburo members	5,000
Ministers	*c.*4,500
High-ranking officers and generals	*c.*2,500–4,500
Professors	2,500–4,500
First regional (*Bezirk*) Secretary of the SED	3,500
General or combine director of an industrial combine	*c.*2,000–3,500
Chairman of a regional council	*c.*2,500

Source: Vortmann, 1985, p. 88.

Table 2.5 Distribution of net disposable employee household income by quintiles, 1960–80/81

Proportion of households	Share in net income			
	1960		1980	
	GDR	FRG	GDR	FRG
Quintile 1	10.4	8.4	11.2	10.2
Quintile 2	15.3	12.6	16.4	14.3
Quintile 3	19.2	16.4	19.8	17.9
Quintile 4	23.4	22.8	23.0	22.6
Quintile 5	31.7	39.8	29.6	35.0
	100	100	100	100

Source: *DIW Handbuch*, 1984, p. 272.

Table 2.6 Average monthly income of fully employed workers and salaried employees in nationalized enterprises according to economic sectors, 1974–85 (Marks)

Year	Total	Industry	Construction	Agriculture and forestry	Transport	Post and telecommunications	Domestic trade
1974	867	865	922	859	954	801	767
1985	1,140	1,147	1,158	1,076	1,241	1,075	1,021

Source: StJB, 1986, p. 129.

Gender Differentiation

The emancipation of women has been a constant goal of the SED since its foundation in 1946. The goal of equality between the sexes was based on the need to repair the shattered social and economic fabric of the country in the immediate post-war years and to ameliorate the acute long-term shortage of labour; but it was also, and still is, derived from the classic works of Marxism–Leninism. Engels's statement on the development of women outside the home provided the ideological underpinning: 'The emancipation of women and their equalization with men is and will remain an impossibility as long as women are excluded from socially productive life and remain confined to their own home' (quoted in Shaffer, 1981, p. 58).

The first constitution in 1949 granted women equality before the law, the right to work and the right to equal pay for equal work. These rights have been realized through the expansion of pre-school institutions for young children, the increased provision of washing machines, laundries and works cafeterias and special women's trade union committees for the development of women workers. The availability of crèches and kindergartens was crucial for enabling women to pursue a career outside the home. Whereas only 20.5 per cent of children aged 3–6 had a place in a kindergarten in 1950, 92.2 per cent did so thirty years later. The degree of care is not so comprehensive in the crèches (72.7 per cent in 1985) and the question of whether the rearing of children below the age of three is better undertaken by parents rather than in the crèche has resurfaced in recent GDR literature.

Indicators of the impressive strides towards greater equality of the sexes include the achievement of parity in higher education (18.6 per cent in 1949, increasing to 50.1 per cent in 1985), women's high rate of participation in employment (49.3 per cent in 1985), and their involvement in political affairs (in 1985 the percentage of women in the regional assemblies was 38.7 and in the district assemblies 42.6) (StJB, 1986, pp. 394, 396). Furthermore, the image of the working woman is firmly embedded in popular perceptions of women's social roles. Numerous investigations by institutions such as the Leipzig-based Central Institute for Youth Research reveal that the overwhelming majority of female respondents expect to go out to work; very few wish to be just a housewife (Dennis, in Wallace, 1981, pp. 98-9).

Despite the many real advances, women still suffer discrimination at work, in politics and at home. They are seriously under-represented in leading state and party positions. No woman has achieved the status of a full member of the SED Politburo; in 1986, there were only two women candidate members, Margarete Müller and Inge Lange. Since Honecker became SED leader, all the First Secretaryships of the party's country executives have been filled by men. The Presidium of the Council of Ministers is a male domain and Margot Honecker, the Minister of Education, has been the only woman member of the Council of Ministers since 1963. Women are also under-represented in management positions in socialist industry. In 1979, according to Inge Lange, female representation on the highest rung, occupied by managers of enterprise or institutions, was only 2.3 per cent. Women's share of level-two posts—for example, deputy managers—amounted to 12.1 per cent. Misgivings about the burdens of responsibility and the nervous strains, the ties and strain of housework and childrearing, and the relative neglect of a systematic development of women cadres all contribute to the lower participation rates of women (Dennis, in Wallace, 1981, pp. 104-5). Moreover, the SED leadership does not appear to be prepared to assign high priority to this issue.

Although women have broken down the male hold over some technical and scientific jobs, women are predominantly the hairdressers, typists, nurses, cooks and nursery teachers but rarely the carpenters, bricklayers and fitters. One consequence of the feminization of so many job categories is a lower earning potential for women. They are heavily concentrated in sectors such as textiles and light industry where earnings are relatively low but they are considerably less visible in the higher-paying construction industry. The wage structure of production workers in 1969, that is before the wage reform of 1976, illustrates the discrepancy: 77.7 per cent of the women as against 21.2 per cent of the men production workers occupied the lowest four wage groups (Dennis, in Wallace, 1981, p. 98). Moreover, traditional stereotypes persist in popular attitudes towards women's employment, especially among men. Young men in the region of Frankfurt/Oder revealed a much lower commitment than did young women (20.5 per cent to 30.7 per cent) to the idea that a woman should continue in full-time employment no matter what the circumstances. A higher proportion of young men (25.1 per cent to 13.7 per cent of women) preferred a woman not to work while children were still young (Dennis, in Kolinsky, 1985, p. 47: 775 young women and 695 young men were involved in the survey).

Despite the exhortation of the 1965 Family Code for men as well as women to bear their share of the upbringing and care of the children and household chores, no serious re-evaluation of the role of men was attempted by the code's draftsmen. Men's contribution was essentially to lighten the burden on their hard-pressed wives. Social welfare legislation sometimes reinforces this image of the working-housewife-mother: the monthly free 'housework' day, a reduced working day and the baby year are all confined to women in employment. Some men—for example, shiftworkers—may enjoy a shorter day but not all three provisions are available to men. Furthermore, the advantages derived from the socialization of housework are partly offset by inferior household appliances and time wasted on queueing. In fact, the amount of time devoted to family tasks does not seem to have undergone any fundamental change: between 1965 and the beginning of the 1980s, it fell from 47.5 hours to 47 hours per week in a four-person household (Enders, in Spittmann-Rühle & Helwig, 1984, p. 45).

Numerous time budgets all point to the persistence of the unequal division of labour within the family. The wife still performs most of the household and childrearing jobs, while some spouses, though by no means all, lend a helping hand. Christel Lane cites one representative survey in the 1970s which established that women perform the housework without assistance in 46.6 per cent of households and men in 1.2 per cent; the whole family shared the work in 46.7 per cent of households and parents helped in 5.7 per cent (Lane, 1983, p. 499). The housework and family burden means that women enjoy less free time than men. This free time deficit, which is not compensated for by women's lower economic participation, has been criticized by one GDR sociologist, Peter Voß, as an expression of women's relative lack of equality (1981, p. 74). As girls, too, are more heavily engaged in household tasks, they have on average one hour less free time per day than boys; and the traditional division of labour within the family is therefore reproduced and reinforced among the younger generation.

Although the state provides generous assistance for women to cope with the triple burden of housework, family and career, the strain may cause women to look for a job with low demands or seek part-time employment. Another alternative is to limit their family to only one offspring. All these 'choices' have drawbacks. From the point of view of the social policy-makers, the births of second and third children are still too few to guarantee the reproduction of the population. Part-time employment (29.4 per cent of women worked part-time in 1980) represents a loss of part of women's labour capacity, hinders their professional development and strengthens the 'traditional' division of labour within the family.

Divorce, too, may offer another alternative to the strain of multiple burdens, although it is not clear to what extent such burdens directly cause the collapse of a marriage. The liberalization of the divorce laws; the gradual erosion of the stigma attached to divorce; women's growing economic independence; all these factors have contributed to the steep rise in the divorce rate (from 1.8 per 1,000 inhabitants in 1971 to 3.1 in 1985). With about one-third of all marriages ending in divorce, the GDR has one of the highest divorce rates in the world. And women are far more likely than men to institute an action for divorce. The increasing number of single mothers and some young couples' preference for free association (*Lebensgemeinschaft*) testify to the questioning of marriage as a 'part of the good life'. Another sign of the changing pattern of the relationship is the increase in the proportion of live births to unmarried mothers from 17.3 per cent in 1978 to 32 per cent in 1983 (Gysi, in *Jahrbuch für Soziologie und Sozialpolitik*, 1984, p. 105).

Conscious that employment does not automatically lead to emancipation and sensitive to the tension and strain arising from the combined demands of home and work, some women are openly questioning the official line on the complementarity of women's various roles. Since the mid- to late-1970s women novelists such as Brigitte Martin, Helga Königsdorf, Helga Schubert, Christa Müller and Hedda Zimmer have given vent to their frustration at the lack of progress in regard to the status of women. In an open and realistic manner their novels depict how women, whether single or divorced, respond to loneliness and isolation and how they are struggling to define their own identity. In another contribution to the debate, Irene Dölling, a lecturer in cultural theory at the Humboldt University in East Berlin, while accepting that socialism has created the basic objective preconditions for overcoming the inequality of the sexes, argues that the fundamental contradiction between women's integration into the productive workforce and their special responsibility for the private sphere of family and home must be overcome by the individual. Society, she claims, cannot offer ready-made answers and rules for the individual's resolution of this particular dilemma. However, as women blue- and white-collar workers with low qualifications tend to subscribe to a conservative female self-concept, Dölling envisages that change is more likely to be initiated by highly qualified women who are more directly affected by the contradictions and tensions arising from the traditional sex-role differentiation (Dölling, 1986, pp. 141–6). Not only should women cease to be passive and acquiescent but it is also argued, notably by Christa Wolf, that they should bring their own qualities and values to bear on the development of society. The adoption of male roles and values is decried as detrimental for sexual equality. This is argued most forcibly by Christa Wolf in her short story, *Self-Experiment*, about the sex-change experience of a woman scientist. After thirty days, she discovers the oppressive nature of masculinity and seeks to break off the experiment. Wolf has identified the fundamental question of the story:

> Is it the goal of emancipation, can it even be worth striving for, that women 'become like men', that is, permitted to do the same things, to gain and increasingly avail themselves of the same rights as men have—when, in fact, men are so greatly in need of being emancipated themselves? [quoted in Fehervary & Lennox, 1978, p. 110]

Social Policy

Until the early 1960s the concept of social policy was rarely used in the GDR as it was associated with attempts to limit the damage caused by antagonisms which capitalism necessarily produces and to deflect the working class from its revolutionary mission. In practice, however, the SED could not dispense with a wide range of socio-political measures covering occupational safety and health, social insurance and the special needs of women and pensioners. 'Social security' was deployed as the umbrella term for these measures. The ideological prejudices against social policy in socialism were gradually eroded in the 1960s. Official acceptance of the term can be dated back to Ulbricht's speech at the Seventh Party Congress in 1967. Two years later, the FDGB created its own department of social policy and in 1978 the Institute for Sociology and Social Policy was founded at the Academy of Sciences. Helga Michalsky regards 1971 as the real watershed: social policy was upgraded in the rhetoric of the political leadership and at the Eighth Party Congress it was incorporated into the SED's overall political strategy. The main task, as pronounced by Honecker, was to raise the material and cultural standard of living on the basis of the growth of socialist production and labour productivity. This was proclaimed as 'the unity of social and economic policy' in that economic and social progress are interdependent (Michalsky, in von Beyme & Zimmermann, 1984, pp. 242–5).

The current GDR conception of social policy is that it constitutes one element in overall policy–making, with the latter remaining the prerogative of the SED. Social policy is therefore an instrument in the hands of the party for shaping socialist society and, as the SED programme states, for creating the prerequisites for the gradual transition to communism. The characteristic features of social policy encompass: the elimination of fundamental differences between town and country, mental and physical work and between social groups; the fostering of a socialist way of life and personality; the improvement of living and working conditions; and a higher standard of living. In detail, this involves, for example, the solution of the housing question as a social problem, the provision of more leisure time, support for families, working mothers, young people and pensioners and the application of the principle of remuneration according to work performance (Autorenkollektiv Manz, 1983, pp. 127–8). As the areas affected by social policy are so numerous, the focus of attention will be on three crucial aspects of operation: housing, the family and youth, leisure and sport.

Housing

In a series of admirable reports Manfred Melzer of the German Institute for Economic Research has pinpointed the 1971 housing census as a turning–point in the SED's housing policy. The survey revealed 'a frightening picture of both the condition of residential buildings and the dwellings' standard of equipment' (Melzer, 1984, p. 78). Only one dwelling in five was undamaged and one in six was totally or almost completely dilapidated; this represented about 11 per cent of the country's total fixed assets.

This situation was the consequence of what Phillip Bryson has criticized as 'a callous neglect' (1984, p. 123) of the housing needs of the GDR populace for many years after 1945. In fact, the immediate post–war housing situation was relatively more favourable in the East than in the West. A higher percentage of dwellings had been destroyed in the three Western zones than in the Soviet zone (24.8 as against 13.0; see Schneider, 1986, p. 736). West Germany soon improved its relative position. At the beginning of 1981, only 35 per cent of the total housing stock in the GDR dated from the end of the war; it exceeded 60 per cent in the West. The Federal

Republic was also far in advance of the GDR in terms of equipage with bath/shower and inside toilet.

At last, in 1973, the SED unveiled a comprehensive housing construction programme 'to solve the housing question as a social problem by 1990'. The 'solution' envisaged an adequately equipped if relatively small dwelling for every family. Housing was thrust to the centre of the country's social policy; it has retained this position despite increases in the price of raw materials and major problems posed by redevelopment in the inner cities and older residential areas. The planners aimed at the construction or renovation of 2.8–3.0 million dwellings between 1976 and 1990. Published data suggest that this target will be fulfilled. If the 1.064 million dwellings to be built (0.593 million) or modernized (0.471 million) during the 1986–90 Five Year Plan are added to the 1.8 million units, including 1.2 million new buildings completed between 1976 and 1985, a figure of 2.9 million dwellings is arrived at (Bartholmai & Melzer, 1987, p. 184).

Much-needed improvements have occurred in the equipage of housing: between 1971 and 1981, the proportion of dwellings with modern types of heating rose from 10.8 per cent to 35.9 per cent and those with a hot water supply from 26.1 per cent to 64.0 per cent (*StJB*, 1985, p. 172). All new buildings have a hot water supply and a bath or shower and virtually all have central heating and an electric cooker. These represent significant achievements, especially as the continuation of the policy of heavily subsidized rents has required the investment of vast sums in construction and modernization as well as in repairs and general maintenance. Melzer estimates that between 1976 and 1980 the state had to find 40 billion Marks for investment purposes and 15 billion Marks for repairs (Melzer, in Gerber, 1985, p. 54). In the capital the tenant of a new building pays only 1.00 to 1.25 Marks per square metre and in the other administrative regions 0.80 to 0.90 Marks. The rents of older dwellings continue to be charged at their 1936 level. In fact, rent payments have accounted for no more than 2.7 to 4.0 per cent of the income of worker and employee households for over twenty years (Melzer, 1984, p. 81).

Regional differences in both the quantity and quality of dwellings are appreciable. East Berlin is the national showcase. Historical buildings and complexes such as the Platz der Akademie were reconstructed for the city's 750th birthday in 1987 and vast new housing developments have been finished or are awaiting completion. The district of Marzahn has 62,000 dwellings and over 200,000 inhabitants; Hohen-schönhausen has 35,000 dwellings; and a further 43,500 are planned for the new district of Hellersdorf by 1990 (Schneider, 1986, p. 740). Berlin dwellings are more likely to be equipped with a modern heating system (47.1 per cent in 1981 as against the GDR average of 35.9 per cent: *StJB*, 1985, p. 172), a hot water supply, a bath or shower and an inside toilet than are those elsewhere in the GDR. Dresden is the backmarker (see Table 2.7). Floor space per inhabitant is highest in Berlin (28.3 square metres in 1985) and lowest in the region of Rostock (22.7), Neubrandenburg (24.1), Schwerin (24.8) and Frankfurt (25.3) regions (*StJB*, 1986, p. 171).

Whether the housing programme, despite the many impressive achievements at a time of serious resource constraints, can be expected to 'solve' the housing problem

Table 2.7 Proportion of dwellings with bath/shower and inside toilet, 1970–90 (per cent)

	Bath/shower			Inside toilet		
	1970	1985	1990	1970	1985	1990
GDR	39	74	86	39	68	79
Berlin	59	84	99	80	93	99
Dresden	33	68	81	32	54	67

Source: *Neues Deutschland*, 18 April 1986, p. 5. Details of the other administrative regions appear in this issue.

is open to question. The American economist, Phillip Bryson, anticipates that the new and remodelled GDR dwellings 'will not be comparable to West German units in terms of contruction quality, variety, general comfort, or size of individual rooms and dwelling units' (Bryson, 1984, p. 126). A comparison of West German data with the material in the 1981 GDR census reveals that the average floor space was 9 square metres per inhabitant less than in West Germany (32 square metres). While 34 per cent of the dwellings in the FRG had only one or two rooms, 41 per cent did so in the GDR. The figures for dwellings with four or more rooms read 36 per cent and 22 per cent respectively (*DIW Handbuch*, 1984, p. 180).

Sociological investigators in numerous GDR cities and towns, including Leipzig, Karl-Marx-Stadt, Erfurt, Halle, Halle-Neustadt, Rostock and East Berlin, shed light on subjective perceptions of these objective data. They reveal a high level of dissatisfaction with the relatively cramped space in newer dwellings (see, for example, Kuhn, 1985, p. 3, and Kahl, 1982, p. 9). The degree of satisfaction varies according to the number of children. In the vast new residential district of Marzahn in East Berlin, parents with one child were more satisfied as well as less dissatisfied with the size of their children's rooms than were parents with two or three children (see Table 2.8). Sociologists have concluded that couples would probably be more willing to have a second or third child if additional dwellings with four or more rooms and larger, three-room dwellings were available (Kuhn, 1985, p. 21). The relative lack of space means that brothers and sisters may still be sharing a room when they reach puberty (Niderländer, 1984, p. 149) and young married couples are sometimes obliged to live with their parents. Data from the city of Leipzig indicate that 25 per cent of married couples lived with their parents in 1975; however, the figure had dropped to 17 per cent seven years later (Voß, 1984, p. 48).

Some people are reluctant to abandon familiar surroundings for the new residential complexes which are often situated on the outskirts of cities. While the modern dwellings enjoy the advantages of superior sanitation, fitted kitchens and

Table 2.8 Parents' satisfaction with the size of their children's rooms (per cent)

Number of children	1*	2	3	4	5	6	7
1	31	18	12	15	15	4	5
2 and 3	19	13	19	16	13	9	11

* Rating: 1 — greatest satisfaction; 7 — greatest dissatisfaction.
Source: Niederländer, 1984, p. 149.

central heating, the vast dormitory satellites tend to be characterized by what Fred Staufenbiel has called a 'technistic monotony'. The environment is dominated by blocks of flats erected according to a standard type, the 'Housing Construction Series 70'. A lack of neighbourliness, anonymity and social isolation are the most frequent criticisms levelled at these satellite towns and the new residential complexes (Neubert, 1986, p. 158). Not surprisingly, a high proportion of urban residents prefer a new or modernized dwelling within their existing neighbourhood once it has undergone reconstruction. Sociological investigations in Sonnenberg, an older residential district in the city of Karl-Marx-Stadt, found that 80 per cent of the inhabitants preferred this solution to relocation (Staufenbiel, 1982, p. 21). This has not been ignored by the political leadership. At a meeting with SED district secretaries in February 1987, Honecker stated that housing construction in inner-city areas 'is moving increasingly into the foreground, the aim being to increase the appeal of old residential districts and make them comfortable to live in' (*Neues Deutschland*, 7 February 1987, p. 6).

While GDR urban sociologists like Alice Kahl and Loni Niederländer deny that life in the new housing blocks is an alienating experience, they acknowledge that residents withdraw into the privacy of their own apartments and that organized bodies such as the tenants' association (*Hausgemeinschaft*) fail to generate primary social bonds within the local community (Kahl, 1982, p. 13; Niederländer, 1984, pp. 137-9). The greater comfort of the modern apartments do not, it is conceded, compensate for the inadequacies of the infrastructure. The problem concerns not only the provision of additional children's playgrounds, nurseries, restaurants, supermarkets, gardens, sports grounds and cultural establishments; it also involves the creation of a social environment which caters for individual tastes and needs. Hence cafés, shops and skittle-alleys are recommended as well as large restaurants, department stores and multi-functional sports complexes (Kahl, 1982, pp. 10–11). More open spaces should be provided close to the housing blocks in order to encourage people to go walking, to relax and to participate in sports activities (Kuhn, 1985, p. 23).

Many families find their own solution: they hasten away at the weekend to their dacha with its small garden. Here they can escape from the monotony of city life and from the burdens of work and public office. This flight to the dacha may not conform to the SED's conception of the primacy of the collective, but by functioning as a safety-valve it does at least have the advantage, from the party's standpoint, of enhancing social stability.

Family and Youth

Despite the rejection of the institution of marriage by some Marxists, the GDR has always recognized the value of both marriage and the family. The GDR family continues to perform the basic functions of reproduction, the socialization of children, and economic and emotional support for its members. Marriage is proclaimed by the 1966 Family Code as a union for life based on mutual love, respect and faithfulness, understanding and trust, and unselfish help for one another. The founders of the GDR sought, however, to modify the traditional relationship between the sexes. For example, the 1950 Law on the Protection of Mother and Child replaced the previous right of the husband alone to make decisions on all marital matters by the joint decision-making right of both partners. In addition, women's employment was regarded as the key to their equality and a 'higher' form of family life. After much delay, a new family model emerged in 1966 with the promulgation of the Family Code.

The code defines the family as the smallest cell in society and proclaims that only socialism, which is allegedly free from the exploitation and material insecurity of bourgeois society, can provide the necessary conditions for family relations of a new and lasting kind. Children receive a good deal of attention in the code. The most important task and duty of parents, to be undertaken jointly, is the upbringing of the children in, it is hoped, a stable and happy environment. The socialization of children and young people is not envisaged as the prerogative of parents but as a cooperative effort between parents, school and state organizations such as the Thälmann Pioneers and the Free German Youth.

The GDR has set ambitious goals for its youth, that is, the 3 million young people aged 14–25. They are to be faithful to the ideas of socialism and to protect socialism against its enemies. Outstanding results are expected of them at work, in their studies and on the sports field. They are also supposed to be intimately involved in the running of the state and in the development of the economy. The 1974 Youth Code, the third such code, presupposes a community of aims and interests between the state and young people. This identity finds expression in the definition of the basic right and basic obligation of young people: 'To help build an advanced society in the German Democratic Republic and to take part in the full-scale integration of the socialist community in firm alliance with the Soviet Union . . .' (Herzig, 1977, p. 58).

State support for the family and young people is extensive. For example, in 1972, a package of social welfare measures improved maternity leave and eased working conditions for mothers in full-time employment. The abortion law of that year gave women the right to decide on an abortion and made abortion available on demand within the first twelve weeks of pregnancy. Four years later, an even more generous set of measures was introduced. Women, after the birth of their second child, were entitled to claim release from work for one year on pay equivalent to 65–90 per cent of their average net earnings (the 'baby year') and maternity leave was extended to twenty-six weeks before and after pregnancy. Finally, Honecker, at the 1986 Party Congress, announced an extension of benefits from 1 May 1986: the baby year was extended to working women after the birth of their first baby; all employed mothers received paid leave to take care of sick children; and loans for young married couples were increased from 5,000 to 7,000 Marks and the age limit was raised from 26 to 30 years. In May 1987, the monthly child benefit was increased from 20 to 50 Marks for the first child, from 20 to 100 Marks for the second child and from 100 to 150 Marks for the third. Honecker estimated that this particular social measure would cost about 2 billion Marks annually (Report of the Central Committee, 1986, pp. 57–8).

The generous support for the family partly reflects broader SED ideological, social and political goals such as the legitimation of its rule, the mobilization of women for work and the reproduction of the population; it also indicates the party's recognition of the vital role of the family in raising young people even in a socialist society with its alternative and complementary agents of socialization. The continuing and strong influence of the family is confirmed by GDR research into career guidance, educational attainment, gender roles and free-time pursuits.

The social class or status of parents is a crucial determinant of their children's careers. According to Barbara Bertram of the Leipzig Central Institute for Youth Research, children from workers' or salaried employees' families usually aspire to skilled workers' careers in industry, whereas those from intelligentsia families express a greater interest in careers requiring a higher level of qualification (in Friedrich & Müller, 1983, pp. 80, 88–9). One of Bertram's colleagues, Gustav-Wilhelm Bathke, has elucidated the significance of social origins for students in higher education at the beginning of the 1980s. Their parents were more likely to be salaried employees than workers and to have an above-average level of qualification. The students enjoyed the double advantage of belonging to a small family which was also well endowed with books. Bathke's observations were supported by an enquiry into the qualifications of the parents of those students who had passed their school certificate (*Abitur*) with distinction: 12 per cent were skilled workers, 16 per cent had acquired a technical college certificate, and 26 per cent had gained a degree (Bathke, in Friedrich & Hoffmann, 1986, pp. 248–9).

Despite its cultivation of the family and young people, the SED is a long way from the realization of many of its official goals, which admittedly are highly ambitious: some goals are difficult to harmonize with each other and the family is frequently resistant to official pressure and doctrine. The SED target of two to three children per family is not easily reconciled with the burdens arising from the full-time employment of a high proportion of women and with the liberal abortion legislation. The happy, stable relationship between partners within marriage, which is central to the Family Code, is a distant, and perhaps receding, target in view of the high divorce rate and the increasing number of live-in couples.

Moreover, the regime's encouragement of multi-shiftworking, in order to secure a more intensive utilization of capital, equipment and machinery, imposes a severe strain on families, especially where there are young children and both parents are on shifts. Shiftworkers discuss school problems with their children less frequently than dayworkers; the weekly care in pre-school institutions, usually necessary if both parents are on shifts, is inferior to that provided in day institutions, and older children are often left alone on Saturdays and Sundays when their parents are at work. Not surprisingly, the school grades of shiftworkers' children are more likely to be below average than are those of dayworkers' children.

Although it is difficult to delineate precisely the attitudes and behaviour patterns of GDR youth, adaptation and accommodation rather than an enthusiastic commitment to the existing system would seem to be the mainstream response. However, the pent-up frustration caused by restrictions on travel and certain forms of self-expression occasionally explodes into open protests, as in June 1987, when clashes occured between youthful rock fans and police in the vicinity of the Brandenburg Gate. The disturbances were triggered off by a rock festival of British groups on the lawn of the nearby Reichstag in West Berlin. Protesters chanted that the wall must come down and indicated their support for *glasnost* by shouting 'Gorbachev' and 'Rosa Luxemburg' (see the report in *The Guardian*, 10 June 1987, p. 8). Despite such clashes and the existence of a minority of dropouts and isolated groups pursuing alternative lifestyles, the SED still appears to enjoy considerable success in obtaining young people's functional support for the system. Material rewards in the form of scholarships and jobs are available in return for demonstrations of political loyalty, such as FDJ membership, even though much of this activity is frequently superficial and ritualistic. Where the SED perceives a threat to its authority, it may resort to repressive measures. One example is the 'decapitation' of the Jena peace community. However, a complex society cannot easily be regulated by issuing degrees from above or by repression. A more flexible approach is required. Not only has the SED devised a relatively liberal social welfare programme for young people, but in the early 1970s it 'capitulated' to their enthusiasm for Western pop music. Watching Western TV is also no longer taboo.

Yet the SED must be worried by the growing involvement of the young people in the unofficial peace groups as well as by youth crime, excessive drinking and a distinctly unsocialist attitude to work. In any one year's qualification group, there exists, according to GDR sources, a core of problem cases of about 10 per cent. These young workers tend not to complete their apprenticeships and are inclined to job switching and loafing at work. They may also require the attention of the youth welfare service. Disillusioned with the undemanding nature of their work, they drift from one job to another (Hille, 1981, p. 339).

From the limited data available, it would seem that the pattern of youth criminality in the GDR is similar to that in other industrial societies. In 1960, young people committed 33.7 per cent of all offences; twelve years later this had increased by over 16 per cent. Certain age groups, 16–18 and 18–21, are more endangered than others. Although criminal actions are confined to only a small minority of young people, West German experts predict that the level of youth criminality will continue to trouble the authorities for the remainder of the 1980s. Indeed, in 1981, the figure of 1,600 offenders per 100,000 young people aged 14–25 was higher than that recorded at the end of the 1960s (Freiburg, 1981, pp. 266–8 and 1985, p. 70).

Young people tend to commit less serious offences than older age groups, although the proportion in which violence is involved remains relatively high. About half of the offences are against public property. Many infringements take place in groups. In 1965, it was officially estimated that 30 per cent of young offenders committed their acts as members of a group; but four years later, Professor Szewczyk of the Department of Forensic Psychiatry at the Humboldt University in East Berlin gave a much higher figure of 60 per cent (Freiburg, 1981, p. 241).

One type of offence which receives considerable attention in the GDR media is 'rowdyism'. Instances of rowdyism include damaging telephone boxes and the furnishings of trams, smashing shop windows, and football hooliganism. One notorious group of hooligans, associated with Rot-Weiß Erfurt football club, attacked fans of other clubs, committed thefts in pubs and made a nuisance of themselves on public transport (Quiesser, 1983, pp. 99, 106).

GDR criminologists, legal scientists and psychiatrists have attempted to explain why crime exists under socialist conditions. One of Szewczyk's associates at the Department of Forensic Psychiatry has identified the preconditions of youth criminality as: a disturbed family setting (an antisocial, broken home, a faulty upbringing, illegitimacy); failure at school or work; alcohol abuse; an unsatisfactory use of leisure; deficiencies in the care of young people after their release from youth welfare institution or prison; and the negative influence of the remnants of pre-socialist forms of behaviour and ideas and attitudes emanating from capitalism (Schering, 1977, pp. 97–8). Problems within the family which Professor Kräupl of the University of Jena identifies as 'criminologically significant' are the overloading of parents by vocational and public activities, insufficient time for family life and childrearing, difficulties in supervising or controlling children's free-time pursuits and the relaxation of social bonds (1980, p. 303). These problems do not only emerge in what Schubring calls a milieu with asocial tendencies but also in families where at least one person holds an important public office with the requisite qualifications. Such parents were found by one investigation to have insufficient time and understanding for their children (Schubring, in Szewczyk, 1982, pp. 230–1). This scholarly research has revealed serious deficiencies in the upbringing of the young people of the GDR not solely as a result of inadequacies on the part of parents but as a consequence of the extensive political and economic mobilization of the population by the state.

Leisure and Sport

The right to leisure and recreation is guaranteed by the constitution and an active pursuit of leisure is expected by the SED to contribute to the development of socialist personality and to the reproduction of labour. Sport, it is hoped, will develop and strengthen such desirable characteristics as discipline, courage, reliability, self-confidence, a sense of responsibility, optimism, joy of living and willingness to defend the fatherland. The regime aspires to a harmonious relationship between leisure and work on the grounds that socialism has abolished the contradiction which exists between the two spheres in capitalism. The populace, however, perceives a clear distinction. In a UNESCO survey of cultural needs, 41.3 per cent of GDR respondents in Freiberg state that 'In work too one finds pleasure and self-esteem. But in leisure, work problems should play no role; one only wants to switch off one's mind and rest' (Gransow, in Wallace, 1981, p. 27). The economic historian Jürgen Kuczynski was prepared, as always, to challenge orthodox positions. He argued in the columns of *Forum* that not only is more free time required but that it is the criterion of social progress (Gransow, in Wallace, 1981, p. 26).

Time-budget surveys, conducted in the 1970s, enable us to identify the main leisure activities pursued after time has been subtracted for work, household chores, the upbringing and care of children and physiological needs. For example, the 1974 national survey of about 6,600 persons revealed the widespread popularity of watching television and listening to the radio and the disadvantaged position of women.

The Leipzig-based Central Institute for Youth Research has conducted numerous careful investigations of young people's leisure pursuits. Watching television and listening to the radio and music, especially pop music, emerge as the most popular activities (see Table 2.10). Since about 1961, watching television has been the major leisure pursuit of GDR youth. According to Walter Friedrich, television viewing has increased among young people by an average of twenty minutes per day over the past ten to fifteen years. The Central Institute's Interval Study data for 1965–76 reveal that the 13–16-year-olds watch more television than any other age group. The favourite programmes are adventure, crime and entertainment films. One result of the growing significance of television has been a decline in cinema-going. Although the cinema audience remains essentially a youthful one (three out of four cinema-goers belong to the younger generation), the appeal of television and discos and the greater availability of motorbikes and cars have reduced attendance figures.

Several aspects of television viewing have been criticized by the GDR's media experts: the 'superficiality' of so much viewing; entertainment programmes have a less positive impact on personality development than information and educational programmes; many children frequently watch television without advice or guidance from their parents; and impressionable youngsters are susceptible to ideological 'diversion' by the Western media (Wiedemann, in Voß, 1981, pp. 134, 137–8). West German television programmes penetrate most of the GDR, with the exception of the Dresden region and part of north-eastern Mecklenburg. Although various

Table 2.9 Leisure activities of male and female workers and salaried employees, 1974 (hours per person per day)

	Average	Men	Women
Education and seeking qualification outside working hours	0.05	0.06	0.04
Societal activity	0.14	0.19	0.09
Visits to cultural events and institutions	0.12	0.13	0.11
Artistic activity and hobbies	0.04	0.05	0.02
Active sports participation	0.06	0.09	0.03
Walking	0.23	0.23	0.23
Visit to sports events	0.02	0.03	0.01
Watching TV and listening to radio	1.26	1.40	1.14
Listening to records and tapes	0.02	0.03	0.01
Reading	0.19	0.23	0.15
Recreation without specific purpose	0.11	0.11	0.11
Taking part in sociable gatherings	0.23	0.24	0.22
Participation in religious activities	0.01	0.01	0.01
Others	0.19	0.19	0.19
Total leisure time	3.44	4.18	3.17

Source: Ministerrat der Deutschen Demokratischen Republik, 1975, n.p.

campaigns were once waged to prevent the reception of Western television, Honecker, in 1973, accepted the *fait accompli* and *de facto* lifted the official proscription of Western television and radio programmes. The University of Bamberg in West Germany conducted an investigation into the television preferences of 205 emigrants from the GDR. Their replies, which cannot however be regarded as GDR-representative, revealed that a high proportion (72 per cent) had never or rarely watched GDR television and that only 10 per cent could be described as regular viewers. Of those who had been able to receive Western television, 82 per cent had watched Western programmes virtually every day. West German news programmes such as *ZDF-Magazin*, and *Heute* and *Tagesschau* were the most popular transmissions (*Berliner Morgenpost*, 12 September 1986, p. 12). Although these findings testify to the keen desire for political information, it should not be forgotten that the Western media are avidly followed by the youthful devotees of beat and rock music.

One surprising omission in the time-budget surveys is any reference to sexual activity. Sexual attitudes and behaviour have undergone a notable liberalization during the Honecker era. Borman and Schille's claim, in 1980, that young people's first sexual experience was taking place one year earlier than a decade ago was

Table 2.10 The structure of the free time of older pupils, apprentices and young workers (hours per week)

Activity	Pupils	Apprentices	Young workers
Watching TV	8.9	7.6	6.3
Meeting friends, colleagues, relations and acquaintances	6.5	5.1	5.6
Listening to radio and music	3.7	3.5	1.8
Active sports participation	3.0	2.2	1.0
Walking	2.4	0.9	2.1
Going to discos and/or other dances	2.2	3.2	1.9
Cultural–artistic and/or natural–scientific–technical activities	2.0	3.7	2.0
Driving a car, moped, motor cycle, cycling	1.3	1.4	0.8
Relaxing	1.1	0.8	0.3
Cards and other games	0.5	0.9	0.6
Visiting restaurants or pubs	0.5	0.8	2.9
Attending sports events as spectators	0.4	0.5	0.2
Visiting the cinema	0.3	0.5	0.2
Visiting other events and exhibitions	0.4	0.5	0.2
Others	3.5	4.9	4.6

Source: Voß, 1981, p. 88.

confirmed by the Partner Studies of the Central Institute for Youth Research. Whereas in 1973 18 per cent of the students had experienced sexual intercourse by the age of 17, in 1980 just over half had done so on reaching this age. The result of the second Partner Study indicated that, at the beginning of the 1980s, the average age at which sexual intercourse started was 16.9 years and, another important change, girls' first experience of sexual intercourse, took place at the same age as that of boys (see Table 2.11). The orgasm frequency rate of young women in the 1980s was higher than ten years before: 42 per cent nearly always experienced an orgasm during intercourse. An increasing number of women experienced multiple orgasm: 30 per cent of the girls and young women, including 55 per cent of the 17-year-olds. However, young men are still far more likely to take the initiative in sexual relations, especially with regard to the first experience of sexual intercourse (Starke & Friedrich, 1984, pp. 96–7, 100–1, 136–7, 147, 187, 194–5. The second Partner Study was carried out between 1979 and 1982 among 5,496 people aged 16–30).

Table 2.11 Age of first experience of sexual intercourse (per cent)

Years	13	14	15	16	17	18	19	20	21	22	Average
Total	1	5	11	27	27	17	19	3	2	1	16.9
Young men	1	5	11	27	26	16	7	3	3	1	16.9
Young women	0	3	11	27	29	19	7	3	1	0	16.9

Source: Starke, in Starke & Friedrich, 1984, p. 137.

GDR youth researchers and sexologists have welcomed these developments, partly because their data indicate that the more fulfilling a sexual relationship based on love, the greater the engagement in political activities and the higher the performance at work and study (Voß, in Starke & Friedrich, 1984, pp. 267–71). However, there is a negative side. Many young people marry but divorce at an early age. The relatively high rate of sexual activity combined with widespread ignorance about the various methods of contraception, fear of the negative effect of the pill and deficiencies in sex education may lead to an unwanted pregnancy. One leading authority, Kurt Starke, estimates that about 10,000 babies are born to girls under 18, that is, about 5 per cent of all births (Starke, 1980, pp. 166–8).

Peter Voß discovered a positive correlation between sports participation and the sexual behaviour of young people. According to the Central Institute of Youth Research's Partner Study, the greater the participation in sport, the more frequent were the contacts with the opposite sex (Voß, in Starke & Friedrich, 1984, p. 270). The SED leadership also perceives a correlation between the achievement of its sportsmen and women and the international standing of the GDR. At the Eighth SED party congress, Honecker declared: 'Our state is respected in the world today not only because of the excellent performance of our top athletes but also because of the unrelenting attention which we devote to physical culture and sports to make them an everyday need of each and every citizen' (Gitter & Wilk, 1974, p. 15).

The GDR's sport representatives have been dubbed 'diplomats in track-suits': they contributed to breaking the diplomatic isolation of their country and they continue to enhance its international status through their outstanding performances. The GDR's tally of medals rose from sixty-nine at the Olympic Games in Munich to 126 eight years later in Moscow. International success is essentially based on an elaborate organizational network and a series of incentives. Highly gifted children are selected early in their school life and are developed at one of the nineteen special sports schools, which combine a normal but usually extended curriculum with intensive training. Talented athletes are concentrated in about thirty large and well-endowed sports clubs such as Dynamo and Vorwärts. The Sports and Physical Education College in Leipzig is world-famous for its rigorous and systematic training of coaches and instructors and for its contribution to the science of sports medicine. The reward for top athletes, including foreign travel and good career opportunities, are attractive but sacrifices have to be made. Reports appear in the Western press of the loneliness experienced by youngsters cut off from their parents and friends and, albeit rarely, of some athletes using drugs to stimulate performance.

However, the GDR aims not only to produce world-class athletes but also to make physical culture and sport a mass activity. Sport is seen as enhancing people's sense of well-being and health and their labour productivity. An elaborate system has been devised to achieve these goals. Mass sport is catered for by the major sports organ, the DTSB (German Gymnastics and Sports Association), in conjunction with the Ministry of Education, the FDGB, the GST, the Free German Youth movement and other state organizations. The DTSB was founded in 1957 and its membership totalled 3,564,852 in 1985. Its 10,000 sports communities (*Sportgemeinschaften*) are usually subdivided into sections, which provide facilities for intensive training and regular competition in a specific sport, and general sports clubs for those members with less specialized interests.

A striking feature of mass sports in the GDR is its competitive orientation. The famous children's and youth Spartakiads are staged each year in the schools, localities and districts, and biannually, though in alternate years, at regional and national level. They stimulate a high level of performance and arouse great interest. The Joint Sports Programme of the DTSB, FDGB and FDJ, a central feature of popular free-time sport, aims to encourage active recreation in the form of walking, hiking and swimming as well as the competitive instinct of participants. The key element is the insignia 'Ready to Work and to Defend the Homeland'. Badges in gold, silver and bronze are awarded for the attainment of set goals. Over 4 million people qualified for one of the medals in 1983.

On balance, the sports functionaries and scientists prefer sport to be pursued within this organizational framework on the grounds that it is more likely to guarantee a life-long participation in sport. Dieter Voigt, formerly a member of the Leipzig Sports and Physical Education College and now at the University of Bochum in West Germany, advances another, and in his opinion more significant, reason: organized sport provides the SED with greater opportunities for controlling free time (Voigt, 1975, p. 124). However, the GDR cannot be described as a large organized sports factory: the widespread pursuit of independent sport, whether individually or with friends, workmates and family members, shows that people are resistant to the functionaries' preferences. For example, research by Hinsching and Thieß has revealed that male pupils engage in independent sport about one and a half times more frequently than in organized forms (in Voß, 1981, pp. 200–1; and see Table 2.11). Moreover, despite Voigt's claim, it is certainly not the aspiration of the SED to discourage people from independent sport and leisure activities.

Although many GDR publications and official pronouncements give the impression of widespread popular participation in sport, time-budget surveys usually reveal a different picture. The rate of participation varies according to age and sex; and disturbingly low rates of activity have been observed among certain groups, especially multi-shiftworkers, apprentices and employed women. As a general rule, participation declines with age, although since about the mid-1960s in has been on the increase among the middle-aged. Heidi Bierstedt, a leading GDR sports official, has recently provided a clear overview, derived from sociological investigations, of participation rates. On average, 47 per cent of all GDR citizens take part in some form of sport at least once a week. Among 15–16-year-olds the participation rate reaches 80 per cent; it then decreases by 20 per cent among the 20–23 age group; and, finally, it declines gently towards the 40th year. Two decisive turning-points in the fall in active engagement in sport occur at around the ages of 40 and then 60 (Bierstedt, 1986, p. 29). Among the major reasons advanced for the fall in participation are: inadequacies in the organization of adult sport, especially for older people; the demands and responsibilities of work and family; the loss of the stimulus of obligatory sport after leaving school or college; the emergence of other free-time interests; and the relative shortage of sports equipment and accommodation.

Women pursue considerably less active sport than their male counterparts. The 1974 national time-budget survey recorded a disparity of 0.06 hours per day between the sexes (see Table 2.8); it also revealed the disadvantaged position of women with at least two children and of those in full-time employment. Whereas men with two children spent 0.22 hours on sport at the weekend, the women were actively engaged for only 0.04 hours (Ministerrat der Deutschen Demokratischen Republik, 1975, n.p.). In general terms, more men (56 per cent) pursue sport as a leisure activity than women (37 per cent) and the men are more involved in organized forms (see Table 2.12).

Table 2.12 Forms of sports participation of men and women (per cent)

	Men	Women
Only organized sports participation	23	19
Organized as well as independent sports participation	15	8
Only independent sports participation	18	10

Source: Bierstedt, 1986, p. 27.

Everyday chores—housework, childrearing—are clearly part of the explanation for women's lower engagement in active sport, especially in the more time-consuming organized forms. Although dissenting voices are sometimes heard, many GDR researchers and sports officials are of the opinion that greater female participation in sport depends to a considerable extent on the availability of more facilities in those types of sport which are supposed to correspond to the sex-specific physiological and psychological characteristics of girls and women. Gymnastics, accompanied by music, is frequently recommended as it allegedly accords well with girls' greater agility, their need for enjoyment and pleasure, their desire for an attractive figure and the close linkage between music and sport in their interest structure. Swimming, handball, basketball and apparatus gymnastics are regarded by Jahnke and Saß as particularly appropriate to the physiological needs of girls, whilst Bringmann and Märker, for aesthetic reasons, advise against girls' participation in boxing, wrestling and the heavy events in athletics. In order to develop the appropriate interests and needs, Jahnke and Saß advocate the continuation of the segregation of the sexes in sports lessons from the fifth grade onward. However, as the West German author Arnim Brux observes, such recommendations and policies, based on the *a priori* bipolarity of the sexes, may well reinforce rather than break down the sex-typing which associates boys with strength and endurance and girls with charm, elegance and grace (Dennis, 1982, pp. 18–20; Brux, 1980, pp. 107–8).

The Standard of Living

No consensus exists on the definition of the term 'standard of living'. The narrow definition encompasses the provision of private households with commodities and services, whereas a broader version extends the term to working conditions, education, leisure and social security. Socialist countries, including the GDR, adhere to a wider definition similar to the quality of life concept used in the West: they posit the notion of the socialist way of life in deliberate contrast to the overemphasis on materialism inherent in the narrow standard of living concept. The socialist way of life, it is claimed, will ultimately not only be richer in material terms than life in capitalist society but it is already more humane. Personal relations are supposed to be characterized by equality, mutual respect and assistance, friendship and optimism. As the socialist way of life is based on social ownership and the means of production and the political leadership of the party of the working class, a higher material standard of living is not regarded as an end in itself but as the means to the realization of the development of the socialist personality and to the satisfaction of social, cultural and intellectual needs (Ruban, in Bethkenhagen *et al.*, 1981, pp. 321–5; Aßmann *et al.*, 1977, pp. 390–7).

Without wishing to deny the importance of the components of a broader definition of standard of living such as education, health, job security and leisure, this section will first focus on private consumption, above all on consumer durables and foodstuffs, before attempting an East–West comparison of respective 'shopping baskets'. Most Western commentators would probably agree that the GDR consumer was usually neglected until the late 1950s and early 1960s and that, although GDR citizens enjoy one of the highest living standards in Eastern Europe, they are often at a disadvantage in comparison with West Germany, especially as regards the range and quality of goods available.

A comparison of per capita consumption of foodstuffs and stocks of durable consumer goods establishes the GDR along with Hungary and Czechoslovakia as the most affluent countries in Eastern Europe (see Tables 2.13 and 2.15). Per capita meat consumption is the highest by far in Eastern Europe and on a par with that of the

Table 2.13 Per capital consumption of foodstuffs in Eastern Europe, 1960–84

	Meat and meat products (kg.)		Eggs (no.)		Potatoes (kg.)	
	1960	1984	1960	1984	1960	1984
GDR	55.0	94.4	197	303	174	146
Bulgaria	29.1	71.0	84	237	35	30
Poland	42.5	57.2	143	210	223	149
Czechoslovakia	56.8	84.5	179	332	100	79
Soviet Union	39.5	60.4	118	256	143	110
Hungary	47.6	75.6*	160	327	98	58

* 1983.

Source: *StJB*, 1986, Appendix I, p. 26.

Federal Republic. Fewer breadstuffs and more protein are being consumed as incomes rise. On the other hand, the per capita fruit consumption of 70.2 kilograms in 1982 was well below that of the Federal Republic (127.1) and the consumption of beer, spirits, wine and cigarettes is on the increase (see Table 2.14). Medical warnings and sanctions against drinking at work and whilst driving and an increase in the price of spirits have not halted the growth in alcohol consumption. Alcoholism is now one of the country's most serious medical problems and excessive drinking is frequently associated with criminal offences.

In 1981, GDR households were well supplied with durable consumer goods. The stock per 100 households was higher than in most Eastern European countries but the GDR endowment of automobiles, televisions and refrigerators is lower than that of the Federal Republic. In 1982, the West German stocks of these goods were 78, 121 and 158 respectively. Although washing machines are more numerous in the

Table 2.14 Per capita consumption of alcohol, spirits and cigarretes, 1960–82

	GDR			FRG
	1960	1970	1982	1982
Cigarettes (no.)	1,069	1,257	1,788	1,829
Wine and champagne (litre)	3.2	5.0	9.7	24.8
Beer (litre)	79.5	95.7	147.0	148.1
Spirits (litre)	3.5	6.6	12.7	6.8

Source: Zimmerman, 1985, p. 815.

Table 2.15 Stocks of durable consumer goods per 100 households in Eastern Europe, 1981

	Radio sets	Television sets	Refrigerators	Washing machines	Motor cars
GDR	159*	109	114	88	40
Bulgaria	90	78	80	73	30
Czechoslovakia	183	113	97	125	44
Rumania	79	66	50	34	23
Soviet Union	89	90	88	70	10
Hungary	153	108	94	97	9
Poland	152	110	98	109	23

* 1982.
Source: *DIW Handbuch*, 1984, p. 420; Zimmermann, 1985, p. 816.

GDR (83 automatic washing machines per 100 households in the FRG in 1982), they tend to be inferior in quality, a judgement which applies with equal force to most other goods, notably private motor cars. The purchase of a motor car has been likened by Marlis Menge of the West German weekly *Die Zeit* as 'a bigger event than birthday, youth conservation and wedding combined' (quoted by Dooley, in Gerber 1981, p. 36). The long delays in the delivery of a vehicle can be circumvented through the *Genex* stores, where Western models and GDR cars may be purchased at lower prices, though in hard currency. Luxury items may, of course, be purchased at the Intershops and the *Delikat* or *Exquisit* shops.

The West Berlin-based German Institute for Economic Research regularly undertakes studies of the comparative purchasing power of the GDR Mark and the Deutschmark which shed light on living standards in the two republics. The Institute devises two shopping baskets, which are representative of consumption patterns, and then calculates how much a typical employee household of four persons and a typical pensioner's household of two persons in both countries would spend on each other's basket. GDR citizens enjoy the advantages of relatively lower prices on basic foodstuffs such as bread, meat, potatoes and vegetables; they must pay more for coffee, spirits and wine. The GDR's policy of stable consumer prices was modified in 1979: the prices of new high-quality industrial consumer goods are expected to cover costs and make a profit; a turnover tax supplements the cost of goods in this category such as television sets, motor cars and washing machines. On the other hand, rents, household electricity, gas and fuels are heavily subsidized and remain well below West German levels. Rents are only one-fifth the level prevailing in the FRG, gas and fuels 30–40 per cent (Melzer & Vortmann, 1986, pp. 261–4 Bryson, 1984, pp. 63–70). Table 2.16 provides an overview of the expenditure patterns of four-person households.

Table 2.16 Relative purchasing powr of the GDR Mark for a four-person employee household, 1960–81 (per cent)

Expenditure on	GDR consumption structure			FRG consumption structure		
	1960	1977	1981	1960	1977	1981
Foods	76	110	114	75	102	93
Tobacco, alcoholic drink, coffee	49	65	56	47	65	50
Housing	133	397	435	133	314	417
Electricity, gas and fuels	137	339	227	135	274	303
Household goods	67	63	77	66	63	52
Clothing	52	62	50	51	58	47
Cleaning and hygiene	100	102	102*	101	94	88
Education and entertainment	105	13	161*	96	81	57
Transport	105	77	n.a	103	66	n.a.
Total consumer outlay	77	103	120	75	90	83

* Not strictly comparable.
Source: Bryson, 1984, p. 68; *DIW Handbuch*, 1984, p. 278.

An examination of the representative GDR shopping basket for a four-person household shows that the GDR consumer's outlay was higher throughout the 1960s than that of the West Germans; however, since 1977, GDR citizens could purchase their own market basket for 3 per cent less of their currency than West Germans would pay for the same basket of goods in Deutschmarks. This improvement has been sustained throughout the early 1980s: in 1981 and 1985, the GDR's advantage is in the order of 20 per cent and 24 per cent respectively (Melzer & Vortmann, 1986, p. 265). The relative purchasing power of the GDR Mark emerges in a less favourable light, however, when the richer and more varied West German market basket is used as the basis for comparison. The GDR four-person household would find that the GDR mark had only 75 per cent of the purchasing power of the Deutschmark in 1960, 90 per cent in 1977, 83 per cent in 1981, and 89 per cent in 1985 (see Table 2.16 and Melzer & Vortmann, 1986, p. 264).

Prices and the purchasing power of the currency represent only one aspect of the GDR's standard of living. Income, too, should be assessed. The German Institute for Economic Research has attempted a comparative analysis of real incomes in the two states. Nominal income, which has risen more rapidly in the West than in the East, is adjusted on the basis of a mixed market basket. The latter is designed to remove disparities in purchasing power as it represents the mean of the results from the two shopping baskets. The calculations of the Institute indicate that real income in the GDR lags well behind that in West Germany: expressed in percentage terms, this was 30 in 1960, 50 in 1975, 55 in 1982 and about 50 three years later (*DIW Handbuch*, 1984, pp. 279–81; Melzer & Vortmann, 1986, p. 268). Thus, despite the many positive aspects of the GDR's social policy, including full employment, and despite its more egalitarian tendencies, the GDR consumer has to pay a price for his country's lower level of productivity and economic performance in comparison to that of the Federal Republic. This price is related to the benefits of the GDR's more egalitarian social welfare system which in turn hampers work incentives and alienates capable employees. To what extent SED policy-makers will increase levels of differentiation and how they will reconcile it with the legitimizing concept of social convergence is one of the major policy questions as the country's fortieth anniversary beckons.

3 The Political System

The Ruling Party and the Social Contract

The Socialist Unity Party of Germany (SED) remains the single most influential and powerful body in the GDR. It describes itself in its 1976 statute as 'the highest form of societal–political organization' and as 'the conscious and organized vanguard of the working class and the working people of the socialist German Democratic Republic' (Fricke, 1976, p. 107). Moreover, in Article 1 of the 1974 Constitution the GDR is proclaimed as 'the political organization of the working people in town and countryside under the leadership of the working class and its Marxist–Leninist party'. As the other four political parties recognize unreservedly the SED's leadership role and are linked to the SED through the bloc system and the National Front, their 'alliance' with the SED is dominated by the ruling party.

The party's justification of its leadership role rests, first, on its claim to have a monopoly on insights into the correct scientific laws governing social progress and hence being singularly well equipped to guide and shape advanced socialist society; and, secondly, on its claim to represent the interests of the working class, the largest and, by definition, the most progressive class.

The party buttresses this theoretical and self-legitimizing position by a tightly-knit network of party organs based on the principle of democratic socialism; by binding all state functionaries, and not only party members, to party decisions; and by means of the transmission-belt activities of the FDGB and other large mass organizations. However, the SED, or rather its apparat, cannot manipulate at will a complex industrial society such as the GDR, especially one which is so highly penetrated by exogenous forces, whether the Soviet Union or the Federal Republic, and which continues to be buffeted by the turbulence in the international economic order. Party leaders are therefore confronted by the onerous task of reconciling or integrating a series of competing and conflicting inputs into the political system. The old, simplistic totalitarian model can no longer do justice to the complexity of the party leadership's management and coordination of a plurality of institutional-ized groups such as the party itself, the armed forces, the enterprise and combine managers and the territorial organs of state as well as to its response to the pressures emanating from the 'autonomous' social forces which have proliferated in the alternative culture of peace and ecological groups. Which of the various theoretical constructs—corporatism, institutional pluralism, limited pluralism, bureaucracy—can best do justice to the nature of group politics in the GDR remains a matter of lively academic controversy; however, there can be no doubt that group involve-ment in politics has increased under Honecker and that the present leadership is more pragmatic, more flexible than in the days of Ulbricht.

The notion of a 'social contract' is applicable to this policy. Although a contract had been emerging in Ulbricht's latter years, it was not fully developed until the Honecker era. In effect, the contract constitutes a tacit and somewhat uneasy compromise between regime and populace: a relatively widespread acknowledgement of the SED's political primacy is complemented by the regime's greater sensitivity to many of the needs and wishes of the population, including a tolerable standard of living. The First Secretary's commitment to a *modus vivendi* with the populace was signalled at the 1971 congress when the SED's 'main task' was defined as raising the material and cultural standard of living on the basis of an adequate economic growth. This was reinforced in the 1976 party programme which explicitly recognized the existence of the different needs and interests of the people. Furthermore, the vast subvention of basic consumer goods in the difficult years of the early 1980s illustrates the leadership's anxiety that a serious decline in living standards might jeopardize the social contract. Other indicators of the leadership's more pragmatic approach include the informal pact with the Evangelical Church, the more flexible policy toward visits and emigration to the West, and the greater tolerance of people's retreat into their own niches. There are limits, however, to this relaxation of political and ideological controls: the SED's political organs represent a highly intrusive actor in the political process and the regime's critics may still be subjected to arbitrary treatment by the instruments of coercion.

SED Membership

The SED is both a cadre and a mass party in that a mass membership comprising a relatively high proportion of the adult population coexists with the highly privileged, full-time professional functionaries. In 1986, the party had 2,199,741 full members and 104,380 candidates (see Table 3.1).

Table 3.1 Membership of the SED, 1946–86

Date	Membership
April 1946	1,298,415
June 1948	c.2,000,000
July 1950	c.1,750,000
September 1953	c.1,230,000
December 1957	1,472,932
December 1961	1,610,769
June 1971	1,909,859
April 1981	2,043,697
April 1986	2,304,121

Sources: Zimmermann, 1985, p. 1185; Fricke, 1986b, p. 629.

The self-image of the SED requires that 'workers' should constitute the mass base of the party; however, this has not always been the case: in 1961, for example, workers represented only 33.8 per cent of total party membership. Consequently, the party organized 'proletarianization' drives to maximize recruitment from this section of the population. Moreover, it is assumed that the SED takes advantage of the imprecise definition in GDR statistics of the term 'worker' to inflate this section of the populace's representation in the party, thereby legitimizing itself as the party of the working class. Official statistics record that the party's social composition at the end of 1985 was: workers 58.2 per cent, of which production workers represented 37.9 per cent; collective farmers 4.8 per cent; members of the intelligentsia 22.4 per cent; white collar employees 7.7 per cent; students and pupils 2.1 per cent; members of production cooperatives and independents 0.8 per cent; and housewives 0.9 per cent (Ammer, 1986, p. 500).

The age structure of the party membership was difficult to delineate precisely from the mid-1960s to the early 1980s, as the relevant data appeared only sporadically. However, the more plentiful data published recently trace a relatively higher proportion of younger members than in the 1960s and a decisive change in the generational profile. The under-30s accounted for 20.3 per cent of members in 1966; twenty years later their share had increased by 3.4 per cent (see Table 3.2). The

Table 3.2 Age structure of SED members and candidates, 1981–85 (per cent)

Age	1981	1985
under 26	12.8	12.9
26–30	11.2	10.8
31–40	18.5	19.3
41–50	22.6	21.1
51–60	17.7	18.2
61–65	4.2	6.7
over 65	13.0	11.0

Source: *Neues Deutschland*, 9 January 1986, p. 3.

group of old functionaries, who belonged to one of the pre-1933 workers' parties, is rapidly dying out and is being replaced by younger comrades whose political experience was acquired after 1945. In late 1985, only 196,058 party members were founder members of the SED or communists before 1946; a further 5,140 veterans had participated in the anti-fascist resistance. Women have gradually increased their share of the party's overall membership: from 31.3 per cent in 1976 to 35.5 per cent in 1985 (*Neues Deutschland*, 9 January 1986, pp. 3–4).

The administration of a relatively sophisticated industrial society requires appropriate qualifications and expertise. A degree or equivalent qualification has become one of the prerequisites for office-holding within the party: in 1981, all secretaries of the regional party executives and district party executives and 93.7 per cent of party secretaries in combines and large enterprises were graduates; and among the rank-and-file more than one in three had successfully completed a course at university or technical college (Zimmerman, 1985, pp. 1186–7).

Specific conditions have to be fulfilled before full party membership can be confirmed by a candidate's local basic party organization. The original application for candidate membership must be supported by two party members. During the probationary period, which usually lasts for one year, candidates must familiarize themselves with the party programme and statute and demonstrate that they possess the personal and political qualities appropriate for membership. The benefits conferred by full membership include the right to elect and to be elected to party office, to discuss all aspects of party policy at meetings and in the party press, to criticize any comrade or party functionary, and to make suggestions and proposals to higher party bodies and to demand a reply (Fricke, 1976, pp. 112–13). In addition to these benefits, a member can often expect to derive an advantage over a non-party member in his/her career. The obverse side of the coin is the considerable drain on members' time represented by attendance at meetings, electoral work and study. Furthermore, members are obliged in principle to accept eleven duties. For example, not only are they committed to protecting the unity and purity of the party but they are expected to work actively for the realization of party decisions, the strengthening of the GDR and its greater economic efficiency, and to safeguard party and state secrets. In general, a party member should aspire to be a model in her/his personal life and at work (Fricke, 1976, pp. 110–12).

Errant members may be censured or even expelled from the SED. Violation of party discipline, failure to behave in a worthy manner in public and private life and the misuse of party membership or office may lead to an investigation by the member's basic party organization or a higher body. Although not 'purges' in the traditional sense of the word, comprehensive membership reviews are carried out periodically. About 4,000 members were expelled in March and April 1980, 3,787 forfeited their membership, and 1,359 resigned as a result of personal talks conducted with all but a small fraction of members and candidates between August and October 1985. The reasons cited for leaving the party ranks included 'no commitment to the party' (74.1 per cent), 'behaviour prejudicial to the party' (19. per cent) and 'unjustifiable personal demands' (6.8 per cent) (Ammer, 1986, p. 498). It has recently become apparent from official SED sources that the turnover of membership is higher than hitherto supposed. A series of reviews led to 63,000 expulsions and 25,000 resignations between April 1981 and the beginning of 1986 (Fricke, 1986b, p. 630).

Party Organization

The organization of the SED is based on the territorial–production principle (see Figure 3.1). The bedrock of the party is the basic or primary organization

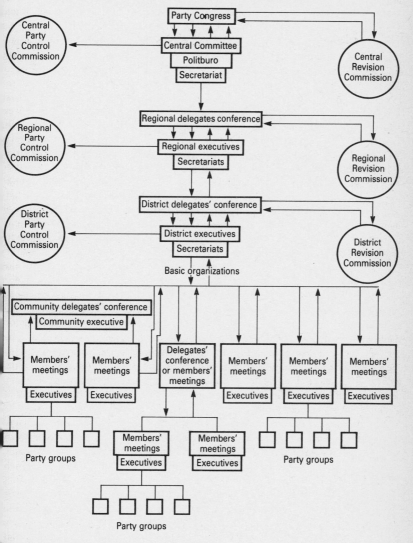

Figure 3.1 Organizational structure of the SED
Source: Völkel, in Erbe, 1979, p. 89.

(*Grundorganisation* —GO), which is established if there are at least three members at a place of work, whether in industry, commerce, education, the armed forces, the police or trade. The party organization at an industrial enterprise is called the enterprise party organization (*Betriebsparteiorganisation*—BPO). Members not in employment come under the auspices of the residential district party organization (*Wohnparteiorganisation*—WPO). If more than 150 members and candidates are attached to a GO, a departmental party organization (*Abteilungsparteiorganisation*— APO) is founded. An APO or GO with less than 150 members or candidates may be further subdivided into party groups (*Partiegruppen*) based on a work collective or brigade. In 1986, the SED rank-and-file was distributed among 59,115 GOs, 23,009 APOs and 96,104 party groups.

The basic organizations are defined by the party statute as bearing responsibility for the ideological toughening of members and candidates and for guaranteeing the SED's political, ideological and organizational influence in all sectors of society. A high priority is given to their mobilization of support for the fulfilment of economic plans, the raising of labour productivity, the application of scientific labour organization and the inculcation of socialist labour discipline. Members' meetings in the smaller GOs and delegates' conferences in the remainder elect the executives of their respective organs as well as the delegates for the district (*Kreis*) conference. In order to coordinate the activities of the party, state and the mass organizations, the GO executives include the chairman of the enterprise trade-union executive, the secretary of the FDJ basic organization and the enterprise manager.

Above the GOs, in ascending order, are the 263 district, the fifteen regional (*Bezirk*) and the central party organizations. At each of these levels the executive is elected by a delegates' conference. As the executives are usually large bodies, between 60 and 100 members in the case of the districts and regions, smaller secretariats are created to conduct the day-to-day business. The districts normally have six full-time functionaries, including the first secretary. The district party organizations ae based on either the territorial (districts, municipalities, boroughs) or the functional (large enterprises, universities, numerous ministries) principle. The 263 district party organizations do not include among their number those NVA party bodies which enjoy this status.

The fifteen regional party organizations (to which should be added the SED organization in the Wismut district) have executives varying in size from between seventy-five and eighty-five full-time members and 15 to twenty candidates. However, as in the districts, actual authority resides in the smaller secretariats, which usually consist of six full-time secretaries. The secretariats frequently conduct enlarged meetings with the chairman of the Regional Council, the chairman of the Regional State Planning Commission and leading representatives of the FDJ, the FDGB and the district party organizations. The first secretaries of the regional party organs, all men, are important personages in the SED hierarchy. Not only do they all sit on the Central Committee but Schabowski (Berlin), Böhme (Halle), Lorenz (Karl-Marx-Stadt) and Eberlein (Magdeburg) are full members of the Politburo. Walde (Cottbus) has candidate status. The Politburo constituted in 1986 thus has more regional first secretaries than any of its predecessors.

The whole organizational structure of the SED rests, as a Marxist–Leninist party, on the principle of democratic centralism, whereby each level in the hierarchy is subjected to the supervision and control of the tier immediately above it. All resolutions of the higher party organs are binding on the lower organizations and the minority as well as the individual must, at least in theory, subordinate themselves in a disciplined manner to the decisions of the majority. Factions are banned. This system is theoretically counterbalanced by the democratic election of all party organs from the base upward and by the regular reports submitted by elected party organs to their constituents. In practice, the results of elections are invariably decided in advance and procedures are determined by the SED's national bodies.

The SED's highest organ is the Party Congress which since 1971 has been held once every five years. It is also possible to convene extraordinary Congresses on the initiative of the Central Committee or at the request of more than one-third of party members. Elected representatives throughout the country assemble at the Party Congress to hear and approve the reports of the Central Committee, the Revision Commission and other central organs. The Congress elects the Central Committee and it is supposed to determine the grand policy and tactics of the party. As is well known, the Congress is too large a body and meets too infrequently to function as an effective policy-making body. It is essentially limited to ratifying policies and directives which have been determined in advance. Delegates are pre-selected by the Central Committee apparat. However, the elections and the numerous speeches at the Congress are used as opportunities for propagating the policies of the party leadership. The most important items of business are the General Secretary's lengthy report and the submission of the directive for the new Five Year Plan. Party spokesmen may use the occasion to identify or underscore changes in the general line of the party. This occurred in 1971 when Honecker unveiled the 'main task'.

The Central Committee, which is encharged by the party statute to carry out the decisions of the Party Congress, is in theory the highest organ of the SED between congresses. It 'elects' the General Secretary and delegates party representatives to the highest management organs of the state apparat and the economy. Moreover, it directs the work of the elected central state organs and the mass organizations by means of the party groups existing within them. A plenum must be held once every six months.

The Central Committee has varied in size under Honecker from 189 in 1971 to its present 165 members and fifty-seven candidates. Women, as usual, are under-represented: they constitute 10 per cent of current members and 18 per cent of candidates (Fricke, 1986b, p. 631). The composition by age group in April 1986 is set out in Table 3.3. The candidates were on average considerably younger than the full members. In comparison to the slightly smaller 1981 Central Committee, the 1986 body had nine more representatives among the youngest age group but an additional ten sexagenarians and three octogenarians.

The breakdown of the Central Committee by occupation reveals a preponder-ance of party and state functionaries but, in view of the party's economic strategy, a surprisingly low representation of economic and scientific-technical interests

Table 3.3 Age structure of the SED
Central Committee, April
1986

Age	Number
30–39	13
40–49	30
50–59	106
60–69	48
70–79	19
over 80	6

Source: *Neues Deutschland*, 22 April 1986,
pp. 4–5.

among the full members. Out of the 165 full members, ten are full-time party and
state functionaries. The full-time party officials, with sixty-three representatives,
constitute by far the largest group. The party chief, Honecker, is the leading figure in
this group. Seventeen of the secretaries of the forty-one departments of the Central
Committee Secretariat enjoy the status of full members. Low-level party officials are
barely visible: only six of the 263 first secretaries of the district party organizations sit
on the Central Committee. The second largest group is formed by the forty-seven
representatives of the SED in the state apparat and the President of the People's
Chamber, Sindermann. The foremost central state organ, the Council of Ministers,
is, as expected, well to the forefront: twenty-seven out of the Council's forty-four
functionaries, including its chairman, Willy Stoph, appear on the Central
Committee. The Defence and Foreign Ministries, too, enjoy a high profile among
the full members.

The thirty-one representatives of the mass organization (sixteen), associations and
academic institutions (fifteen) comprise the third group of members. Their much
higher representation since Honecker's first Central Committee signifies the party's
attempt to raise their status, in particular that of the FDGB which contributes seven
full members. The FDJ sends three and the Writers' Union five full members. Both
the FDGB chairman, Harry Tisch, and the FDJ Central Council First Secretary,
Eberhard Aurich, sit on the Central Committee.

Finally, the fourth group of full members is composed of sixteen representatives
from industry, agriculture and other occupational spheres: six general directors of
combines, including Professor Wolfgang Biermann of Carl Zeiss, one head of a
combine department, four agricultural functionaries and two team leaders
(*Brigadiere*) in enterprises. However, this group is more conspicuous among
candidates: eight foremen (*Meister*) and team leaders, two general directors, seven

enterprise management personnel, six agricultural functionaries, four academics and the director of a major hospital (*Neues Deutschland*, 22 April 1986, pp. 4–5; Bundesminister für innerdeutsche Beziehungen, 1986a, pp. 9–12).

The range of party interest groups represented on the Central Committee probably justifies labelling it as a mini-parliament for discussing and advising on party matters. Party leaders use it to gauge elite reaction to policies and the published extracts from reports to the plenary sessions frequently contain critical assessments by Politburo spokesmen of the country's domestic and foreign policies. However, the Central Committee meets too infrequently to perform a policy-making function and it has undergone little change since the elaborations of its essentially consultative role within what the West German political sociologist Peter Christian Ludz defined as 'the consultative authoritarianism' of the 1960s. The SED's supreme decision-making bodies remain the Central Committee Secretariat and the Politburo.

The Secretariat of the Central Committee, which is elected by the Central Committee, is responsible for the direction of current work, above all for the implementation and supervision of party resolutions and for the selection of party cadres. The eleven members of the Secretariat are each responsible for a particular area of policy. For example, Günter Mittag is in charge of economic affairs and the only woman secretary, Inge Lange, deals with women's questions. Honecker's most likely successor, Egon Krenz, is in charge of security, youth and sport. The Secretariat meets once a week and the General Secretary, Honecker, takes the chair. It also supervises the work of the departments (*Abteilungen*), with, it is estimated, a staff of about 2,000. The departments' control over access to vital information ensures that the Secretariat has a key role to play in the overall decision-making process. However, the precise nature of the relationship between the Secretariat and the Politburo remains somewhat obscure.

The Politburo, though the main decision-making body of the SED, receives only two lines in the party statute, where it is described as being elected by the Central Committee to discharge the political work of the Central Committee between its plenary sessions (Fricke, 1976, p. 124). In practice, as it concerns itself with the basic questions affecting the SED, the government and the economy, it is the functional equivalent not only of the political executive of a Western-style political party but also of the Cabinet in Britain. Like the Secretariat, which deals with ongoing party work, it assembles once a week. Ten out of the eleven members of the Secretariat are also full Politburo members; the only female secretary, Inge Lange, is a candidate. Decisions within the Politburo are probably reached by consensus rather than by recourse to voting; Honecker, however, is undoubtedly *primus inter pares* (Gaus, 1983, p. 148).

The size of the Politburo has fluctuated between fourteen and twenty-seven, if members and candidates are counted together. Whereas its 1981 predecessor numbered seventeen members and eight candidates, the Politburo elected after the Eleventh Party Congress consisted of twenty-two members and five candidates. The average age of the new Politburo was 62.7 years (April 1986). Only two women,

Margarete Müller and Inge Lange, sit on this august body; both have been candidates since 1963 and 1973 respectively. No woman has yet attained the status of full member, a surprising omission in the light of the party's commitment to the equality of women.

Eight of the members of the Politburo at the time of their re-election in 1986— Honecker, Axen, Hager, Mielke, Mückenberger, Neumann, Sindermann and Stoph—were septuagenarians. Honecker, Mückenberger and Stoph are the longest-serving members. Stoph entered the Politburo as a full member in 1950, the same year as the other two were appointed candidates. Clearly, this generation, whose political beliefs and values were refined in the pre-war KPD and in the struggle against fascism, must soon give way to a generation whose roots lie solely or primarily in the GDR and the SED, not in an all-German past. Its departure may be accelerated by the shock waves of a reformist leader in the Kremlin and his general impatience with bureaucratic inertia. At the 1986 Party Congress, which Gorbachëv attended, the SED leadership revealed itself as highly cautious and reluctant to engage in the kind of political reforms advocated for the Soviet Union by the CPSU leader. Significantly, the SED organ, *Neues Deutschland*, has carefully refrained from giving detailed coverage of Gorbachëv's commitment to *glasnost* (openness). Whether this ultimately benefits Egon Krenz, who has obviously been groomed as Honecker's successor, remains to be seen. Krenz, born in Kolberg in 1937, acquired his political spurs as the First Secretary of the Free German Youth (appointed in 1974). He joined the Politburo as a candidate in 1976 and was upgraded to full member as well as a Central Committee Secretary in November 1983; he is currently in charge of the politically important posts of Central Committee Secretary for security and for youth and sport. Except for a lack of expertise in economic matters, he appears to have acquired most of the necessary skills in party management and although he is not a scintillating public speaker, this handicap did not prevent Ulbricht and Honecker from attaining high office.

Various institutions and interests are represented on the Politburo: the armed forces by the Minister of Defence, General Heinz Keßler, born 1920, and a founder member of the FDJ; the state security apparat by its veteran minister, Erich Mielke; and the FDGB by its chairman and experienced trade-union functionary, Harry Tisch. Gerhard Schürer, born in Zwickau in 1921, occupies the post of chairman of the State Planning Commission. Günter Mittag, five years younger than Schürer, is an economics specialist who, in the 1960s, was one of the main proponents of the New Economic System. The chairman of the Council of Ministers, the experienced and taciturn Willy Stoph, headed the economic policy section of the Central Committee in the late 1940s and served as Minister of Defence from 1956 to 1960.

The current Politburo was reshaped not so much by the elections in 1986—Keßler and Böhme were the only new appointments—but by the eighth and eleventh plenary sessions of the Central Committee in May 1984 and November 1985. The changes in the Politburo's composition undoubtedly reinforced Honecker's control over and authority within the party's main policy-making body. His foreign policy and the economic intensification strategy were also reaffirmed. In 1984, Paul Verner, who, it was speculated, may have harboured doubts about Honecker's policy toward West Germany, was retired; Werner Jarowinsky and Günter Kleiber, both advocates of the New Economic System, were promoted from candidates to full members. In the following year, 1985, Konrad Naumann, allegedly a critic of Honecker's pursuit of inter-German détente and of Honecker's relatively pragmatic domestic and cultural policy, was removed from the Politburo and was replaced as First Secretary of the Berlin regional party organization by the former editor of *Neues Deutschland*, Günter Schabowski, a man whose loyalty to Honecker has hitherto not been in doubt. Remarks attributed to Naumann reveal a rare glimpse into the existence of strains within the Politburo which must arise from time to time over difficult policy-making decisions. In November 1982, with probable reference to the GDR's approaches to Bonn for a large credit, Naumann declared that 'the political principles of the GDR are not wares to be haggled over, they cannot be bought with dollars and in other ways' (quoted in Baylis, 1986, p. 416). Naumann, it has been alleged, travelled to Moscow in the autumn of 1984 in an attempt to depose Honecker as party leader by the next SED congress (*Der Spiegel*, 31 August, 1987, p. 339). Schabowski, aged 58, has risen rapidly: he did not enter the Central Committee until 1981, the same year as he became a Politburo candidate; promotion to full member occurred four years later. Three other regional party first secretaries—Gerhard Müller, Werner Eberlein and Siegfried Lorenz—achieved candidate status in 1985 (Fricke, 1985, pp. 1251–3).

The SED elite in the Politburo is reliant on the organizational talents and political loyalty of a multitude of cadres to implement and monitor party and state policy in all areas of society. Their number was estimated at 195,000 by Starrels and Mallinckrodt in the mid-1970s (1975, p. 85). Whereas political loyalty was originally the indispensable prerequisite of a cadre, toward the end of the 1950s, but especially after the introduction of the New Economic System in 1963, cadres were also required to master the technical skills entailed in the administration of society. Thus in addition to ideological training at a variety of party schools, specialist skills and knowledge must be acquired in the requisite social sciences, sciences or engineering. An elaborate system of further training enables cadres to keep abreast of new developments in management techniques, party policy and their own specialist subjects. The key positions in all areas of society are controlled by the SED through the nomenclature, a list of positions at three levels, which require the direct or indirect approval of the appropriate SED department before they can be filled. The level-one nomenclature cadres of the SED include the heads of department of the Central Committee apparat, while that of the state covers ministers and the chairmen of the regional and district councils (Glaeßner, in Erbe, 1979, pp. 104–6).

The Allied Parties

The four allied parties—CDU, LDPD, NDPD and DBD—unswervingly follow the leadership role of the SED. As we saw in Chapter 2, the CDU and the LDPD pursued an independent line in the late 1940s; however, since the early 1950s all four parties have essentially performed a transmission function. That is, they transfer the policies and decisions of the ruling party to groups of people not under the direct organizational control of the SED in order to secure their support for official policies. Needless to say, the preservation of the outward appearance of a multi-party system is also a useful legitimizing device both at home and abroad. The CDU and the LDPD perform a modest role as a bridgehead between similarly named parties in the Federal Republic. For example, a representative of the West German Free Democrats, Wolfgang Mischnick, attended the 1987 Party Congress of the LDPD. In addition, all four allied parties provide modest opportunities for political participation outside the confines of the SED and they possess attenuated rights to articulate the needs, views and grievances of their members.

The DBD's basic constituency is the cooperative farmer, but the recent upgrading in the status of the VdgB, one of the mass organizations, has undermined its role as the mouthpiece of the farming community. The NPDP, which once numbered over 230,000 members (1953), was originally conceived of as a political home for former national socialist members and soldiers. The party chairman, Heinrich Hohmann, was himself a former member of the NSDAP and a major in the Reichswehr. Whilst in captivity in the Soviet Union, he joined the National Committee for Free Germany. The social profile of the NDPD is now similar to that of the CDU and the LDPD. In 1985, 32 per cent of its members were recruited from white-collar employees and 22 per cent from among artisans and tradespeople. The intelligentsia account for 17 per cent but workers only 4 per cent of membership (see Bundesminister für innerdeutsche Beziehungen, 1986b, p. 10). The interests of shopkeepers, sections of the intelligentsia professionals and self-employed craftsmen are also represented by the CDU and the LDPD. Although these two parties acquiesced in the transfer of a large proportion of existing artisan cooperatives into nationalized enterprises in 1972, the SED's subsequent reappraisal of the value of private and cooperative artisan enterprises (in particular those performing services and repairs) revived their flagging fortunes. In general terms, the SED leadership's recognition that its allies have a role to play in representing the needs and wishes of a variety of groups in a highly differentiated socialist society suggests that the small parties have a guaranteed if relatively modest future. Only the DBD would seem to be under any threat.

Membership has risen in recent years. In 1987, the DBD's membership stood at 115,000 (an increase of 11 per cent since 1982); the NDPD attracted 110,000 and the LDPD 104,000. The latter figure represented an increase of about 25 per cent over the preceding five-year period (see Lapp & Löwis of Menar, 1987, pp. 728–30).

The largest allied party, the CDU, is supposed to act as the political voice of Christians in the GDR. It has normally enjoyed limited 'elbow room'. In 1972, several CDU parliamentary deputies opposed the new abortion law and in 1964, partly as a result of pressure from Christians in the CDU, the SED conceded the right of conscientious objectors to serve in construction units during national service. However, the CDU adheres to the official line on peace and security: in the

1980s, it has, for example, supported the SED campaign for defence education in schools and it has not embraced the autonomous peace initiatives.

All allied parties are represented in the national and local assemblies but, significantly, they are denied permission to establish their own political organizations in the NVA, the enterprises and the universities. A special SED Central Committee department for relations with friendly parties oversees developments in the allied parties and ensures that they do not compete with the SED for members among the working classes. Although a member from each party is a deputy chairman of the Council of State and Council of Ministers, the parties' representatives are conspicuous by their absence among the departmental heads of the Ministry of Foreign Affairs, the chairmen of the regional councils and the members of the State Planning Commission.

The Constitutional Arrangement

The GDR's first constitution, adopted in 1949, represented a compromise between the SED's socialist aspirations and the bourgeois conception of the other political parties. In some respects it was patterned on the Weimar Constitution of 1919. It contained a section on the limits of state authority, including a catalogue of liberal-democratic basic rights. It envisaged a system of election by proportional representation and the right of representation in government of all parties with at least 10 per cent of the seats in the People's Chamber. The newly created ceremonial office of President, the head of state, was occupied by the veteran Communist and co-chairman of the SED, Wilhelm Pieck.

Three significant changes were made later to the 1949 constitution: the five *Länder* were replaced in 1952 by a system of fifteen regional administrative units (*Bezirke*); military service was introduced in 1955 and made compulsory seven years later; and in 1960, on the death of Pieck, a Council of State was created to replace the office of President.

By 1967, it was decided to introduce a new constitution which would take account of the many fundamental socio-economic and political changes which had occurred since 1949. For example, the 1967 law on a separate GDR citizenship clashed with the 1949 constitution's proclamation of a common German citizenship. A draft constitution was submitted to popular discussion and came into force in April 1968.

The new constitution embodied many basic rights, including the right to work and an equal right to education; men and women were granted equal rights and legal equality in all spheres. Although freedom of assembly and freedom of speech were guaranteed, they were both circumscribed by the phrase 'according to the principles of the constitution'. Several rights embodied in the first constitution were modified or removed completely. The right to strike and the right to emigrate both disappeared and work was defined as a duty as well as a right.

The principle of the unity of powers was retained in the 1968 Constitution. Article 48 states that the rights of the People's Chamber cannot be restricted and that it 'is guided in its activities by the basic principle of unity of decision and execution'. The liberal–democratic concept of checks and balances achieved, at least in theory, by the separation of the judicature, legislature and executive was regarded as incompatible with a socialist society in which the fundamental interests of the working class tally, it is alleged, with those of the overwhelming majority of the people. Led by its Marxist–Leninist party, the working class holds political power and unites the entire working population around itself. Political unity is supposedly derived from the social unity achieved through social ownership of the means of production which, according to Marxist–Leninist theory, enables 'public and personal interests to be harmonized . . . and offers people an equal right to take part in political life' (*Introducing the GDR*, 1976, p. 57).

Considerable attention is paid to the structure of the state. Article 47 lays down that 'The sovereignty of the people, realized on the basis of democratic centralism, is the sustaining principle of the administrative structure of the state'. In other words, all organs of state power are bound to respect the plans drawn up, the laws passed and the decisions taken by the next higher body. The state organs include elected assemblies at local and central level, the legal and security system and national bodies such as the Council of Ministers and the National Defence Council. However, Article 1 left no doubt where final control lay: 'The GDR is the political organization of the urban and rural working people who are jointly implementing socialism under the leadership of the working class and its Marxist–Leninist party'. The SED, through the Politburo and its other major organs, defines the political priorities and monitors the decision-making process. The institutions of state are therefore instrumental in the implementation of party-determined policies. In addition, the state organs provide opportunities for political participation not only by SED loyalists but also by the many citizens who do not belong to the ruling party, and the state acts as a mechanism for resolving conflicts and for furthering the integration of society. This theoretical complementarity of party and state is not, of course, always achieved in practice.

Although membership of state and party positions frequently overlaps, the 'withering away of the state' is not on the political agenda. If the possibility of the disappearance of the state was an item for discussion in the 1960s, the Honecker era has witnessed a firm rebuttal, at least until that distant day when a classless communist society materializes. The Marxist–Leninist theory of the state now in favour in the GDR calls for a strengthening of the state in the present stage of the further shaping of 'the developed socialist society' (Akademie für Staats- und Rechtswissenschaft, 1979, p. 85). State institutions perform a wide range of complex tasks: the promotion of scientific–technical progress and the raising of labour productivity; the protection of the rights and liberties of the citizens and the safeguarding of socialist property; the provision and organization of educational and cultural facilities; the realization of social welfare goals; the development of socialist consciousness; and the further 'perfecting' of socialist democracy (Zimmermann, in von Beyme & Zimmermann, 1984, pp. 34-9; Akademie für Staats- und Rechtswissenschaft, 1979, pp. 152, 221-2, 266-7, 287, 307-8).

The Honecker era has experienced not only an amplification of the role of the state but also a major revision of the 1968 Constitution. Although only 66 of the 108 articles of the 1968 Constitution were not reframed, the 1974 document is regarded by the GDR as no more than an amendment to Ulbricht's constitution. The major changes concern: the GDR's conception of itself as a separate nation; the revision of Ulbricht's notion of socialism; and the redistribution of powers in favour of the Council of Ministers and the People's Chamber at the expense of the Council of State.

The description of the GDR in Article 1 of the 1968 Constitution as 'a socialist state of the German nation' was amended to 'a socialist state of workers and farmers'. The ties with the Soviet Union were bound even more firmly by Article 6: 'The German Democratic Republic is for ever and irrevocably allied with the Union of the Socialist Soviet Republics'. These new articles underscored the demarcation policy of the early 1970s. It was, however, an indication of the regime's uncertainty on the sensitive national question that the constitution did not refer explicitly to the GDR as a new socialist nation, a concept which the SED leadership was then employing to distinguish the GDR from the 'capitalist nation' in the FRG. Honecker's influence on the new constitution can also be traced in the reintroduction of the term 'communism' and the removal of the references to 'the societal system of socialism'. Instead, the GDR was described as a 'developed socialist society' (Article 2), which was progressing toward communism, thereby refuting Ulbricht's view of socialism as an autonomous social formation.

Organs of State Power

The People's Chamber

The unicameral People's Chamber (*Volkskammer*), the GDR Parliament, is defined in the 1974 Constitution as the supreme organ of state power in the country. It elects the members of the Council of State, the Council of Ministers, the Chairman of the National Defence Council, the President and the judges of the Supreme Court and the Procurator-General. In addition, it 'determines the aims of the development of the GDR through laws and resolutions which are binding on everyone' and it ratifies state treaties. Since 1971, deputies have been elected for a period of five years; previously they had served for four years. The Chamber compromises 500 deputies (463 until 1963), including forty from the capital, who in 1981 were elected directly instead of being nominated, as hitherto, by the city parliament. Between 1963 and 1986, the five political parties and four of the mass organizations were represented in the Chamber and the distribution of seats, determined in advance in a unitary list of candidates prepared by the National Front, was fixed at: SED—127, DBD—52, CDU—52, LDPD—52, NDPD—52, FDGB—68, DFD—35, FDJ—40, and KB—22.

Then in 1986, as part of a campaign to raise the profile of the rural community and agriculture, the Farmers' Mutual Aid Association (VdgB) re-entered the Chamber after an absence of twenty-three years; it recouped its seats from the FDGB (seven), the FDJ (three), the DFD (three) and the KB (one). Membership of the parliamentary contingent of a mass organization does not preclude membership of a political party: in 1986, fourteen of the twenty-one deputies of the KB were also SED members; and, *in toto*, about 90 per cent of the mass organizations' deputies belonged to the ruling party (Lapp, 1986, p. 681; Bundesminister, 1986c, pp. 9–10).

The social composition of the Chamber has not altered perceptibly since 1971 (see Table 3.4). Workers represent the largest social group; women remain under-represented, constituting 32.4 per cent of the deputies in the 1981–6 period and 32.2 per cent in the newly elected Chamber.

Table 3.4 Social structure* of People's Chamber deputies, 1971–91

Social group	1971–76	1976–81	1981–86	1986–91
Workers	219	235	236	271
Members of agricultural cooperatives, small farmers, horticulturalists, fishermen	77	60	52	31
White-collar workers	102	127	89	69
Intelligentsia	101	76	115	126
Others	1	2	8	3

* According to vocational training or first job.
Source: Neugebauer, in Zimmermann, 1985, p. 1440; *Junge Welt*, 14–15 June 1986, p. 4.

Competitive elections in the Western sense are dismissed as unnecessary as the key question, the acquisition of political power by the party of the working class in a society free from exploitation, has been resolved. As unity has been established there is no need to seek it by means of the Western pseudo-democratic process. What then is the purpose of a general election in the GDR? The main purposes would appear to be: to demonstrate outwardly the legitimacy of the regime; to enhance the integration of society; to involve citizens in a particular form of political participation without the risk of 'spontaneity'; and to propagate governmental and party policies by means of meetings of the electorate with the candidate and so forth.

The National Front, to which all political parties and mass organizations belong, is responsible for the conduct of elections to the People's Chamber and the other representative assemblies. The election programme, which is drawn up by the National Front, is based on the overall policy of the SED. All candidates for election to the People's Chmaber must have received the prior approval of the appropriate SED cadre department before they are nominated by their work collectives. The collectives may exercise the right to check the suitability of candidates. The next stage in the process is the presentation of candidates to representatives of the electorate at public meetings organized by the National Front. Although the electoral representatives can propose the rejection of a candidate, the final decision rests with the National Front. The single list of candidates, which is ultimately presented to the electorate, is identical with the result of the election. Since 1965, the list has contained more candidates than there are seats. In 1986, 203 successor candidates were nominated in addition to the 500 candidates for election to the People's Chamber. No example is known of the order of candidates being reversed by the voters. The successor candidates are allowed to take part in the work of the Chamber and the other representative assemblies but they do not have the right to vote. Parliamentary deputies perform various functions outside the Chamber. Although they are expected to continue in their full-time jobs, they are required to conduct surgeries for their constituents. Secondly, they carry out political communication between the government and the citizen. They are obliged to acquaint their electors with government policy and to encourage their participation in the political process. The flow of information is not one way: the deputies are expected to inform the full-time state apparat of the needs, wishes and grievances of their constituents (Lapp, 1984, pp. 26–57; Zimmermann, 1985, p. 1447).

As elections are perceived by the authorities as a general ratification of the existing system, no effort is spared to ensure the highest possible turnout. Voters are encouraged to proceed to the polls not as individuals but together with other members of their work collective or *Hausgemeinschaft* (tenants' community). Although separate booths are provided at the polling stations, the pressure to cast votes openly rather than risk drawing attention to oneself by using a booth, persuades the vast majority of voters to perform the simple act of folding and dropping their ballot paper into a box. The paper does not even identify the party or organization to which a candidate belongs. Moroever, only if the names of all the candidates are crossed out is this regarded by the electoral commissions as a negative vote against the unitary list drawn up by the National Front (Lapp, 1984, pp. 79–88). During the 1986 Volkskammer elections, observers of the peace movement in East Berlin observed that where voters had entered 'idiots' by the names of candidates of the National Front list, this was interpreted as positive as the names had not been crossed out. A report from Jena revealed that individuals suspected of 'deviant activity' had been crossed off the electoral register (*DDR-heute*, December 1986, n.p.). Given these conditions, it is not surprising that the electoral participation rate is extremely high and negative voting a rare occurrence. In the elections of the People's Chamber in June 1986, 99.74 per cent of the electorate turned out to vote and 99.4 per cent cast their vote in favour of the National Front's list. As in the past, the highest percentage of negative voters (0.17–0.21) was recorded in several East Berlin constituencies (Lapp, 1986, p. 680).

Once constituted, the People's Chamber elects a Presidium which directs the Chamber's business and the plenary sessions according to standing orders. Horst Sindermann has been the President since 1976. Twelve of the fifteen standing committees each have jurisdiction over a specific area of public life, such as industry, education and foreign affairs; the other three deal with citizens' petitions, standing orders and the supervision of mandates. The committee enjoy the right to discuss bills and check on the implementation of laws. Although committees which are involved in the less sensitive political areas appear to play an active role in shaping legislative proposals, the attempt to upgrade the Chamber has, as might be expected, met with little success. In other words, it remains essentially a confirming body. This is not surprising when one considers that the committees meet on average only three times per year and that plenary sessions of the Chamber are so infrequent (see Table 3.5). These sessions usually last for only one or two days, and no discussion takes place of economic plans or draft legislation. All bills have been approved unanimously except in 1972 when fourteen CDU deputies voted against the proposed abortion law and eight abstained.

Table 3.5 Number of plenary sessions of the People's Chamber, 1950–81

Legislative period	Number of sessions
1950–54	49
1954–58	36
1958–63	27
1963–67	27
1967–71	20
1971–76	18
1976–81	13

Source: Neugebauer, in Zimmermann, 1985, p. 1443.

Local Government

For administrative purposes, the GDR has been divided since 1952 into fifteen regions (*Bezirke*), each of which is named after its major city; however, East Berlin's separate status has not been formally recognized by the three Western powers. Below these large administrative units are the thirty-six urban and 191 rural districts which are in their turn divided into 7,550 communities or municipalities. Each tier has a representative assembly, an executive organ, an elected council and a standing committee. The principle of democratic centralism underpins this structure. A higher-ranking body is entitled to rescind the resolutions of a lower-level organ if these impinge on its competencies.

The manifold functions of the local authorities include: the maintenance and modernization of the housing stock; the provision of consumer goods and facilities for recreation; and the organization of the public transport system. Furthermore, since the 1985 law on Local People's Representative Bodies, local authorities have become co-responsible for the intensification of economic performance in their territory, in particular for the management, planning and organization of rationalization programmes (*Neues Deutschland*, 5 July 1985, p. 3).

All deputies, with the significant exception of full-time state and party officials, perform their functions on an honorary basis. By combining a full-time job with representative duties, the deputies, so it is argued, are able to keep in touch with their electorate. A closer and trustful contact between citizens and their elected representatives and local government bodies has been proclaimed as one of the major objectives of the new local government law. However, serious problems exist. Even the Council of State has admitted that the insensitive and bureaucratic behaviour of some functionaries has been detrimental in the past to the realization of this goal (Probst, 1985, pp. 788–90). This highlights the advantageous position of the executives and the full-time state administrators *vis-à-vis* the ordinary deputies. The effectiveness of the deputies is likely to be impaired by the fact that they have a regular job in addition to their representative duties. In order to counteract these and other negative tendencies, deputies are supposed to be recruited from among the 'best representatives' of the workers, cooperative farmers and intelligentsia. They should have distinguished themselves as activists, innovators or heads of research collectives and enjoy a high reputation in their work collectives for their political and vocational achievements (Büchner-Uhder, Hieblinger & Poppe, 1986, p. 6). Efforts are also made to mobilize young people, women and production workers.

There are almost 200,000 deputies from regional to community level. Women and young people are well represented in the district and community assemblies (see Table 3.6). The relatively high proportion of deputies with a degree or technical college certificate indicates the importance of a formal qualification for access to these bodies, although the proportion declines from the People's Chamber downward.

While it is acknowledged that their myriad tasks give large numbers of people some experience, as deputies, in the running of affairs, especially at local level, most of the real power lies with the full-time functionaries and professionals. Moreover, the formalism of so much political participation, including the election process, has been a regular target not only of dissident intellectuals like Robert Havemann and Rudolf Bahro but also, though far less radical, of a number of critical social and political scientists such as Uwe-Jens Heuer who have argued that the conflict of interests between classes, groups and individuals can only be resolved by increasing individual political participation within the framework of socialist democracy (Heuer & Mollnau, 1983, pp. 548–9). Subjectivism and bureaucratism must be overcome, contends Heuer, by more worker participation in economic and political

Table 3.6 Composition of regional assemblies, district assemblies, community assemblies and borough assemblies

	County assemblies*	District assemblies†	Community assemblies	Borough assemblies
According to mandate				
SED	806	5,125	59,698	781
DBD	320	1,903	13,656	137
CDU	316	1,974	10,325	285
LDPD	316	1,911	5,825	285
NDPD	316	1,948	5,409	284
FDGB	444	5,930	23,006	1,174
DFD	255	2,632	17,217	385
FDJ	286	3,844	17,116	664
League of Culture of the GDR	113	705	1,806	96
VdgB	–	1,045	11,715	13
Consumer Cooperative Societies	–	506	5,286	71
Total	3,172	27,523	171,059	4,175
According to sex				
Men	1,944	15,801	108,050	2,453
Women	1,228	11,722	63,009	1,722

According to age			
18–24 years	550	6,107	25,332	950
25–30 years	316	3,116	18,188	579
31–40 years	600	5,846	36,246	1,029
41–50 years	890	7,353	48,192	1,037
51–60 years	720	4,464	34,712	498
61 years and over	96	637	8,389	82
According to social status				
Workers	1,595	16,306	83,220	2,781
Members of LPG, GPG and PGB	376	3,461	42,986	24
Office employees	986	6,488	35,598	1,220
Members of PGHs, commission agents	108	363	1,503	36
Tradesmen, self-employed craftsmen, freelance workers	78	442	3,294	56
Other deputies	29	463	4,458	58

County assemblies: as of 14 June 1981. District assemblies, community assemblies, borough assemblies: as of 6 May 1984.

* Including the City Assembly of Berlin, capital of the GDR.

† Including town assemblies of urban district and borough assemblies of Berlin, capital of the GDR.

Source: StPB, 1985, p. 19.

affairs, albeit as part of a dialectical unity of discipline and democracy (quoted in DDR *Report*, no. 11–12, 1983, p. 694. I owe this reference to Krisch, 1985, p. 175).

Of course, the SED political elite cannot remain impervious to demands made from 'below', whether by the professional groups of scientists, managers, economists, military and security experts and writers, or by the citizenry at large. It recognizes the need to consult various groups in order to obtain the information, ideas and recommendations necessary for the identification of priorities and the finalization of policy decisions. Indeed, the speeches of party leaders rarely fail to acknowledge the importance of popular participation in the policy-making process. For instance, in his address in February 1987 to the assembled first secretaries of the SED district organizations, Honecker expressed his satisfaction that 'ever broader sections of the people are to be involved in running the state and public affairs in responsible offices', and he reminded his audience that 'Nothing provides so wide and direct an impact on people's lives as the results of local policies' (*Implementing the resolutions*, 1987, pp. 91, 92). He warned, furthermore, that the complaints and petitions of the people 'must be handled in an unbureaucratic fashion' (*Implementing the resolutions*, 1987, p. 93).

Yet this is extremely circumspect language: the SED leader, in contrast to his Soviet counterpart, prefers a more pragmatic approach to domestic politics, a cautious 'perfecting' or 'improvement' of the system; not for him the boldness of Gorbachëv's democratization campaign and his harsh criticisms of: the lack of proper control over executive organs; the abuse of office and favouritism; party and state officials' intolerance of independent action and thinking by subordinates; and the usurpation of the functions of elected bodies by executives (see, for example: 'Gorbachëv Addresses Party', 1987, pp. 8–14).

Obviously, individual members of the Honecker team may, like the Brezhnev gerontocracy, find themselves prematurely out in the political cold if Gorbachëv's wind of political change reaches the GDR. However, any policy changes are likely to be within the framework of the present order, especially in view of the undoubted success of Honecker and his colleagues in maintaining political and social stability in such a highly sensitive political arena as the GDR and in surviving, with considerable adroitness, the formidable military and economic challenges of the 1980s. And it should be remembered that, as yet, the Soviet process of regeneration does not entail the rejection of democratic centralism or the power prerogative of the party in Soviet society, two principles which underpin the GDR political system.

The Government Structure

The Council of State

The Council of State was created as a 'collective head of state' immediately after the death of the GDR President, Wilhelm Pieck, in 1960. Until his resignation as party secretary in 1971, Ulbricht extended the State Council's powers at the expense of the

Council of Ministers. Article 79 of the 1968 Constitution proclaimed the Council of Ministers as functioning not only on the basis of the laws and decrees of the People's Chamber but also of the decrees and decisions of the Council of State. The latter's decrees and decisions enjoyed legal force and its activities embraced all important domestic and foreign affairs. Ulbricht used his position as Chairman of the State Council to enhance his own power and authority. For example, Article 69 empowered the Chairman to direct the work of the Council and to represent the People's Chamber in international relations.

Despite his enforced resignation as First Secretary in 1971, Ulbricht managed to cling on to the post of Chairman until his death in January 1973. However, in the year prior to his death, the Council was downgraded as a legislative body, a change that was confirmed by the 1974 revision of the constitution. It managed, on the other hand, to retain certain rights and functions, although these are mainly ceremonial: it announces the elections of the People's Chamber and of the other representative assemblies; it exercises the right of amnesty and pardon; and it ensures the permanent supervision of the constitutionality and legality of the Supreme Chamber and the Prosecutor-General on behalf of the People's Chamber. Members of the National Defence Council are appointed by the Council of State and the two bodies cooperate with each other in organizing the defence of the country. As titular head of state, the Chairman of the Council of State appoints the diplomatic representatives of the GDR to other states and receives the credentials and letters of recall of accredited foreign representatives.

The Council of State elected in June 1986 consisted of twenty-eight members, including the Chairman, eight deputy chairmen and representatives from the allied parties and the mass organizations. The chairmen of the four allied parties are all deputy chairmen and Honecker, as Chairman of the Council of State since 1976, is therefore both head of state and SED party leader.

The Council of Ministers

The Council of Ministers resumed its function as the government of the GDR in 1971. The reallocation of authority between the Council of State and the Council of Ministers was finalized by the 1974 constitutional amendments. Under the leadership of the SED the Council of Ministers performs a wide variety of tasks. It formulates the broad lines of governmental domestic and foreign policy on behalf of the People's Chamber. It organizes and supervises the implementation of government policy in the political, economic, cultural and social welfare spheres in addition to those defence functions which are allocated to it. Furthermore, it directs the work of the central ministries and the regional councils and it submits bills and drafts of decrees to the People's Chamber. This proliferation of tasks accounts for the Council's large membership (forty-five in 1986) and for the numerous organizational changes since its creation in the early 1950s.

The Council's main field of action lies in the planning and supervision of the economy. A major task is the preparation and coordination of the annual, five-year and long-term economic plans. The State Planning Commission, the Office for Prices, and the Workers' and Peasants' Inspectorate assist the Council in its planning of the national economy. A smaller group, the Presidium, currently numbering fourteen members, is usually regarded as the 'economic cabinet' and the real decision-making centre of the Council.

Article 80 of the constitution defines the Council as a collective organ. Ministerial proposals are discussed, coordination decisions reached, reports received and decisions of the Presidium confirmed at weekly meetings of the whole Council. Members are elected by the People's Chamber for a period of five years and the Chairman is nominated by the largest political group in parliament. Willy Stoph, an experienced and talented administrator, occupied this position between 1964 and 1973; after a brief spell as Chairman of the Council of State, he returned to his old post in 1976, replacing Horst Sindermann. All except four out of the current forty-five members belong to the SED; seven sit on the Politburo. As an essential requirement of membership, technical expertise in a specific field would, apart from several obvious exceptions, appear to rank ahead of political skills. Most of the constituent ministries or offices have responsibility for a specific sphere of the economy: light industry, finance, foreign trade, coal and fuel, electrical engineering and electronics, glass and ceramics, heavy engineering, the State Planning Commission and the Office for Prices. Excepting Stoph and his two first deputy chairmen, Werner Krolikowski and Alfred Neumann, who have no specific portfolio but have held important economic posts, twenty-nine of the remaining forty-two members are involved in the administration of the national economy. The 'classical' ministries are not entirely ignored; they are represented by justice, education, health, foreign affairs and defence. Erich Mielke, the Minister of State Security, occupies a place on the Council.

The Ministry of State Security (MfS)

The major function of the Ministry of State Security, or 'Stasi' as it is more commonly known in the GDR, concerns fending off what the regime conceives of as threats to national defence and security posed by foreign or domestic subversion. This entails the investigation of major crimes, controlling dissident elements and the observation or interception of foreigners useful for espionage. The Ministry's domestic role was enhanced by the opening-up of the GDR after the Four-Power Agreement on Berlin (1971) and the Basic Treaty (1972). Party leaders make no secret of their approval of the external activities of the Ministry. Honecker has referred to the need for 'socialist spies on the invisible front'. The external activities, directed above all against the Federal Republic, are controlled by the Ministry's Main Department for Reconnaisance (*Aufklärung*).

A secret police establishment was created in the Soviet zone soon after the end of the war but a separate Ministry of State Security was not founded until 1950. The nucleus of the new body was the Main Department for the Protection of the National Economy in the Ministry of the Interior. The direct involvement of the first two ministers, Zaisser and Wollweber, in attempts to overthrow Ulbricht created considerable turmoil in the organization of the state security service. However, the appointment of Erich Mielke as minister in 1957 inaugurated an era of stability and organizational efficiency but tighter control by the party leadership. Mielke, born in 1907, had been attached to the security apparat of the old KPD. He was involved in a political murder in 1931 and spent most of the war in Moscow, probably performing military and security tasks (Fricke, 1984a, pp. 213–16).

Symptomatic of the close cooperation between party and MfS in the Honecker era is Mielke's entry into the Politburo in 1971 and his upgrading to full member five years later. Other leading MfS officers are to be found in the party's leading organs: one of Mielke's deputies, lieutenant-general Rudolf Mittig, and the chief of the MfS party organization, major-general Dr Horst Felber, are both full members of the Central Committee. All MfS officers are probably SED members; however, this is almost certainly not the case among the rank-and-file.

The political direction and control of the MfS is the immediate responsibility of the Central Committee department for security questions and the security section of the Central Committee Secretariat presided over by Egon Krenz. A grand celebration of the Ministry's role as 'shield and sword' of the SED was held on its thirty-fifth anniversary in February 1985. At the unusually well-publicized 'secret policemen's ball' at the Palace of the Republic attended by top party and MfS leaders, Mielke reaffirmed his Ministry's 'unshakeable loyalty' to the SED and paid tribute to the purposeful leadership of the party of the working class as the decisive basis for the successful development of the MfS into a fighting-fit organ of state firmly rooted in the nation and feared by the class enemy (*Neues Deutschland*, 7 February 1985, p. 2).

While the MfS is undoubtedly a vital instrument of SED rule, such a secretive organization may well develop considerable autonomy or, as in the 1950s, it may be employed as a power base by the minister against the party leadership. Ulbricht's lingering suspicions of the MfS may be one reason why Mielke failed to gain entry into the Politburo until Honecker's accession. The presence of the veteran head of the 'Stasi' in the GDR's most important political body is one reason why, even under Honecker, the organization is in a favourable position to escape subjugation to the Central Committee Secretariat's security section whose own head, Krenz, is less experienced than Mielke. And, finally, the clandestine *modus operandi* of the MfS provides it with additional elbow room (Fricke, 1984a, p. 78).

The main Western authority on the MfS, Karl Fricke, estimates that the Ministry's full-time staff, excluding the 6,000–7,000 men in the Guards Regiment Felix Dzierzynski, has risen from about 4,000 in 1952 to perhaps 20,000 in the early 1980s (Fricke, 1984a, pp. 50–1). Moreover, it can draw upon about 60,000 to 80,000 unofficial informers in all areas of society who are active not only in the factories, institutes and the armed forces but also at meetings and sports events. The motivation for becoming an informer is manifestly mixed: political conviction, financial reward, professional advancement all play a role; but coercion and blackmail, too, are sometimes used to obtain recruits (Fricke, 1984a, pp. 103–7).

Mielke once attempted, in the SED's official monthly *Einheit*, to justify cooperation with the MfS on the grounds that the party

> regards safeguarding the state security of the GDR not just as a task of specially designated organs but as a matter of concern for the whole state and the whole of society. It is in the interest of the socialist state and every citizen to take an active part in constantly strengthening and protecting the workers' and peasants' power. [Mielke, 1980, p. 156]

As well as collecting information for the personal dossiers of individual citizens, the MfS performs typical police work, including house searches and arrests. It possesses two central pre-trial detention establishments in Berlin-Lichtenberg and Berlin-Hohenschönhausen and additional prisons in the capital and the other fourteen major regional cities. In the 1950s, it was involved in kidnapping many former GDR citizens living in the West. Heinz Brandt, a former secretary of the SED's regional party organization in East Berlin, suffered this fate in 1961. Sentenced to thirteen years' imprisonment, Brandt was eventually 'pardoned' in 1964 and permitted to return to the Federal Republic (Zimmermann, 1985, p. 910). Finally, the surveillance of mail and telephone conversations is the responsibility of special MfS units. No special effort is made to keep this activity secret, an indication of one form of psychological pressure which is used to encourage citizens to conform.

Although MfS activities create a climate of uncertainty, excesses are by no means so widespread or common as in the 1950s and the present regime is much more tolerant of critical discussion among, for example, the autonomous peace and ecological groups and creative artists. Perhaps, as Karl Fricke contends, most citizens have come to regard the MfS as an unavoidable nuisance (1984a, p. 222). Nevertheless, the MfS occasionally acts in an arbitrary manner, not only against political dissidents but also against some of the citizens who lodge an official request to leave the GDR. Anyone attempting to leave the GDR without official permission faces a charge of illegal crossing of the frontier. If, however, citizens persist in applying for official permission to leave, they may face political charges such as 'defamation of the state'. Of the approximately 200 political prisoners in the GDR adopted by Amnesty International in 1981, over 160 had been imprisoned on account of unauthorized or legal attempts to leave the country (Ammer, 1985, pp. 950–1). According to official West German sources, there were at least 2,000 political prisoners in the GDR (Fricke, 1987, p. 160) before the amnesty in July 1987.

The Mass Organizations

Although the SED has over 2 million members, it must, in addition to the governmental system, rely on a series of mass organizations to implement and rally support for party policies. These organizations, while catering for the specific interests of their own members, act as 'transmission belts' for the SED. Moreover, they provide a source of information about people's attitudes, which can be used to shape party policies and propaganda, and they represent a training ground for management cadres in the party, state and economy. Although membership of the organizations is voluntary, SED members form the nucleus of the executives. The chairmen and secretaries of the most important mass organizations at the various organizational levels are simultaneously members of the corresponding SED executives. All mass organizations recognize in their statutes the leading role of the SED and their organization is governed by the principle of democratic socialism. However, the mass organizations should not be written off as mere conduits for party directives. The larger bodies, notably the FDGB and FDJ, perform essential advisory and consultative functions within a complex decision-making process and they enjoy a limited scope for the articulation and representation of their members' interests.

The most important mass organizations and their membership figures are given in Table 3.7. Only the first six are formally represented in the GDR's elected assemblies.

Table 3.7 Membership of selected mass organizations, 1985

Confederation of Free German Trade Unions	9,375,922
Free German Youth	2,300,000 (1981)
Democratic Women's Association of Germany	1,500,000
Farmers' Mutual Aid Association	529,497
Consumers' Cooperative Societies	4,559,951
League of Culture of the GDR	263,874
Society for German–Soviet Friendship	6,000,000
Ernst Thälmann Pioneer Organization	1,340,557
People's Solidarity	2,093,260
Chamber of Technology	275,236
Association of Allotment Gardeners, Settlers and Breeders of Livestock	1,358,994
German Sports and Gymnastics Association	3,564,852

Source: *StJB*, 1986, pp. 321, 403–6.

The Confederation of Free German Trade Unions (FDGB)

The FGDB was founded in February 1946 as an integrated trade-union organization which was intended to encompass working people of various political persuasions. The creation of the FDGB was a crucial step toward the later merger of the KPD and SPD as it deprived the socialists of their traditional base in the free trade unions. From 1947 onwards, the SED intensified its efforts to convert the FDGB into a 'transmission belt' of the party. A decisive element in the assertion of institutional control over the workforce was the dissolution in November 1948 of the workers' enterprise councils and the transfer of their rights of worker representation to the more pliant enterprise trade-union organizations. The democratically elected enterprise councils were regarded as an obstacle to the realization of SED goals, partly because they comprised many non-SED members: in the council elections of 1948, independent candidates received over 50 per cent of the workers' votes (Fricke, 1984b, p. 84). The completion of the SED's administrative control over the unions was achieved at the FDGB's third national congress in 1950: the FDGB recognized the leading role of the SED and accepted democratic centralism as its basic organizational principle (Zimmermann, in Zimmermann, 1985, p. 461).

This did not, however, guarantee a quiescent workforce. Conflict erupted over the imposition of autocratic union officials over the workers, the implementation of technological work norms (TAN), and the introduction of an annual enterprise agreement (*Betriebskollektivvertrag*). These agreements, which deprived workers of many of their rights over the setting of production norms, encountered fierce resistance in many factories, especially in such traditional centres of the working-class movement as the Leuna and Zeiss-Jena works (Fricke, 1984b, p. 85). The collapse of the June uprising did not terminate worker opposition: it returned to the factory, manifesting itself in passive opposition to work norms and planning targets. Gradually, however, after the construction of the Berlin Wall and with the introduction in 1963 of limited decentralization in the New Economic System, both union officials and the workforce developed a less adversarial relationship, helped by an expanded role for the FDGB in economic activity and an extension of workers' participatory rights in the factories. The FDGB's slow evolution from essentially a transmission belt of the SED to 'something of an active junior partner' at the workplace (Reuschemeyer & Scharf, in Pravda & Ruble, 1986, p. 61) culminated in the 1972 Law on the Council of Ministers which envisaged joint decisions and decrees between the FDGB and the Council in areas such as social welfare and income policy.

All sixteen trade unions in the GDR are united under the umbrella of the FDGB. The eight industrial unions and the unions for areas such as health, education and civilian employees in the NVA do not enjoy autonomous status; they can be dissolved by the FDGB Presidium. The Congress, the supreme body of the FDGB, is convened once every five years. Between congresses, trade-union affairs are managed by the elected Presidium. The FDGB is based on the territorial and production principle. Trade-union branches or organizations are formed at enterprises and institutions wherever there are at least ten FDGB members.

Over 97 per cent of the workforce, with the exception of the cooperative farmers, troops and the self-employed, belong to the FDGB. Over 2.5 million activists perform trade-union functions as shop stewards, sports organizers, labour safety officials, and so forth. Posts at the local level are filled by volunteers, who are usually non-SED members. These functionaries are normally elected for a term of two and a half years, whereas the central trade-union bodies are elected for a period of five years.

The high rate of participation in the various bodies of the FDGB is impressive but much of this activity reflects SED policy to confine and integrate working people into the existing political order and to forestall autonomous trade-union activity. The SED exercises a tight control over key personnel for though most trade-union functionaries do not belong to the ruling party, the leadership positions are held by SED officials. The FDGB Chairman, Harry Tisch, his deputy, Johanna Töpfer, and all the chairman of the regional organizations are recruited from the ranks of the SED. Furthermore, the trade unions and their enterprise committees are engaged in the fulfilment of official goals: the achievement of production targets; the raising of labour productivity; the involvement of the workforce in the formulation of the annual economic plans; and the operation of the Labour Code provisions concerning wages, labour safety and worker training. Finally, despite extensive co-determination rights in areas such as the dismissal of workers, the allocation of bonuses and the setting of work norms, the trade unions do not possess these rights in the decisive area of economic decision-making and they lack institutional influence over the appointment of an enterprise manager (Biermann, 1978, p. 108).

The FDGB's wide range of activities, on the other hand, make it an indispensable actor at the workplace. In addition to the tasks mentioned above, it administers the social insurance programme and provides package holidays for workers. In 1984, it arranged holiday tours for over 1.8 million citizens. The FDGB and the enterprises own more than 1,600 holiday homes and hotels. Places in such homes are in great demand and are available to FDGB members at only 30 per cent of the actual cost.

The trade unions are also involved in the work of the conflict commissions which settle small labour disputes and minor violations of the Labour Code and socialist work discipline. Conflict commissions are set up at enterprises with at least fifty employees. The eight to fifteen lay assessors are proposed for election by the enterprise trade-union executive. The commissions meet in open sessions and appear to represent an effective form of popular justice administered by workers on their fellow workers. Although the commissions can impose fines and public reprimand, they are not empowered to imprison offenders. This reinforces their educative function.

Western commentators have observed a conscious effort since the early 1970s to raise the status of the FDGB above that of the other mass organizations. One expression of this aspect of SED policy was the 1978 Labour Code's amplification of the FDGB's co-determination rights. The numerous activities of the Confederation and its functionaries also reinforce its key position within the system and undeniably provide it with some leverage at the workplace. However, its expanded role as a channel for worker participation and as a representative of workers' interests is circumscribed by its other role as a transmission belt of the SED. These two roles are by no means easy to reconcile: workers have to be convinced rather than merely informed—the latter is a standard complaint—that, for example, labour rationalization schemes and multi-shiftworking schedules will not be detrimental to their working and living conditions. Here is the basic dilemma of the FDGB in the 1980s and beyond: the credibility of the trade unions will be emasculated if they are perceived, in the final analysis, as a co-intrument of management and party policy.

The Free German Youth (FDJ)

The Free German Youth was founded in 1946 not as the youth organization of the SED but as the democratic, anti-fascist movement of all young people, no matter what their religious or political affiliation. The gradual transformation of the FDJ into a socialist youth organization was initially resisted by those FDJ members and officials who came from CDU, LDP and Church circles. However, by 1950, this resistance had evaporated and two years later the new FDJ constitution openly acknowledged the leadership position of the SED. The FDJ and the affiliated Ernst Thälmann Pioneers for children 6–14 are the only youth organizations permitted in the GDR.

Membership of the FDJ is open to all young people aged 14–25. In 1982, its 2,300,000 members constituted 77.2 per cent of all young people in that age group. The participation rate varies according to age and activity: whereas virtually all pupils in the eighth to twelfth grades at school, apprentices and young soldiers belong to the FDJ, membership is much lower in rural areas and small enterprises. In general terms, participation falls rapidly after completion of an apprenticeship and entry into the FDGB. Only about one-third of the 18–25-age group belongs to the FDJ (Freiburg & Mahrad, 1982, p. 99).

The organizational structure of the FDJ follows the usual GDR model. Every school, enterprise and university has an FDJ organization. There were 28,191 primary or basic organizations in 1983. The main organ is the Parliament which meets once every five years. The parliamentary deputies elect the FDJ Central Council, which had 123 members and twenty-nine candidates in 1981; it meets three times per year. *De facto* political control is exercised by the Bureau of the Central Council. About 670,000 people (in 1983), or about one-third of all members hold an office in the organization (Freiburg, in Zimmerman, 1985, pp. 453–4). These officials constitute a supply of young cadres for the SED and the state bureaucracy. Egon Krenz, a former First Secretary of the Central Council, is a full member of the Politburo and Erich Honecker was the FDJ's first chairman.

The FDJ's 1976 statute depicts the movement as 'an active helper and reserve force' of the SED. In conjunction with the other agents of socialization—the family, school and mass organizations like the GST—it strives to mould young people a socialist personalities whether at work or school or in their leisure time. No effort i spared in the realization of this goal: young people sit as FDJ deputies on popula representative bodies at all levels; 8,865 youth clubs (1983) cater for leisure interests and special youth projects tie young people to the state's economic and socia objectives. The FDJ's 'Berlin Initiative' is part of the capital's rebuilding programme and another project covers the development of industrial robots. Young Innovators Fairs (*Messe der Meister von morgen*), launched by the FDJ in 1957, are held throughou the country for the exhibition of young people's scientific and technologica achievements. The FDJ is an active participant in the military training programmes which are regarded as indispensable for the ideological upbringing of young socialists. The Hans-Beimler contests rank among the FDJ's most important military training activities. Organized by the FDJ, the GST and the schools, these events are the major form of military sports education for pupils in the eighth grade at secondary school. Finally, the public order groups (*Ordnungsgruppen*) represent a kind of FDJ police force for maintaining order and discipline at sports events, dances, youth meetings and so forth. In 1982, about 40,000 members were engaged in these groups (Freiburg, in Zimmermann, 1985, pp. 455-8).

The FDJ and Thälmann Pioneers obviously enjoy much success in reaching the vast majority of young East Germans, in obtaining new recruits for the SED and in training a nucleus of politically active young people to take over political functions. Like the FDGB, the FDJ has at its disposal an array of material incentives and mechanisms for ensuring at least the functional support of most young people for the GDR's social and political system. In addition to the tens of thousands of youth clubs and discos, the FDJ's tourist agency arranges holiday trips for about 500,000 young people (in 1984). Exemplary work in the FDJ may be vital for obtaining a much coveted university or college place; the FDJ has the right to participate in decisions on access to higher education.

Yet severe limits remain on the extent to which the FDJ articulates and caters for the interests of young East Germans. Many do not wish to pursue their interests within the framework of an 'official' organization: they prefer to spend their free time in informal peer groups, listening to music, dancing or simply having a 'natter'. A minority turn to the unofficial rock and punk groups, gigs in church halls or old tenements and imitate Western skinheads, punks and new romantics. Furthermore, time-budget surveys reveal that young people spend relatively little time on political activities and GDR youth researchers admit that ritualism characterizes much overt FDJ activity such as political meetings and demonstrations. It should be stressed, however, that idealism and a healthy criticism of bureaucracy and secretiveness are found among some young FDJ functionaries (Hanke, 1986, p. 32).

The Interlocking Relationship: Party-State-Mass Organizations

As has been seen, the SED exercises close political control over the socialist state and the mass organizations. The SED effectively controls the electoral process by means of the National Front; broad questions of national policy are determined by the party's top bodies, the Politburo and the Central Committee Secretariat; party members in the state organs and mass organizations are formally obliged to follow party instructions; party groups at various levels of the state system monitor governmental performance; and the approval of the appropriate SED department is required for the appointment of cadres to leading positions in the nomenclature. Another important mechanism of SED control is the interlocking membership of posts in the party, state and mass organizations. Table 3.8 illustrates the relatively

Table 3.8 SED Politburo representation on leading state bodies and mass organizations, June 1986

Name and date of birth	Party		State					Mass Organizations	
	Politburo	Secretariat	People's Presidium	People's Chamber Committee Chairman	Council of Ministers	Council of State	State Planning Commission	FDGB	GDR-Soviet Friendship Society
Axen, H. (1916)	X	X		X					
Böhme, H-J. (1929)	X								
Dohlus, H. (1925)	X	X							
Eberlein, W. (1919)	X								
Felfe, W. (1928)	X	X				X			
Hager, K. (1912)	X	X		X		X			
Hermann, J. (1928)	X	X							
Honecker, E. (1912)	X	X				X			
Jarowinsky, W. (1927)	X	X							
Keßler, H. (1920)	X				X				
Kleiber, G. (1931)	X				X				

Name						
Krolikowski, W. (1924)	X	X			X	
Lorenz, S. (1930)	X			X		
Mielke, E. (1907)	X	X		X	X	
Mittag, G. (1926)	X	X		X		
Mückenberger, E. (1910)	X	X	X			X
Neumann, E. (1909)	X	X		X		
Schabowski, G. (1929)	X	X				
Sindermann, H. (1915)	X	X	X	X	X	
Stoph, W. (1914)	X	X	X	X		
Tisch, H. (1927)	X	X		X	X	X
Lange, I. (1927)	X					
Müller, G. (1928)	X					
Müller, M. (1931)	X			X		
Schürer, G. (1921)	X	X		X	X	
Walde, W. (1926)	X				X	

Source: Compiled by author.
Note: Dates of birth are taken from Buch, 1982.

high representation of Politburo members and candidates in the leading organs of state and mass organizations; Honecker, Hager, Mittag, Mückenberger, Sindermann, Stoph, Tisch and Schürer all hold two positions in addition to their seat on the Politburo. The total SED representation on prestigious state bodies is conspicuously high, especially on the Council of Ministers, where forty-one out of forty-five members belong to the party; furthermore, thirty-one out of these forty-one sit on the SED Central Committee. Sixteen of the Council of State's thirty members, including the head of the chancellery, and seven of the thirteen members of the Presidium of the People's Chamber are recruited from the leading party. The SED is highly visible elsewhere: according to Ammer (1986, p. 499), 590,000 functionaries of the FDGB, 185,000 FDJ officials and 133,000 deputies in all representative assemblies are party members. The SED is not only the strongest political group in the People's Chamber (127 deputies) but the vast majority of the deputies of the mass organizations belong to the party.

Despite the elaborate network of party controls and the overlap of personnel, the state and the large public organizations should not be dismissed as simply the pliant executors of an omniscient party apparat. Although the SED's political primacy is unchallenged, a highly educated and occupationally diversified society, the growing complexity of policy-making, and the need to incorporate the millions of non-SED members into the existing system are some of the considerations which preclude the SED from ruling by fiat. The SED leadership organs simply cannot issue instructions or directives from above for automatic transmission downwards by the myriad regional and local bodies. Local officials have to exercise a degree of initiative in responding to the particular interests and needs of their community, needs which cannot always be encompassed by central policy directives. Moreover, throughout the state system cadres have acquired the technical expertise and access to information which are essential for the shaping of long-term strategy and national policy by the SED's political leadership and central bureaucracy.

The SED's leading organs must therefore consult and draw upon a plethora of advisory bodies and individuals to assist them in questions relating to the shaping of policy on economic growth, scientific-technical progress, culture and education. The New Economic System in the 1960s provided specialists with an early opportunity to exert a limited influence on the policy process. Since Honecker became party leader, but above all since the launching of the economic modernization strategy in the 1980s, experts—whether natural scientists, engineers, economists or sociologists—have been drawn into a more extensive network of consultation and cooptation. The politicians draw upon social scientists for advice on key issues such as the social implications of new technologies, the motivation of the workforce and the raising of labour productivity. The inherent complexity of these issues provides key specialists with greater scope for influencing decisions but, at the same time, also generates disagreement among the experts themselves. Antonia Grunenberg has identified one such cleavage between a group of dogmatic Marxist–Leninist scholars, often philosophers, and a group of more flexible economists, labour scientists and legal scientists. This conflict can be discerned, for example, in the current debate about the need for the active cooperation of all sections of the workforce in the planning and the implementation of new forms of work organization in industry. (The debates can be followed in the specialist journals such as *Sozialistische Arbeitswissenschaft*, *Arbeit und Arbeitsrecht* and *Deutsche Zeitschrift für Philosophie*.)

This does not mean that a Western-style pluralism has emerged: certain groups, above all the party and state bureaucracy but also the military and the MfS, still occupy an advantaged position in terms of access to the key decision-making groups. And despite recurrent attempts by Western scholars to inflate the political status of some groups of experts (the most recent is Clemens Burrichter's thesis on the emergence of a 'knowledge elite' of social scientists, writers, engineers and natural scientists), one should be careful not to overstate their influence by identifying them as a junior partner of the party elite. The political influence of the experts remains severely restricted by the comprehensive party–state complex outlined in this section. Furthermore, whilst consensus-building and a widening of the parameters of the policy-making process have become easier than in the politically more volatile 1940s and 1950s, the party does not refrain from what Starrels and Mallinckrodt refer to as 'an occasional resort to selective coercion when confronted by group and individual opposition to its policies' (1975, p. 198).

Political Dissent

The authoritative dictionary of political terms, the *Kleines politisches Wörterbuch*, asserts that: 'No objective political or social basis exists for the existence of an opposition in socialist states, for the working class—in alliance with all other working people—is the class which not only exercises power but is also the main productive force in society' (1978, p. 652). As for the need for a parliamentary opposition, another official publication reassures its readers that none of the five political parties would wish 'to exchange the well-established practice of working together for an "opposition role"' (*Freedom, Democracy, Human Rights*, 1976, p. 24). Who, the pamphlet asks, 'would wish to oppose the peace policy of the government or socialist system which guarantees all sections of the population a secure existence today and tomorrow?' (p. 24).

Official dogma notwithstanding, opposition has proved endemic to GDR society, especially in the early days when SED plans for the construction of socialism were opposed by religious and political groups and, most seriously of all, by the industrial workers in June 1953. And until 1961, emigration to the West was available to those who rejected the new social and political order.

Unfortunately, no agreement exists on a definition of the term 'dissent' in socialist societies and where the line, if any at all, should be drawn between opposition and dissent. Dissent is treated here as strong disagreement or dissatisfaction with established ideas or values. However, it is recognized that the fluidity of the legal and political parameters, the tactics both of the regime and the dissidents themselves, outside pressure and so forth make classification problematic. Judged by

Gorbachëv's recent pronouncements, today's Soviet leader would have been yesterday's dissident. This verdict might have been passed on Ulbricht in the later 1960s when he committed himself to a limited decentralization of the economy and a modest revision of the notion of developed socialism.

In the following pages, Bahro and Havemann will be treated as exemplars of anti-systemic dissidence of a traditional Marxist pedigree. The autonomous peace movement illustrates the complexity and the growing diversity of dissidence in the 1980s (ecological protest is examined in Chapter 5). The small peace, ecological, gay and women's groups have managed to secure a niche outside the confines of the established political system; however, at times, they overlap with the official value system and with certain state and party bodies. They are classified here as critical dissidence within the framework of what has been termed an alternative political culture. As critical dissidents, members of such groups as well as individuals deviate from official positions and tend to focus on specific issues such as peace and the environment. However, critical dissidence, at one end of the spectrum, may well border on the more fundamental and comprehensive rejection of the existing political system of the intra-Marxist intellectuals. At the other end of the spectrum it is linked to debates in official circles (as are some of the ideas of Bahro and Havemann) on the development of a more humane socialism at work, the protection of the environment and the role of the individual in society.

Finally, emigration will be examined in this section. Although individual emigrants are not necessarily dissidents, they constitute, together with the even larger number of applicants for official permission to leave the GDR, a significant challenge to and deviation from the regime's aspirations to create effective as well as functional support for the GDR 'socialist fatherland'.

The Autonomous Peace and Ecological Groups

The emergence of an autonomous, grass-roots peace movement critical of official policy constitutes a new and unexpected departure in GDR politics. Tim Garton Ash testifies to the significance of this development:

> When I lived in East Berlin in 1980, it was hard to imagine that within two years there would be independent, voluntary groups all over the country in which young people could get together and actually say what they thought about the most urgent political concerns of the day … this itself is a moral and psychological breakthrough for countless individuals. [1983, p. 250]

Since 1978, when the introduction of compulsory theoretical and practical pre-military training in schools for pupils aged 14–16 triggered off widespread protest on the part of the clergy and parents, autonomous peace groups have become more outspoken and more visible on the political landscape of the GDR. In the early 1980s, peace initiatives have attracted considerable popular support, above all among young people. The rapid growth of these initiatives can be attributed in part to the influence of the debates in the FRG on the deployment of Cruise and Pershing

II missiles and to an awareness of the activities of the peace movements in Western Europe. However, the GDR-specific preconditions should not be overlooked or underestimated: the growing militarization of life not only at school but in the Thälmann Pioneers, the FDJ and the GST; the desire for freedom of expression; and the 'shelter' provided by the Evangelical Church for discussions about and practical support for peace initiatives.

The Evangelical Church, especially since the informal pact with the state in 1978, has provided considerable space for the articulation of 'unofficial' views (see Chapter 5). For example, at a conference of Evangelical Church Directorates in July 1982 the production, testing and deployment of nuclear weapons was denounced as a moral evil. The major open event has been the annual Dresden Peace Forum, notably that of February 1982, which was attended by about 5,000 people, despite the authorities' attempts to suppress news of the event and hinder travel to Dresden. At the Forum, speakers called for the introduction of obligatory peace education in schools. The authorities forcibly suppressed the wearing of the famous 'Swords into Plough-shares' emblem whose popularity mushroomed after the 1982 Forum. Students and apprentices who wore the badge faced expulsion from college.

Other activities include, since 1980, the Peace Weeks and the Peace Workshops which attract thousands of young people. The Peace Weeks, organized each November, encompass services, discussions, poetry and music. These events are not confined to peace groups: the Peace Workshop held at East Berlin's Church of the Redeemer in July 1983 was attended by women's, gay and ecology groups. The East Berlin pastor Rainer Eppelmann, who has been a focal point of the peace movement since the beginning of the 1980s, organizes highly popular blues masses. The masses consist of blues and rock music, meditation and reading. In 1984, about 6,000 mainly young people attended the blues mass at Eppelmann's church in East Berlin. This may, however, have represented a turning-point since numbers declined sharply to about 2,000 participants in 1985 and then to over 1,000 in the following year; a waning interest in the blues masses themselves rather than pressure from the state and the church authorities seems to be the main reason for the fall in attendance (Röder, 1986, p. 106).

A few young men refuse military call-up: Wensierski estimates that about 100 did so in 1982. Penalties can be severe: in November 1985, about forty men, mainly total conscientious objectors, were imprisoned for several weeks before church intervention secured their release towards the end of the month. Since the Construction Soldiers decree of 1964, conscripts can serve in a construction unit as an alternative to formal military service. The number of young men choosing this option varies from 350 to 700 per year. Although not engaged in formal military duties, the construction soldiers are obliged to wear their own uniforms with a spade emblem on the epaulette (Wensierski, 1983, p. 12; Sandford, 1983, pp. 28–32; Henkys, 1986a, p. 30). In 1981, a group in Dresden proposed a more radical solution: a community peace service as a civilian alternative to military service. Those performing this kind of service would be employed in homes for children, old people and the physically and mentally handicapped, in auxiliary service in hospitals and community care.

Despite the support of the church synods for the proposal, the authorities refused to contemplate it. Werner Walde, a Politburo candidate, countered that the GDR itself was a community peace service.

Small women's peace groups have been formed in several cities under the protective cover of the autonomous peace movement. When in March 1982 the new Military Service Law was passed providing for the conscription of women aged 18–50 in the event of an emergency, several hundred women signed a letter of protest to Honecker. In their letter, in October 1982, they contended that army service for women was not an expression of equality but in contradiction to their being female (Hundreds of Women Make Pacifist Protest, 1982–83, p. 39). Bärbel Bohley and Ulricke Poppe, two leading figures in 'Women for Peace', were arrested in December 1983 but released soon afterwards.

Rainer Eppelmann, a co-author of an even more far-reaching document, the 'Berlin Appeal', has also suffered brief imprisonment for his views. It was in January 1982 that Eppelmann, in conjunction with Robert Havemann, launched the 'Berlin Appeal' calling for the withdrawal of all 'occupation troops' from the GDR and the FRG and the conclusion of a peace treaty between the victors of the Second World War and both German states. The former allies, it was proposed, should then agree on guarantees of non-intervention in the internal affairs of the two German republics. The authors of the document, after having broken a taboo by referring to the occupation forces and the limited sovereignty of the GDR, next sought to identify the internal preconditions of peace. They proposed a great debate on peace in an atmosphere of tolerance and they urged the renunciation of the production and sale of military toys, the introduction of a community peace service and the replacement of defence studies in school by lessons about problems of peace (Sandford, 1983, pp. 95–6). Within the short space of three months the Appeal attracted 2,000 signatures.

Independent peace activists opposed the deployment of Cruise and Pershing II missiles in Western Europe and the stationing of Soviet nuclear weapons in the GDR and Czechoslovakia. The 'Rostock Appeal', initially attracting 100 signatories, 'noted with abhorrence the announcement of the National Defence Council of the GDR on 25 October 1983 concerning the deployment of operative–tactical Soviet missile complexes' (the text is in *Labour Focus on Eastern Europe*, Winter 1984, p. 22). In the town of Weimar slogans were daubed on walls: 'SS-20s—No thank you' (Hartmann & Urban, 1985, pp 143–4). Even the SED leader intimated his concern: in November 1983, he defended the need for Soviet counterdeployments to the installation of missiles in the FRG but commented that these measures had 'evoked no joy in our country' (Asmus, 1985, p. 748). He also stressed his desire to limit the damage to East–West relations following deployment. On the other hand, he could not have been expected to respond positively to a petition drawn up by members of the peace movement which, in April 1986, called for a policy aimed at the medium-term withdrawal of the GDR from the Warsaw Pact, the departure of all foreign troops from the GDR, and the conclusion of a peace treaty between the two German states (*GDR Peace News*, Summer 1986, p. 3).

Although peace activities and concerns are certainly not confined to the Evangelical Church and Christians, the church, as the only 'self-supporting' institution outside the control of the party and state, provides the essential sanctuary. It is, however, a difficult and taxing relationship for all concerned. The church hierarchy desires to embrace the autonomous peace movement but without jeopardizing its fragile compact with the state by becoming the centre of an overt political opposition against state and party. This delicate balancing act leaves church leaders open to charges of expediency from the more impatient peace activists. Tension also exists within the church over to what extent the peace groups, which contain many non-church members, should be incorporated more firmly into the organizational framework of the church (Krusche & Passauer, 1985, p. 160).

The SED has adopted a 'carrot and stick' approach toward the unofficial peace movement. It occasionally resorts to open repression, as in the 'decapitation' of the Jena peace community in late 1982 and early 1983. The organization of a one-minute silence for peace in Jena town centre precipitated numerous arrests and the subsequent expulsion from the GDR of several of the group's leaders. On the other hand, the regime tries to undermine the movement by more subtle means: by staging official rock-for-peace concerts and designing attractive headbands and emblems similar to those of the autonomous groups. The FDJ has been assigned the crucial task of mobilizing young people's support for slogans such as 'Make Peace Against Nato Weapons', a deliberate counter to the autonomous movement's rallying cry of 'Make Peace Without Weapons'. Quite clearly, the SED leaders are reluctant to crush the peace groups by force as they are aware of the repercussions such a course of action would have on the regime's image and interests in the West as well as its credibility within the GDR itself. And while the church remains the main shelter and conduit for the autonomous peace initiatives, the regime is probably confident that it can contain what is still very much a minority movement.

It is generally agreed that adherents to the autonomous peace movement are to be numbered at the very most in tens of thousands, not hundreds of thousands. In 1986, one well-informed GDR source estimated that there existed 'about 200 peace groups with a few thousand members who are active on peace issues inside and outside the Church (*GDR Peace News*, Summer 1986, p. 4). It would seem that university students and pupils in the extended secondary schools are under-represented as participation threatens their career prospects. Most support probably comes from among the manual or semi-skilled workers and apprentices (Mushaben, 1984, p. 131).

Although the movement lost some of the *élan* of the early 1980s, it did at least manage to survive the crisis of the installation of missiles in Western Europe, Czechoslovakia and the GDR. And there remains a sense of participating in a vital cause, not only in East Berlin but in the provinces too (*GDR Peace News*, Autumn 1986, p. 45). Yet symptoms of depression have been observable. At the Spring 1986 Synod of the Evangelical Church of Berlin-Brandenburg, Bishop Forck identified the causes of resignation: the missile installations; the lack of progress on a community peace service; the failure of problems of the Third World to generate as much interest as questions of peace and justice in GDR society; and the widespread indifference to ecological issues (*Chronik*, 1986, pp. 135–6). Hope, however, has been rekindled by Soviet and American initiatives on the dismantling of medium- and short-range nuclear missiles.

Considerable overlap exists between peace and ecology groups symbolized by the slogan painted on the wall of the Gethsemane Church in East Berlin, 'Jesus lives—Jesus is green' (Büscher & Wensierski, 1984, inside cover). Ecology groups, which are frequently attached to the Evangelical Church, have become increasingly active since the late 1970s, spreading information about the high level of environmental degradation in the GDR and how it can be combated. In June 1986, in the wake of the Chernobyl disaster, autonomous peace and ecology groups sent the appeal 'Chernobyl is Everywhere' to the People's Chamber and the Council of Ministers, calling for a halt to the construction of the Stendal nuclear power station and to reliance on nuclear power (for further details on the ecology movement, see Chapter 5).

The Intra-Marxist Intellectual Critics

Under Honecker elaborate theoretical critiques of real existing socialism, as the GDR likes to characterize itself, have been confined to a handful of highly publicized intellectual dissidents, notably Robert Havemann, a survivor of the Ulbricht era, and Rudolf Bahro, who both found official dogma and practices deficient in the light of their interpretation of Marxian texts. Literary and artistic dissent, of varying degrees of criticality, has been voiced by, among many others, Volker Braun, Wolf Biermann, Stefan Heym, Reiner Kunze and Christa Wolf.

Robert Havemann, born in Munich in 1910, joined the KPD in 1932; in December 1943, he was condemned to death for high treason. After the war he became a Professor of Physical Chemistry at the Humboldt University in East Berlin and from 1950 to 1963 served as a deputy to the People's Chamber. His series of public lectures during the Winter semester of 1963–64, in which he aspired to a regeneration of dialectical and historical materialism, aroused the ire of the party authorities and led to his expulsion from his university post in 1964. Although he was placed under house arrest in 1976 after protesting against the expatriation of Biermann, he did manage to smuggle his writings out of the GDR. His basic argument was that Stalinism as practised in the Soviet Union and elsewhere in Eastern Europe

> so absolutely and profoundly contradicts the nature of Socialism that it has not only impeded the progress of Socialism in the Socialist states but has prevented the development of any society which one can call unreservedly Socialist.
> [Havemann, 1973, p. 43]

Havemann lamented the general lack of trust of the population in the SED and the government and the servile imitation of the West. Instead of an open, creative life, a *petit-bourgeois* egotistical life had taken root in the GDR. People's status, he argued, was based on the possession of Western goods. What socialism should be striving for was not greater consumption but the offer of greater liberty and personal development. In fact, 'freedom' and the socialist way of life, so frequently propagated in the media, had degenerated in Havemann's view into an atmosphere of jealousy and suspicion, into a basic division of society into exploiters and exploited, and into massive corruption at the workplace with detrimental consequences for labour morale and productivity (see 'Interview with Robert Havemann', 1978, pp. 42–8).

On the other hand, with the abolition of private property in the relations of production, a decisive condition for the realization of socialism had been achieved. But the no less decisive second stage, the one which was lacking in the GDR, was, according to Havemann, the development of socialist democracy. The Prague Spring, he contended, proved that socialism and freedom could be combined. Freedom should embrace speech, information, place of work and residence and the formation of associations, organizations and parties. Among his concrete suggestions were: the establishment of an independent opposition party and a newspaper critical of the regime; competitive elections to the People's Chamber; the lowering of the age limit for visitors to the West; and the abolition of censorship (see Havemann, in Jäckel, 1980, p. 202). If the suppression of the Prague Spring by Warsaw Pact troops was a sad disillusionment, Havemann derived comfort before his death in 1982 from the ideas of Eurocommunism and from the activities of young people in the peace movement. Indeed, as one of the co-authors of the Berlin Appeal, he came to favour a neutralized and reunited Germany. Despite his many criticisms of the GDR, he continued to insist that

> it represents decisive progress in German history, and ... the part of Germany which can make an all-important contribution to the defeat of capitalism and Fascism in Germany as a whole. [Havemann, 1973, p. 210]

Rudolf Bahro, born in 1935, was a philosophy student at the Humboldt University, the deputy editor of the FDJ student weekly *Forum*, and a labour expert at a factory in East Berlin. The Prague Spring convinced him of the ideological bankruptcy of real existing socialism. His comprehensive analysis of 'the general crisis of the socialist system', *The Alternative in Eastern Europe*, was not published in the GDR but Western television and radio programmes ensured that his views reached an East German audience. Excerpts from the book appeared in the Hamburg weekly magazine, *Der Spiegel*, in August 1977. Bahro was arrested in the same month and eventually sentenced, in June 1978, to eight years' imprisonment on trumped-up charges of betraying state secrets. An international campaign secured his release in 1979 as part of an amnesty to mark the GDR's thirtieth anniversary.

Real existing socialism, Bahro insisted, is a fundamentally different social organization from that outlined in Marx's socialist theory. Despite the relative stabilization of the mid-1970s, the system faced a burgeoning crisis rooted in the contradiction between the modern productive forces and the relations of production which had become a hindrance to them. The abolition of private property in the means of production had not resulted in their transformation into the property of the people. Instead, argued Bahro:

> the whole society stands property-less against its state machine. The monopoly of disposal over the apparatus of production, over the lion's share of the surplus product, over the proportions of the reproduction process, over distribution and consumption, has led to a bureaucratic mechanism with the tendency to kill off or privatize any subjective initiative. [Bahro, 1978, p. 11]

At the head of the political bureaucracy stands the Politburo, which Bahro attacked as 'a grotesque exaggeration of the bureaucratic principle, in as much as the party apparatus subordinate to it is at the same time both church hierarchy and superstate' (Bahro, 1978, p. 244). An irreconcilable conflict exists between this dictatorship of the Politburo and the masses. The alternative to this system Bahro perceived as 'maturing in the womb of actually existing socialism' (Bahro, 1978, p. 14]. The massive 'surplus consciousness', that is, energetic mental capacity which is no longer absorbed by the immediate necessities of human existence, can be mobilized against the dictatorship in the interests of a general emancipation. 'Absorbed consciousness', in contrast, represents mental expenditure which is tied up in the hierarchy of bureaucratic knowledge as well as in the routine functions of daily production and reproduction.

The task of releasing and directing the emancipatory interests of all strata and groups is allotted by Bahro to a League of Communists, to replace the former party. The League would be open to all social forces, thus precluding 'any kind of exclusive sectarianism, any power-secrecy behind closed doors' (Bahro, 1978, p. 367). Central to his whole programme was a redivision of labour: functionaries and intellectuals must spend some of their time—four to six weeks per year—in 'direct participation in the condition of the majority who are largely disadvantaged in the present division of labour and education, and the distribution of income as well' (Bahro, 1978, p. 392). In addition to this engagement of functionaries and the intelligentsia in routine and low-skilled work, Bahro proposed the elimination of work norms and piecework, which in his view were both degrading for the worker and inefficient, and he advocated the equalization of incomes, though with due allowance for onerous and unpleasant work and restrictions on shirkers (Bahro, 1978, pp. 393–8).

Bahro admitted that these views on general emancipation represented 'the least secure and most inadequate portion' of his book. Indeed, many Western critics have criticized him for what they perceive as his utopianism: in particular, his assumption that most people are capable of attaining the necessary high level of intellectual sophistication and that they will be favourably disposed toward his anti-consumerist values. He has also been taken to task for his lack of precision on how the League of Communists would displace the ruling SED elite. But not only has he been criticized for the obfuscation of his institutional design for his new political system; he has also been identified by Ivan Szelenyi as a Leninist, albeit 'a noble and honest one, certainly more noble and honest than most of those rather cynical ones who are currently bossing East European bureaucracies' (1980, p. 120). By positing an intellectual elite as the mono-organizational agency of the initial democratization of society, Bahro is accused of pursuing a democratic goal along a clearly non-democratic road. Arato and Vajda contend that the real alternative to Bahro's neo-Leninism should be 'the reconstruction of civil society, that is, the system of needs, laws, pluralities and public spheres' (1980, p. 175).

Bahro's call for a League of Communists appeared to have been answered when, in late 1977, a 'Federation of Democratic Communists of Germany' drafted a Manifesto which was published in *Der Spiegel* in January 1978. The Manifesto demanded the abolition of the one-party dictatorship and the introduction of an independent parliament and judiciary. Scurrilous attacks were made against top SED leaders such as Honecker, Lamberz and Herrmann, though it spared so-called technocrats like Mittag and Stoph.

> our politbureaucrats are morbidly vain—count their titles: We, Erich & Co, by the Grace of Brezhnev King of Prussia, etc, etc. Count the personal eulogies the arse-lickers and boot-lickers lavish on them at every Central Committee, Parliament, Regional and Local Council meeting; count the 'works', collected of course, of these puffed-up frogs . . . [Szajkowski, 1978, p. 307]

The foreign policy goals of the Federation were wide-ranging: the departure of Soviet and American troops from Germany; the withdrawal of the two German states from their respective military alliances; and a reunited Germany in which social democrats, socialists and democratic communists would prevail over conservative forces.

A major controversy immediately erupted over the question of the Manifesto's authenticity: some observers claimed that it was sponsored by a small group of management cadres on the top and middle levels of the party apparat; the GDR authorities dismissed it as the fabrication of the West German intelligence service; and others saw it as the hand of the 'Stasi' at work, in an attempt to disrupt inter-German relations. Although members of the Federation did not emerge from the political shadows, the Manifesto's intimate knowledge of the internal situation in the GDR convinced many Western observers that it was a genuine, though theoretically confused and inconsistent document (see the interview with Hermann von Berg, a former advisor to Willy Stoph, in *Der Spiegel*, 19 May 1986, pp. 66, 69).

Creative writers and intellectuals have represented a source of critical thinking throughout the GDR's history, even though the literary establishment has tended to be a privileged section of the relatively self-contained intellectual elite of GDR society. In more recent years, however, contact has been established between the unofficial peace movement and intellectuals such as Havemann and Heym. The grand old man of the GDR's dissident writers is Stefan Heym. Born in Chemnitz in 1913, Heym fled Germany in 1933. During the war he served as an officer in the American army. Obliged to leave the United States in the McCarthy era, he arrived in the GDR in 1952 as a convinced socialist. He was given permission during the cultural thaw of the early 1970s to publish two novels, *The King David Report* and *The Queen Against Defoe*, which, though set in the past, were attacks on the perennial problems of the misuse of power and the suppression of critical thinking. He did not, however, find a GDR publisher for *Five Days in June*, which dealt with the June 1953 uprising, and *Collin*, a critique of corruption among the cultural and political elite of the GDR. Heym spoke for many of his colleagues when he defended the rights of writers to make criticisms, not in outright opposition to the SED, but as a contribution to the development of socialism in their own country (Heym, 1974, p. 5).

This commitment to socialism was put to a severe test in 1976 when the critical poet and singer, Wolf Biermann, a friend of Robert Havemann, was forbidden whilst on a concert tour of West Germany, to return to the GDR. He was accused of 'gross violation of his civic duties and a hostile public performance against our socialist state' (quoted in Childs, 1983, p. 223); his citzenship was revoked. The expatriation of Biermann immediately elicited an open letter of protest to *Neues Deutschland* from twelve well-known writers, among them Christa Wolf, Volker Braun, Heiner Müller, Franz Fühmann, Stefan Heym and Stephan Hermlin. Within a few days, over 100 writers and artists had joined the chorus of protest. The regime reacted harshly: prominent intellectuals such as Christa Wolf, Volker Braun and Ulrich Plenzdorf were removed from office in the Berlin section of the Writers' Union. Some lesser-known figures were imprisoned; and numerous writers, including Sarah Kirsch, Günter Kunert and Jurek Becker, subsequently left the GDR either permanently or on long-term visas. Another public dispute occurred in 1979 when the harassment of Stefan Heym for violating new currency regulations on contacts with Western publishers elicited a letter of protest from fellow writers.

Despite the open clashes between writers and SED cultural functionaries in the late 1970s, the pragmatism of the regime has made it possible for critically minded writers to tackle and publish on controversial themes. Christa Wolf's *Cassandra* (1983) challenged orthodox positions on women's equality and warned of the threat of annihilation by nuclear war. Shocked by the Chernobyl disaster, she addressed the question of the self-destructive urge in civilization in *Störfall* (1987); her theory of human aggression is difficult to reconcile with socialism's optimism on social progress. Nor is the party spared in some of the novels of the 1980s: Günter de Bruyn's *Neue Herrlichkeit* and Volker Braun's *Hinze-Kunze-Roman* both attack the corruption and mindless behaviour of party officials. An earlier novel by de Bruyn, *Märkische Forschungen*, exposed the duplicity of party academics. Finally, the writer Stephen Hermlin was granted permission in 1981 to hold a meeting in East Berlin of ninety-two writers, mainly from the two Germanies. GDR writers working in the West discussed problems of peace and security with colleagues who had stayed in the GDR. If the regime had been hoping to mobilize general support for the official line on peace and security, it must have been taken aback by the candour of several of the 'home-based' writers. Hermlin, Braun and de Bruyn, for example, urged toleration of the unofficial peace groups in the GDR.

Emigration to the West

The construction of the Berlin Wall neither deterred East Germans from making illegal attempts to escape to the West nor did it halt the movement of GDR citizens with official permission. Over 38,000 risked life and limb, according to official West German sources, to leave the GDR between August 1961 and 1983 (Zimmermann, 1985, p. 419). The GDR's entry into the United Nations in 1973 and Honecker's signing of the Helsinki Final Act in 1975 encouraged groups within the country to apply for official approval to leave. The most notable collective attempt was the 1976 'Petition for the Complete Attainment of Human Rights' signed by thirty-three citizens of the town of Riesa; all of them had previously made applications to move to the West. Seven signatories, including one of the organizers, Dr Heinz Nitschke, were imprisoned; they were, however, eventually allowed to go to the Federal Republic.

It has been estimated that between 200,000 and 500,000 exit applications had accumulated by the end of 1983 (Fricke, 1984b, p. 171). Then, suddenly, in the spring of 1984, the regime permitted a sharp rise in emigration to the West, prompted in part, no doubt, by the wish to defuse the internal political pressure building up behind this high number of applications, but also, it has been argued, as an informal political payment in return for financial support from the Federal Republic. In the first half of 1984, 31,194 GDR citizens were allowed to depart, and the figure had risen to 42,316 by the end of the year. In 1985, 18,000 emigrated and a further 23,752 between January mid-November 1986. The 1985 figure represented a return to the 'normal' outflow of the early 1980s when emigration was running at between 15,000 and 18,000 per annum (Woods, 1986, p. 33; Martin, 1986, p. 98; Statistisches Bundesamt, 1986, p. 80).

In addition to the emigrants, many GDR citizens undertake personal trips to the West: in 1986, according to Honecker, the total number was over 1.5 million retired people and a further 573,000 on 'urgent family business', a category which is now being interpreted in a highly flexible manner by the GDR authorities. The West German magazine *Der Spiegel* reported Honecker as stating that only 0.2 per cent did not return to the GDR (23 March 1987, p. 17). It is anticipated that over one million will undertake such visits in 1987, a tenfold increase in a matter of only three years (*Der Spiegel*, 31 August 1987, p. 33). This sharp increase in short-term visits obviously represents an attempt by the regime to meet popular aspirations for greater freedom of movement and to curb the rate of permanent emigration. It is also another example of the denser network of communications between the two German states.

The motives for emigration have been studied in depth by two West German institutes on the basis of a representative sample of the 1984 emigrants (see Table 3.9). Political motives—the 'lack of freedom of expression' and 'political pressure'—enjoyed a marginally greater weighting than material motives. Among the emigrants from the Dresden region, who were over-represented in the 1984 emigration wave, material motives, including limited opportunities for travel, were a more significant

Table 3.9 Reasons and motives for leaving the GDR*

	Percentage of the emigrants	
	Total	Dresden region
Lack of freedom to express opinion	71	71
Political pressure	66	62
Limited opportunities to travel to other countries	56	68
Supply situation	46	59
Lack of or unpromising prospects	45	46
Relatives in the FRG (reuniting family)	36	31
Making a fresh start	28	28
Unfavourable career opportunities	21	21

* Multiple responses possible.
Source: Köhler & Ronge, 1984, p. 1282.

factor than among other groups. The West German researchers attributed this difference not to the inferior supply situation in Dresden but to the fact that the Dresden emigrants tended to come from less well-endowed, lower social strata. In terms of their overall social profile, the 1984 emigrants were younger than the GDR population as a whole and a high proportion (almost 90 per cent) were in employment. The representative sample of the spring 'exodus' revealed that 37.7 per cent of the adults (over 18) were under 30 years of age, whereas this age group's share of the total population of the GDR was 23.5 per cent. Men (59 per cent in the sample), too, were over-represented (Köhler & Ronge, 1984, p. 1281). A 1984 survey of the attitudes of about 2,000 West Germans toward their East German 'brothers and sisters' shed some light on the current debate on the reopening of the German question and German reunification. Only 26 per cent of the sample welcomed the emigrants unreservedly as against 22 per cent who were absolutely antagonistic. In between these two poles were the 26 per cent who were personally quite well disposed toward the emigrants but opposed the granting of financial assistance to them, and the 25 per cent whose strong reservations were determined by fears of greater competition for jobs and espionage (Köhler, in Wiedenfeld, 1985, p. 162).

The Significance of Opposition

Opposition, though not commanding a large following and in general successfully contained by the regime, is, nevertheless, an increasingly heterogeneous phenomenon encompassing individual intellectuals, emigrants and members of grass-roots peace, ecology and women's groups. Human rights issues, notably curbs on freedom of expression, association and travel, tend to run as a common thread through these various manifestations of opposition. Despite the SED's almost complete monopoly on the official GDR mass media and obstruction by the authorities, the Berlin Appeal and events like the annual Dresden Forum succeed in attracting the open support of several thousand people. It must also be a matter of some concern for the SED that the young people on whom it has expended so much effort in raising as socialist personalities form the popular base of the activities of the autonomous groups. Another worry for the regime is the threat by a minority within the peace movement to reopen the 'Pandora's box of German nationalism', a question which lies at the very core of the GDR's identity and the SED's legitimacy.

It is, of course, extremely difficult to measure with confidence the degree of disaffection and the potential support for opposition positions, although it is well known that low-key dissent is widespread among ordinary citizens desirous of improvements in the quality of the mass media and the service sector and annoyed at the ban on travel to the West. One frequently cited general indicator of popular attitudes in the GDR is the opinion poll conducted in 1975 by the now defunct SED Central Committee Institute of Public Opinion. The poll revealed that 25 per cent of those interviewed accepted and 21 per cent opposed the GDR political system; 15 per cent were indifferent and 37 per cent had adapted to the situation (McCauley, 1981b, p. 18). Woods has drawn attention to several Western surveys of popular attitudes in the GDR during the 1960s which produced estimates of support ranging from 7 to 15 to over 50 per cent (Woods, 1986, p. 43). Although such wide discrepancies serve as a warning against facile generalization, the findings do at least provide a crude indication of the existence of a mismatch between the aspirations of the regime and their realization as well as the social and economic preconditions for a movement which might just possibly shake the stability of SED rule. It should, however, be stressed that the prospect of popular dissatisfaction spilling over into mass unrest is exceedingly remote.

Another way of testing the significance of opposition positions is to assess whether the criticisms of the maverick intellectuals enjoy a resonance elsewhere in society (see also Woods, 1986). The repudiation by Bahro and Havemann of the SED's leadership's consumerist orientation and the competition with the West in economic growth and the consumer stakes obviously strikes a sympathetic chord among the ecology groups and Evangelical environmentalists such as Heino Falcke (see Chapter 5). But an overlap also occurs with debates in which might be termed the 'official' circles of party and academe. Bahro and Havemann's concern for the environment; their awareness of the ambivalence of scientific and technical progress; their attack on the wastage of human intellectual potential, on the repetitiveness and standardization of certain tasks in industry and on low labour productivity: all these issues are echoed in critical discussions taking place among natural and social scientists in the universities and academic organizations attached to the party. The under-utilization of workers' skills and experience; the delay in transferring research results into marketable products and processes; the rigid technical division of labour;

the impoverishment of work content at automated workplaces (for details of the GDR sources, see Dennis, in Gerber, 1986, pp. 61–72); environmental degradation (Paucke & Bauer, 1979); the continuing disadvantaged position of women in politics, at home and in employment (Dölling, 1986); the need for more effective stimuli for enhancing productivity and creativity (Lötsch, 1984); the alienation of labour in certain work processes (Schirmer, in 'Rundtischgespräch', 1983, p. 323); and the social and personal disadvantages of multi-shiftworking schedules (Wendt, in 'Rundtischgespräch', 1983, p. 325): these debates underline the pertinence of many of the criticisms voiced by Bahro, Havemann and others. Furthermore, the 'new thinking' in international affairs is producing, particularly among political scientists and philosophers, a reassessment of the application of just war theory to nuclear war (Schmidt, 1986). Yet it should be stressed that intractable differences remain between 'unofficial' and 'official' positions (although even this dichotomy is becoming more fluid), notably on the question of reform and the democratization of the political system.

Nor does the top leadership remain aloof from the debates: Honecker issues frequent warnings against nuclear disaster; he castigates low productivity and poor labour discipline; and he goads scientists and engineers to achieve top international standards. Moreover, the present leadership has at times granted its various 'unofficial' critics greater latitude. While the widening of the parameters of 'permissible' criticism undoubtedly reflects the Honecker regime's more flexible social integration policy, it is also part of a well-tried strategy pursued with varying degrees of success and sophistication by socialist regimes toward their political critics. The components of this strategy have been described by Robert Sharlet as: pacification through consumption; repressive tolerance; differentiated political justice; and suppression by force.

The extreme method, the use of force, was employed by the beleaguered Ulbricht in 1953 with the assistance of the ultimate guarantor of SED rule, the troops of the Soviet Union. Another instance of this kind of technique was the forcible closing of the border in August 1961, although it was undertaken with a minimum of physical confrontation. Differentiated political justice is applied when the regime 'perceives itself to be significantly challenged by individuals or groups at any vulnerable point' (Sharlet, in Curry, 1983, p. 12). Examples of the use of this method include: Biermann's expatriation; the granting of long-term visas to troublesome writers and artists; the export of dissidents, sometimes forcibly as in the case of leaders of the Jena peace movement, to West Germany; bureaucratic harassment and house arrest (Havemann); designation as hooliganism; punitive legislation (the 'Lex Heym' of 1979); and imprisonment. The state security apparat is the main instrument of this policy.

A more sophisticated technique is repressive tolerance, which is a form of 'benevolent paternalism' usually applied to the potentially troublesome intelligentsia. It allows them a limited social space in which to express their views. Restricted publication runs in the GDR or permission to publish in the West exemplify this method, as in the case of Reiner Kunze, Volker Braun, Stefan Heym,

Christoph Hein and many others. It has also been extended to the unofficial peace and ecology movements. Yet while the 'space' has grown quite appreciably in the 1980s, it remains a contested terrain between regime, the Evangelical Church and activists, for whereas the last two seek to expand the territory, the regime, albeit with a careful eye on potential domestic and international reactions, may attempt to contract it or re-employ the weapons of repressive tolerance.

Finally, the favoured technique of the Honecker era is pacification through consent, described by Sharlet as 'the most benign, efficient and politically cost-effective method of governing mass publics and quieting social unrest in the European communist states' (Sharlet, in Curry, 1983, p. 10). The GDR, though having the highest living standards in Eastern Europe, does, of course, experience the special problem of a neighbouring German society which continues to act as a source of attraction for many GDR citizens. The existence of a second currency in circulation in the GDR, the 'capitalist' Deutschmark, can sometimes have a destabilizing effect in the form of minor strikes by workers seeking partial payment in hard currency (see *DDR-heute*, March–April 1987, p. 19 for a recent report on a strike by workers in a combine in the Karl-Marx-Stadt region). Nevertheless, the vast subsidies for basic consumer items, a generous social welfare system, access to more consumer durables, trade-union involvement in social policy, and so on have helped maintain the social compact in the difficult 1980s, at a time when it collapsed in Poland. The success of the strategy also highlights a serious limitation on the appeal of Bahro, Havemann and the environmentalists, namely, the strength of consumer values among East Germans.

Other significant factors in the regime's overall success in containing opposition include: the relatively underdeveloped institutional and communication network of the opposition groups; the regime's successful cooption of the scientific-technical intelligentsia (despite the strains between 'experts' and 'ideologues'); the absence of internecine disputes within the top SED leadership since the failure to unseat Ulbricht in the 1950s; differences regarding methods, priorities and policies among the regime's critics (for example, between the younger peace activists and the more cautious Church hierarchy); and the regime's use of the West German safety valve to divest itself of 'unpalatable' dissidents. However, while the regime has been relatively successful in its containment policy, this does not mean that it has always played a skilful and consistent hand: the expatriation of Biermann backfired. It must, of course, always be sensitive to major economic crisis endangering the social compact and causing the divergent strands of discontent and opposition to coalesce. Moreover, it can never rest easily while the concept of German reunification contributes to what a Western observer has referred to as a 'kind of national schizophrenia' regarding its accomplishments (Mushaben, 1984, p. 134).

4 The Economic System

The Economic Position in 1945

The Potsdam Conference established the principle that the whole of Germany should be treated as a single economic unit. This concept did not long survive the conference: it was undermined by the four military commanders' exercise of sole command within their own zone and by disputes over Soviet reparations. The collapse of the Allied Control Council, the inclusion of the Western zones in the Marshall Aid Plan and the introduction of two separate German currencies in 1948 finally destroyed the concept of the economic unity of Germany.

The Soviet zone's economic potential was seriously reduced by extensive war damage. About 650,000 houses had been totally or partially destroyed (in percentage terms, this amounted to 80, 65 and 25 in Dessau, Berlin and Leipzig respectively) and over 40 per cent of industrial capacity had been lost due to the direct and indirect effects of war. Agriculture, too, suffered heavy losses: the pre-war levels of cattle, sheep and pigs were reduced by 900,000, 3,000,000 and 1,100,000 respectively (Barthel, 1979, pp. 40–1, 44, 47). The situation was exacerbated by Soviet dismantling activity, representing perhaps a 26 per cent loss of capital assets in industry. Dismantling continued for two years after Marshal Sokolowski had declared it completed on 21 May 1946. Entire plants, parts of plant and equipment were removed. In May and June 1945, for example, about 460 Berlin enterprises were completely dismantled and transferred. Moreover, reparations payments out of current output continued to be made until 1953 (about 34.7 billion Marks at 1944 prices) and 213 enterprises, worth 2.5 billion Marks, were seized in 1946 and converted into Soviet joint stock companies (Pohl, 1979, p. 1; Straßburger, in von Beyme & Zimmermann, 1984, pp. 112–13; Zimmermann, 1985, pp. 1121–2).

The losses suffered as a result of the various types of payments to the Soviet Union between 1945 and 1953 may have amounted to $15.8 billion. Yet this was still not the final statement: partially dismantled factories remaining in the zone were of little use. Levies on current production between 1945 and 1948 exceeded gross investment expenditure, thereby inhibiting investment activity, reducing the export capacity of the zone and impairing the raw material base. Estimates vary but the total industrial capacity lost as a result of dismantling and reparations may have been in the order of 40–50 per cent of pre-war capacity (Pohl, 1979, p. 2; Bröll, 1974, p. 14).

A further burden was the separation of the Soviet zone's economy from its major sources of raw materials and semi-finished products in the Western zones. In 1936, the present GDR territory had produced only 5 per cent of Germany's total production of iron ore and 2.3 per cent of hard coal, whereas machine tools accounted for 50 per cent, textile machinery 68 per cent and office machinery

82 per cent. As the pre-war pattern could not be restored, it was necessary to build up the zone's own basic materials and capital goods sectors. Foreign trade, too, had to be reorientated: in 1936, 82.7 per cent of the foreign trade of what became the territory of the Soviet zone had been conducted with the capitalist West (Bröll, 1974, p. 11; Barthel, 1979, p. 85).

The Development of the Economy

A new economic order gradually took shape in the early post-war years, an order characterized by the expansion of the social ownership of the means of production and central planning of the economy. SMAD and SED played the role of political mentors.

The first step toward a reform of the relations of production, albeit not with the goal of immediately establishing a Soviet-type system, was the promulgation of a land reform in September 1945. About 600,000 hectares of land were seized from former Nazis and war criminals and all estates of over 100 hectares were expropriated (about 2.5 million hectares). The agricultural land was distributed among about 500,000 peasants. The creation of nationalized estates (VEGs) laid the foundation for the later socialization of agriculture. Industrial reform was inaugurated by several orders of SMAD in October 1945 and legitimized by a referendum in Saxony in the following year. Some 4,000 industrial enterprises were seized.

The socialization of agriculture and industry gathered momentum during the 1950s after the launching of the planned construction of socialism at the Second Party Conference. The collectivization programme in agriculture, instituted in 1952, was virtually completed in 1960, by which time over 90 per cent of agricultural land was divided up among agricultural producers' cooperatives (LPGs) and VEGs. By 1965, well over 80 per cent of industry had been nationalized. The GDR's first medium-term economic plan, the two-year plan for 1949–50, aimed to restore industrial production, to provide the population with consumer goods and to meet Soviet reparations requirements. The development of basic industries enjoyed priority. The 1951–5 Economic Plan, the country's first five-year plan, continued the emphasis on basic industries in order to increase the supply of fuel and power, steel and iron to the chemical and investment goods industries. Production targets were attained but at the expense of the consumer. After the uprising in June 1953, the authorities stepped up the supply of consumer goods, a policy which was facilitated by the end of reparations payments and by an increase in Soviet credits.

The policy of favouring the consumer could not be pursued consistently as it proved difficult to harmonize investment in the consumer goods industries with the promotion of basic industries. The seven-year plan for 1959–65, nevertheless, sought to reconcile competing interests. The principal economic task of the plan was stipulated as catching up with and overtaking the Federal Republic's per capita consumption of most consumer goods and footstuffs by the end of 1961. This highly ambitious target, which was to be achieved by raising labour productivity and by lowering costs, soon proved to be unrealistic. The rate of economic growth fell from 12 per cent in 1959 to 4 per cent in 1961 and at the end of the decade private per capita consumption still lagged 25–30 per cent behind that of the Federal Republic. The final stage in the collectivization of agriculture in 1960 and the international political crisis exacerbated the situation and accelerated the flow of refugees to the West. The erection of the Berlin Wall resolved the latter problem; the New Economic System was designed to tackle the economic crisis.

In 1962, the SED leadership, influenced by the Liberman debate in the USSR, undertook a reassessment of the system of central planning which had steered the GDR through the period of reconstruction in the 1950s. The requirements for economic growth based on qualitative factors such as greater efficiency and labour productivity had been obstructed by the rigid price system, overcentralization and the 'tonnage' ideology. Incentives were lacking for technical progress, initiative and rational investment decisions.

The New Economic System of Planning and Management, announced by Ulbricht at the Sixth SED Congress in January 1963 and elaborated in detail by a Council of Ministers resolution in July, endeavoured to remedy these deficiencies. Central planning was to be redirected toward long-term goals; and so-called economic levers were to facilitate indirect control of the enterprises. Costs, prices, profits and wages functioned as direct levers; the bonus and performance funds as indirect levers. Newly established Associations of Nationalized Enterprises (VVBs) became the main economic bodies of their respective industries. Enterprise managers were granted greater decision-making powers and they were encouraged to make profits. Investments were to be financed, within limits, from these profits as well as from bank credits. In order to establish economic criteria for assessing performance and for improving the indirect steering mechanism, fixed assets were revalued in 1963 and depreciation rates were increased in 1964. A general reform of industrial prices, to be realized in three stages, was launched in 1964. In the late 1960s, the SED leaders, Ulbricht in particular, anticipated that modern scientific methods such as electronic data processing would have a positive effect on management and planning techniques as well as on economic growth.

The NES, though extending enterprise decision-making powers, did not constitute a sweeping decentralization of the economic system. Renate Damus has characterized it as a form of indirect centralization in which decisions were transferred downwards only in so far as they did not call into question the existing decision-making structures (1973, p. 50). Despite early success (economic growth averaged 5 per cent per annum in the five years after the introduction of NES) and despite modifications in 1967–8 (the Economic System of Socialism), it was abandoned *de facto* at a Central Committee meeting in December 1970. At the end of the 1960s, serious dislocations had become apparent. The selection, between 1968 and 1970, of structural key projects in specific branches of the economy—instrument-making and the chemical industry—led to imbalances in the overall development of the economy. The privileged branches were unable to meet their targets because of bottlenecks in supplies from non-priority areas. Bottlenecks were particularly acute in the energy sector. Unfavourable weather conditions and increasing foreign indebtedness compounded the problems. As the imbalances derived to a considerable extent from the failure to reconcile the limited initiatives permitted the enterprises and selected economic sectors with the structural policy concept of the central authorities, a more traditional, centrally administered system was reinstated (Leptin & Melzer, 1978, pp. 66–94).

The return to a more direct management of the economy involved an increase in enterprise plan indicators and a shift in enterprise decision-making powers to higher state bodies such as the Council of Ministers, the State Planning Commission and the industrial ministries. The indecisive efforts to make prices more dynamic were finally abandoned in 1971. After a delay of one year, a new five-year plan for 1971–5 was approved by the People's Chamber in December 1971. The plan's economic targets were relatively cautious: an annual growth of 5 per cent in produced national income. Dislocations and bottlenecks were to be eliminated by improving the supplier industries and the technical infrastructure, by expanding the power and raw materials base and by raising export performance. A notable feature of Honecker's initial five-year plan was the amelioration of living standards.

The balance sheet of the 1971–5 plan was encouraging; virtually all targets were overfulfilled. Produced national income rose by 30 per cent, retail trade turnover by 28 per cent and the net money incomes of the population by 27 per cent. This period of consolidation and improvement in the standard of living was disturbed and then disrupted by the explosion of raw material prices, especially those of crude oil. The full impact on the GDR was not felt immediately. However, serious difficulties were experienced by 1975 at the latest when the Soviet Union increased its prices for raw materials traded within COMECON. The existing deficit with the West since 1970 was consequently compounded by a deficit with the Soviet Union, the GDR's main source of raw materials. The country's terms of trade underwent a serious deterioration: between 1972 and 1975 the prices of GDR exports rose by 17 per cent and her import prices by 34 per cent. This was a worrying situation for a highly industrialized country with limited raw materials. The country's growing dependence on foreign trade intensified her difficulties: by 1975, exports as a proportion of gross national product had attained the same level as that of the FRG, 25 per cent. The net indebtedness of the GDR mounted rapidly, reaching a peak of $11.66 billion in 1981, second only to Poland among COMECON states (*DIW Handbuch*, 1984, p. 45).

Despite the harsh economic climate in the late 1970s, the SED leadership did not initiate a fundamental reform of the economic system. Planning amelioration and industrial reorganization became the central features of economic strategy. In 1979–80 the organization of the industry was overhauled. Hitherto the Associations of Nationalized Enterprises (VVBs) had been the main link between the ministries and the individual enterprises (VEBs). This three-tier structure was abolished and combine formation, especially in industry and construction, was accelerated. Whereas only forty-five combines existed in 1975, the number had risen to 316 in all branches of the economy ten years later. A total of 129 combines have been created in centrally managed industry and ninety-five under regional management.

Each combine is formed by the amalgamation of several legally and financially independent enterprises with similar production lines formerly linked to one or more VVBs or ministries. Supplier enterprises and research centres are often located within the combine. The size of an industrial combine varies from twenty to forty VEBs and between 2,000 and 70,000 employees. The average number of employees of the combines under central management is 25,000; however, the regional-managed combines sometimes employ less than 1,000 workers (Erdmann, 1985, pp. 75-6; *DIW Handbuch*, 1984, p. 89; Melzer, in Nove, Höhmann & Seidenstecher, 1982, p. 78). SED leaders had great expectations of combine formation. Honecker described it in 1978 as 'the most important step towards perfect management and planning' (quoted by Melzer, in Jeffries, 1981, p. 97). The combines were to be so structured as to achieve major benefits in economies of scale, a more rational division of labour between enterprises and ministries, the more rapid diffusion of scientific and technological research as a result of closer links between the combines and research institutes, and an increase in exports by means of more effective market research and the affiliation of foreign trade enterprises (Melzer, in Nove, Höhmann & Seidenstecher, 1982, p. 78). In short, combines are in a better position than the old VVBs to achieve a more integrated reproduction process from R & D through to the sale of products, whether at home or abroad.

Western specialists are of the opinion that the general director is the key figure in a combine's operation. Pieter Boot has dubbed them 'crisis managers' with responsibility for restructuring enterprises, for downgrading and promoting division managers and for determining the organization of research, investment and market research. According to *The Economist*, 'They are supposed to be champions of innovation, interpreters of the party's grand economic strategy, and can-carriers if things go wrong' (*The Economist*, 22 February 1986, p. 60).

Top general directors like Biermann of Carl-Zeiss Jena and Erich Müller of the Leuna Works are full members of the SED's Central Committee; Wolfgang Jacob and Otto König have candidate status. These officials unquestionably enjoy greater decision-making powers than did the old VVB management: Honecker, in 1979, advised that ministers should concentrate only on 'major questions' (quoted by Melzer, in Nove, Höhmann & Seidenstecher, 1982, p. 79); and some general directors are known to use their party connections to further the interests of their combines against the wishes of the industrial ministries (*DIW Handbuch*, 1984, p. 92). These are clear indicators of the cautious decentralization of decision-making which has been introduced into the economic system since the wave of combine formation in the 1980s.

There are, however, restrictions on the autonomy of the general directors. They remain subordinate to their minister; he can appoint and dismiss them. The term 'major questions' is open to varying interpretation and strategies: while some combines determine their own production targets, others are recipients of detailed planning tasks from the appropriate ministry. In order to 'rein in' the combines, a decree was issued in 1983 which requires general directors, enterprise managers and foreign trade companies to submit detailed annual reports to their superiors on their economic performance in areas such as R & D, investments, export profits and materials consumption (Cornelsen, Melzer & Scherzinger, 1984, p. 217).

Planning

The principle of a centrally planned economy has survived the emergence of the combine structure. The strategic decisions are taken by the higher organs of the SED, notably the Politburo. The Council of Ministers continues to function as the major governmental organ for the implementation of these decisions. Its members include the heads of the industrial ministries, the State Planning Commission and the State Bank. The State Planning Commission is responsible for the preparation of structural policy, the operationalization of the decisions of the Council of Ministers, and the drafting and implementation of the economic plans. The individual ministries receive aggregated output targets from the State Planning Commission; all are responsible for the execution of plans within their particular area. The combines are located immediately below the ministries; the enterprises represent the bottom tier of these functional units. Regional and district planning commissions coordinate measures affecting labour supply, housing, communications and so forth with the central planning organs.

The broad guidelines of economic policy are laid down in perspective plans over a period of ten to fifteen years; the medium-range or five-year plans are enacted into law by the People's Chamber. As it is not feasible to regulate for all eventualities over a five-year period, short-term plans are issued to determine annual targets. The drafting of the annual plan follows a set procedure according to a precise chronological schedule over a period of twelve months. The State Planning Commission plays a key role: it evaluates and determines what kind of adjustments should be made to the medium-term goals and, after the enterprises, trade unions, local authorities, combine directors and ministries have submitted and coordinated their proposals, the Commission undertakes the final aggregation. After confirmation by the Council of Ministers, the annual plan is then presented to the People's Chamber for formal approval and legal enactment.

An important supplement to the production plan is a highly complex system of balancing which determines the allocation of materials, equipment and consumer goods. A separate balance was established for energy in 1981 and for industrial plant two years later. About 4,540 individual balances existed in 1982. The central organs such as the Council of Ministers, the State Planning Commission and the ministries work out balances affecting 76 per cent of production, over 87 per cent of exports and imports and about 70 per cent of consumer goods for domestic use (for further details, see *DIW Handbuch*, 1984, pp. 96–7, and Rytlewski, in Zimmermann, 1985, pp. 1000–1). Party leaders are hopeful that the computerization of the balancing system will improve coordination between combines, ministries and the State Planning Commission.

Planning indicators (*Kennziffer*) are yet another form of direct steering of the economy. They represent major instruments of the central planning authorities for the regulation of the production programme. The indicators determine production targets, resource inputs and permissible costs (e.g. materials, wages, investments), efficiency (e.g. labour productivity and the utilization of plant and equipment) and economic incentives; they are binding on combines and enterprises. Despite its obvious deficiencies, 'commodity production' functioned as the chief indicator for the assessment of the efficiency of production until the end of the 1970s. As part of a wholesale campaign to improve the planning process, the system of indicators was revised in the early 1980s. Commodity production lost its position as a 'main indicator' in 1983. Since 1984 the 'main indicators' have been net production, net profits, goods and services for private consumers, and exports. The introduction of exports into the system of indicators highlights the importance of foreign trade for the GDR economy. 'Further important qualitative indicators' have also been introduced: labour productivity, costs and material costs per 100 Marks of commodity production, and the production of economically important and high quality goods. These eight 'main and important' indicators constitute the crucial elements in the more highly integrated and complex ensemble of planning indicators which are intended to provide the central authorities with more rigorous mechanisms of cost accounting. Other measures have been implemented to tighten up the system of control. Duty booklets allow for the stricter supervision of scientific and technical innovation. Enterprise norms and state normatives set ceilings on the consumption of materials and raw materials (*DIW Handbuch*, 1984, pp. 98–9; Cornelsen, Melzer & Scherzinger, 1984, pp. 203–5).

The plethora of direct planning mechanisms is complemented by indirect steering mechanisms or, as they were called during the period of the New Economic System, economic levers. These monetary mechanisms—costs, profits, credits, state levies, enterprise funds and price setting—are also employed as devices to facilitate central planning control over the combines and enterprises. While the significance of indirect mechanisms declined after the abandonment of the New Economic System, the intensification strategy and the changed economic situation of the 1980s stimulated their more active deployment. The enterprises enjoy less autonomy, however, than they did in the 1960s.

The production units dispose of a variety of funds which are financial resources derived from net profits. The allocation and use of the funds are regulated by legal prescriptions. Among the major funds are those for science and technology, investments, performance, bonuses, wages, risks, repairs and current assets.

The increasing importance of monetary mechanisms can be illustrated by the new role of profits in stimulating economies in resources; until the 1980s the main function of profit was to ensure that the production units had sufficient funds to be able to meet the financial requirements of the economic plans. However, if combines and enterprises now succeed in exceeding planned profits, they are permitted to make higher contributions to their funds and the net profit levy to the state budget may be less than the half which hitherto had been mandatory. Another example of the more exacting regulations of the 1980s, designed to promote greater efficiency, is the requirement, which came into force in 1986, that the production levy (a tax on the capital of the enterprises) be calculated according to net value, not the gross value of capital assets. Moreover, the basic 6 per cent charge was abandoned in favour of a rate to be determined during the planning year. Such arrangements, in the opinion of Kurt Erdmann, whilst favouring modernization and rationalization instead of the accretion of new investment, introduce an element of uncertainty for combines and enterprises (Erdmann 1985, pp. 102–3; also Cornelsen, Melzer & Scherzinger, 1984, p. 210).

An important innovation is the 'contribution to the societal funds' which came into operation in January 1984 for centrally-managed industry and in 1985 for the construction industry. This is the fourth type of levy paid by enterprises into the state budget. The combines and enterprises are required to pay 70 per cent of their total wages bill to the state. This sum is earmarked as a contribution to housing, education, health and other social services. The real purpose of this new levy is, by increasing labour costs, to encourage enterprises to economize on labour and to deploy workers in a more effective manner. The levy operates in the following manner. Enterprises may increase the projected prices of new products by 70 per cent. If they reduce their manning levels and, therefore, their total wage costs during the actual plan period, they are permitted to pay a lower absolute 'contribution to societal funds' (though still 70 per cent of the final wages bill), but they do not need to revise the prices of their products. They acquire, as a result, a larger net profit. Whether enterprises will be prepared to reduce their manning levels in order to obtain short-term gains whilst, perhaps, jeopardizing future plan fulfilment remains to be seen (Barthel, 1986, pp. 381, 383, 388).

Both the direct and indirect steering mechanisms are supervised by central state control organs. These organs check and assess the execution of the economic plans and enterprise compliance with legal norms. They make recommendations on how to correct planning deficiencies and how production units can improve the planning process. The decline in the significance of the central organs during the New Economic System period was reversed during the recentralization after Honecker came to power. Since the end of the 1970s their powers have been sharpened and new bodies created. They form an important counterweight to the growth in influence of the combines. Among the new control organs created in the 1980s are the State Balancing Inspectorate, attached to the State Planning Commission, and numerous special inspectorates for supervising the utilization of energy, raw materials and materials. In addition, the powers of the director of the price department in the combines and the authority of the banks have been increased (DIW Handbuch, 1984, pp. 117–19; Cornelsen, Melzer & Scherzinger, 1984, pp. 212–15).

The many changes in the system of economic planning during the 1980s constitute planning improvement through a tighter system of management and accounting; they do not amount to comprehensive decentralization. The emphasis lies in 'perfecting' existing mechanisms in order to promote economic growth and greater efficiency. Some positive results have been recorded. By cutting out the middle management level, combine formation has improved the economy's information system. Research, investment, sales, market research and production can be coordinated more effectively.

Industry

Industry is easily the most important economic sector: in 1982 its share of gross national product was 45.4 per cent and in 1980 it accounted for 43.2 per cent of all employees. Private enterprise is virtually non-existent, the final blow occurring in 1972 when most of the surviving 3,000 private enterprises were transferred into public ownership. The regional distribution of industry is characterized by a high concentration of the industrial centres—Leipzig, Halle, Karl-Marx-Stadt and Dresden—in the relatively densely populated southern districts (*DIW Handbuch*, 1984, pp. 150–2; Alton, in Joint Economic Committee, 1985, pp. 89, 100). The structure of industrial production is shown in Table 4.1.

The electrical engineering, electronics and instrument sector has an indispensable role to play in the modernization of the other economic sectors and in enabling the country to meet its export targets. Microelectronics occupies a central position in the

Table 4.1 Sectoral structure of GDR industry, 1950–82 (per cent)

Sector	1950	1975	1982*
Fuel and energy	11.7	5.1	9.9
Chemicals	11.2	15.1	20.5
Metallurgy	6.2	7.9	7.9
Building materials	2.3	2.0	1.5
Mechanical engineering, vehicle construction	17.4	24.2	20.8
Electrical engineering, electronics, instrument construction	4.4	11.2	8.9
Light industry	14.7	11.3	9.7
Textile industry	10.2	6.6	6.1
Food processing	21.9	16.6	14.1
All industry	100	100	100

* 1950 and 1975 values are calculated on the basis of gross output at 1967 prices; the 1982 value is based on industrial goods production and is not comparable with previous years.

Source: Plötz, in Zimmermann, 1985, p. 607.

strategy to enhance productivity and competitiveness. The intensive promotion of microelectronics was resumed in 1977–8, after earlier developments in the 1960s had been allowed to flounder. Microprocessors were imported from American firms like Intel and Texas Instruments. However, the GDR also built up domestic production at such centres as the Microelectronics Combine Erfurt and the Robotron Combine in Erfurt. An important microelectronics research centre, with a staff of over 7,000, is located in Dresden. The GDR intends to produce most of its own microprocessors, and the 1986–90 Economic Plan envisages the further expansion of microelectronics and the more rapid application of industrial robotics and CAD/CAM (see the section on 'Economic Performance and the Outlook for the 1990s').

Production in mechanical engineering is not planned to rise as rapidly as in electrical engineering and electronics. However, mechanical engineering and vehicle construction has the largest workforce (973,283 in 1985) of any economic sector and it is by tradition the most important source of GDR exports. Its share of exports at current prices was 51.3 per cent in 1980 and 46.6 per cent in 1985. Most of the commodities exported are absorbed by the socialist countries; the more technically demanding and competitive Western markets are difficult to enter. For example, most of the exports of machine tools are destined for the Soviet Union and the rest of COMECON; only 20 per cent reach Western markets. Within the mechanical engineering sector clear discrepancies exist with respect to levels of sophistication and investment priorities. Motor vehicle construction has long been notorious for its technological backwardness, whilst automation has progressed more rapidly in machine tools than in other branches. In 1981, 30 per cent of machine tools were of the CNC type; by the end of the decade, machine tools equipped with electronic systems are planned to account for up to 80 per cent of total output. A potential boost to production in motor vehicles is the agreement signed with Volkswagen of West Germany allowing the GDR to import equipment for the production of engines for personal cars. The agreement runs from 1989 to 1993 (Zimmermann, 1985, p. 875; *DIW Handbuch*, 1984, pp. 170–1; *StJB*, 1986, p. 239; Five-Year Plan Act, 1986, p. 23).

The chemical industry is concentrated in the eastern part of the Halle region; another important centre, the Schwedt petro-chemical combine, is located in the Frankfurt/Oder region. The industry, which recorded high growth rates in the 1960s and early 1970s, is heavily dependent on imports of raw materials. In the mid-1960s, oil began to replace domestic lignite as a raw material and oil processing was expanded at the Schwedt and Leuna combines. As virtually all of its crude oil had to be imported, the industry was hit hard by the increase in world oil prices and by the Soviet Union's cutback in its oil exports in 1982. Adjustments to the new situation have included the expansion of the carbo-chemical industry on the basis of domestic lignite and importing semi-processed chemicals from Czechoslovakia. One positive development was the expansion of capacity in the mineral oil industry at Schwedt and Leuna (Zimmermann, 1985, pp. 253–4). However, this strategy has been jeopardized by the recent fall in world prices of oil and in the value of the dollar and by the relatively high cost of Soviet oil. This probably accounts for the sector's poor performance in 1986 when net production grew by 4.8 per cent instead of at the planned rate of 9.3 per cent.

The consumer goods and food–processing industries have traditionally been low growth areas and investment has been below average except in textiles. However, the political leadership has recently proclaimed increases in new consumer goods for domestic and foreign consumers. The output of consumer durables is to be increased by 40 per cent by 1990 and that of newly developed consumer goods by 45 per cent. The annual innovation rate in the consumer goods sector is expected to attain 30–40 per cent. Combines which specialize in consumer goods will obviously have to increase capacity and combines which hitherto have concentrated on the production of capital goods are being encouraged to create specialized departments for the development of major consumer goods lines (Five-Year Plan Act, 1986, pp. 58–60).

The construction industry, which in 1985 employed 593,955 persons (*StJB*, 1986, p. 163), is affected by the SED's intensification strategy in that it has been expected to reduce material outlays and to make more frugal use of costly materials for reconstruction and modernization. Since Honecker's accession to power, investment has increased in this sector (see Chapter 2 for further details).

The energy and fuel sector employs 225,300 workers and accounts for 12.2 per cent of industrial goods production (1985). This sector, at a time of turbulence in the price of fuel, obviously occupies a central role in the SED's economic strategy and is one where savings are imperative. The average annual growth rate of 35 per cent between 1970 and 1982 was lower than that of industry as a whole; and it is extremely capital-intensive, fixed assets per worker being three times higher than the GDR average (*StJB*, 1986, p. 139; Bethkenhagen, in Zimmermann, 1985, p. 349). The GDR has no significant supplies of bituminous coal or oil. Domestic output of natural gas is insufficient for domestic requirements and has to be supplemented with imports from the Soviet Union. It is, however, the world's largest producer of lignite; this reduces the country's dependence on imported energy but at the cost of considerable damage to the environment (see Chapter 5). About 70 per cent of the GDR's primary energy requirements were supplied by lignite in 1984.

At the beginning of the 1970s, the GDR leadership, which hitherto had concentrated on domestic sources, encouraged energy imports, above all from the Soviet Union. In quantitative terms, imports increased tenfold between 1970 and 1980. The Soviet Union accounted for about 80 per cent of the GDR's energy imports and by the end of the 1970s Soviet oil, gas and bituminous coal constituted about 30 per cent of the country's primary energy needs. This policy was revised at the start of the 1980s as a consequence of the reduction in Soviet supplies of crude oil and a sharp increase in its price. Supply fell from 19.0 million tonnes in 1980 to 17.1 million tonnes in 1983. A Soviet–GDR agreement in October 1985 allows for an average annual supply of 17.1 million tonnes in the period 1986–90. The production of domestic lignite was increased to deal with the new situation: raw lignite extraction rose from 256.21 million tonnes in 1980 to 312 million tonnes in 1985. A target of 335,000 million tonnes has been set for 1990, by which time the GDR, it is anticipated, will be covering 78-80 per cent of its primary energy requirements from its own resources (Bethkenhagen, 1985, pp. 579, 581; *Neues Deutschland*, 23 April 1986, p. 5).

Nuclear power is also expected to relieve the energy problem. Whereas in 1982 the two nuclear power stations, at Rheinsberg and at Lubmin, accounted for 10.5 per cent of the generation of electricity, compared to 82 per cent by lignite-fired stations, nuclear energy's contribution is to be raised to 15 per cent by 1990. In 1982, the percentages for the USSR, FRG and USA were 5.1, 17.3 and 11.5 respectively (*DIW Handbuch*, 1984, p. 146; Stinglwagner, 1985, p. 67).

The GDR once entertained high aspirations for nuclear energy. In 1957, it was announced that about twenty nuclear power stations would be in operation by 1970. The Rheinberg station came into operation in 1966 and that at Lubmin, in the Greifswald district, seven years later. The Lubmin station has a total capacity of 1,760MW, Rheinberg, 70MW. A third nuclear power station, at Stendal near Magdeburg, has been planned for a long time but is not expected to come on line until 1991. The reactors and the enriched uranium are supplied by the Soviet Union. Western sources indicate that though high pressure reactors are in use at Rheinberg and Lubmin, containment and additional emergency systems have not been built according to Western safety standards; the new reactors to be constructed at Stendal will, however, incorporate these standards (Stinglwagner, 1985, pp. 63, 92-6; 1986, p. 636; Bethkenhagen, 1986b, p. 310).

The per capita consumption of primary energy in the GDR is very high by international standards. In 1978, an international survey of eighteen countries revealed that the 196 giga-joules per head of population put the GDR above the USSR (176) and the other five Eastern European COMECON states, Great Britain (145) and the Federal Republic (171), but below the United States (346) (Stinglwagner, 1985, p. 162). The same survey revealed that the GDR had a high wastage rate (39.8 per cent) in the conversion and transfer of primary into final energy for commercial, state and private users. The Federal Republic and the USSR recorded losses of 27.2 per cent and 18.2 per cent respectively. The GDR's high wastage rate is attributed to technically outdated equipment, the low proportion of liquid and gaseous primary energy sources, the extensive generation of electricity and, above all, the widespread utilization of solid fuels in primary energy consumption (Stinglwagner, 1985, pp. 162, vii). These factors also account for the relatively low labour productivity in the energy sector, despite its absorption in recent years of about 30 per cent of total investments in GDR industry. According to Cord Schwartau of the German Institute for Economic Research, per capita performance attains only about 45 per cent that of the Federal Republic, even though the worktime of the labour force in this sector is on average 17 per cent longer than in West Germany (1987, p. 257).

Since 1979, however, some success has been recorded in energy economies as a result of the introduction of new consumption normatives, an increase in enterprise energy prices, lower room temperature norms and careful investment policies. An energy inspectorate of the Central Energy Commission supervises the implementation of the regulations. Heavy sanctions can be imposed on enterprises which exceed price and consumption standards. In 1982, economic growth in the GDR coincided, for the first time, with an absolute decrease in energy and raw materials consumption. However, the greatest savings have been made in industry, not in private households, where energy consumption increased in the early 1980s. The lower world energy prices have not yet had any impact on the GDR's medium-term planning and it remains to be seen whether adjustments will be made in the course of the 1986–90 Economic Plan (Cornelsen, 1985, pp. 44–5; Meyer, in Gerber, 1985, p. 73).

Agriculture

Agriculture is basically organized into collective forms and accounts for about 11 per cent of the economically active population. The labour force declined throughout the 1970s from 997,119 in 1970 to 878,489 in 1980 but then, exceptionally for an advanced industrial society, climbed to 992,166 in 1984. The amount of useful agricultural land has declined steadily from 6,526,554 hectares in 1950 to 6,224,804 hectares in 1984, a reflection of industrial and urban requirements (*StJB*, 1986, pp. 180, 184; Kurjo, 1986, p. 77). The degree of self-sufficiency is high, ranging from 85 to 90 per cent. Except for fruit and vegetables, domestic requirements are fully met by GDR production. On the other hand, imports are needed to cater for one-fifth of animal feed and some grain imports are also required (*DIW Handbuch*, 1984, pp. 195, 197).

The model of cooperative and state ownership in agriculture was inherited from the Soviet Union. Three types of agricultural producers' cooperatives were established according to the degree of socialization of the means of production. Type III, in which all the agricultural means of production (land, livestock, machinery, buildings) are collectivized, emerged as the dominant form (see Table 4.2). By 1975, about 98 per cent of agricultural land farmed by cooperatives was worked in LPGs III; their average size was 1,180 hectares. Members of all three types of cooperatives are allowed to work a small plot of 0.5 hectares for their own consumption and to sell the produce themselves (Lambrecht, in Bethkenhagen *et al*., 1981, pp. 95–7, 100).

Towards the end of the 1960s, the SED leadership decided to undertake a reorganization of agriculture in order to raise productivity through the application of industrial methods. The 'industrialization' of agriculture required, it was believed larger and more specialized units. A reorganization of the entire system commenced in the early 1970s. Specialized crop-producing and cooperative farms (KAPs) were created by combining the land, equipment and so forth of LPGs and VEGs.

By 1975, about 1,210 KAPs had been created, accounting for 85 per cent of total agricultural land. These KAPs proved to be transitional forms as between 1976 and 1979 most of them were transformed into specialized LPGs. It was decided to separate animal production and to create large specialized and independent

Table 4.2 Socialist agricultural enterprises, 1960–85

Year	Nationalized estates (VEGs) of which:			Agricultural producers' cooperatives (LPGs) of which:		
	Total	Crop farming	Animal husbandry	Total	Crop farming	Animal husbandry
1960	669	—	—	19,313	—	—
1975	463	—	—	4,621	47	4,574
1985	465	77	314	3,905	1,144	2,761

Source: *StJB*, 1986, p. 181.

production units which would utilize industrial methods to a greater extent than the KAPs and the VEGs. In 1984, only fourteen KAPs remained, whereas 1,140 special crop-farming cooperatives (LPG–P), seventy-five special crop-farming nationalized estates (VEG–P), 2,792 special animal husbandry cooperatives (LPG–T) and 320 nationalized estates specializing in animal husbandry (VEG–T) had been created. The average size in 1982 of the LPG–P was about 4,700 hectares of useful agricultural land, employing on average 320 persons; the LPG–T worked on average about 23 hectares (Eckart, in Gerber, 1985, pp. 16–18; Eckart, in Zimmermann, 1985, pp. 807–8).

Specialization was reinforced by the expansion of inter-enterprise cooperatives for animal husbandry and about thirty-three large animal-fattening stations, the first of which was established in 1968. Agro-chemical centres emerged as independent units after the 1971 Party Congress. The 264 centres have a labour force of 24,749 and specialize in fertilizers and pest control (*StJB*, 1986, p. 191).

By 1980, it had become apparent that the agricultural 'industrialization' policy of the 1970s would have to be modified. Crop yields had not fulfilled expectations and large quantities of feeds were being imported. Farming costs and state subsidies had risen dramatically, the latter amounting to almost 1,000 Marks per hectare in 1981. The general economic situation at the beginning of the new decade exacerbated matters. Consequently, the new agro-political leadership duo of Werner Felfe and Bruno Lietz revised their predecessors' emphasis on vertical specialization and concentration in animal husbandry and crop production. Greater importance has been attached since 1984 to the 1,193 councils of cooperations or inter-farm complexes (KOR) as mechanisms of horizontal integration (Hohmann, 1985b, pp. 127–9).

The cooperation councils are emerging as the key administrative units. They have fifteen to twenty members and meet once a month. Each council is empowered to coordinate and determine the funds, the planning, the norms and the guidelines for comparing the performance of the crop and animal husbandry enterprises within a cooperation. Honecker has described the cooperations and their councils as providing the 'optimum conditions . . . for ensuring that the separation of crop and livestock production that has occasionally prevailed is overcome for the benefit of the farmers' (*Report of the Central Committee*, 1986, p. 45). Until 1984, the LPGs received plan targets directly from the competent district council and then had to defend their plans before the council. Subsequently, the cooperation councils have operated as an additional coordination, planning and management tier between the individual enterprise and the district council. The cooperation councils, on which the LPGs and the VEGs are represented, allocate the plan indicators of the cooperation from the district council to the individual enterprise. The cooperation council must ultimately defend the aggregated cooperation plans before the district councils. Despite the allocation of coordination and management functions to the cooperation councils, Western scholars doubt whether the SED intends to use them in the near future as the basis for the formation of mini-agrarian combines (Hohmann, 1985b, pp. 132–3).

Another new element in SED agricultural policy is the encouragement of private production especially since 1979. Private plots accounted for 240,000 hectares or 3.8 per cent of useful agricultural land in 1976. The cultivation of small plots is no longer restricted to LPG members; employees and workers on the cooperatives can also work small fields. The restrictions on the number of animals which may be raised on private plots have been removed. Allotment gardens are no longer deprecated as relics of the past. In 1982, the private plots and the Association of Allotment Gardeners, Homesteaders and Small Stock Breeders, numbering 1.2 million members, supplied 40.1 per cent of eggs, 29.4 per cent of fruit and 11.2 per cent of vegetables delivered to the state and 11.9 per cent of animals delivered for slaughter (Zimmermann, 1985, p. 597). Such initiatives have been described by Honecker as 'a very effective supplement to social production' (*Report of the Central Committee*, 1986, pp. 46–7).

An agricultural price reform was introduced in 1984 to stimulate production and, as elsewhere in the economy, encourage economies of scale. State subsidies for fodder, machinery, fuels, building materials and building work were abolished. Between 1983 and 1984, the prices paid by the state to producers of agricultural products were raised by between 40 and 60 per cent, including that for wheat from 35 Marks to 64 Marks per 1,000 kilogrammes. However, as the consumer has been protected from increases in the price of basic foodstuffs, state subsidies of consumer foodstuffs prices have rocketed from 11.16 million Marks in 1981 to 23.00 million Marks in 1985 (Eckart, in Gerber, 1985, pp. 22–3; Hohmann, 1985b, p. 139; Kurjo, 1986, p. 79).

The long-term trend in agricultural output has been positive, although fluctuations, partly determined by weather conditions, have occurred on several occasions. The German Institute for Economic Research in West Berlin estimates that, on the basis of average market production for the years 1956–60, the annual growth rate, until 1982, was in the region of 4 per cent (*DIW Handbuch*, 1984, p. 195). The final two years of the 1981–5 plan period witnessed a 5.4 per cent increase in animal production and a record 11 per cent growth in crop production (Hohmann, 1986, p. 55). Good results were obtained in crop production in 1986, too: a record harvest of 11.7 million tonnes was achieved. Favourable weather conditions accounted in part for these higher yields but so too did the stimulus of the sharp increase in procurement prices (Kurjo, 1986, pp. 78–9; *Report by the Central Statistical Office*, 1987, p. 29).

As one would expect in a country with a high standard of living and a high foodstuff consumption, animal products, especially milk and pigmeat, constitute a much higher proportion of total market production than vegetable products (76.1 per cent and 23.9 per cent respectively in 1981–2). The production of grain is therefore vital for the supply of both bread and animal feed. Over half of the arable land is devoted to grain crops and half of that to feed grains. The SED has been anxious to increase grain production in order to reduce its dependence on imports, especially of feed grains. In 1981, Honecker declared: 'Today the urgency of the grain problem is quite comparable to that of the oil problem' (quoted in Krisch, 1985, p. 103).

The cause of Honecker's concern lay in the average increase in grain imports of about 500,000 tonnes per annum in the period 1976–80 in comparison to the average for the preceding five-year period and, with the exception of 1977 and 1979, in the virtual termination of Soviet deliveries since 1975. The GDR was, therefore, obliged to cover its import requirements on the world capitalist markets, especially from the United States and to pay in hard currency, thereby exacerbating its indebtedness (Hohmann, 1985a, pp. 17, 20–1). Relatively modest but realistic increases in production and yields were envisaged for 1981–5 to cope with this problem. Although the targets were surpassed and grain imports fell sharply in 1981 and 1982, the country did not achieve self-sufficiency and imports rose again in 1983. Consequently, the 1986–90 Economic Plan aims 'to achieve a grain output of 11.9 million tonnes by 1990 in order to render grain imports superfluous' (Five-Year Plan Act, 1986, p. 27).

Agricultural productivity in the GDR has exhibited a steady long-term growth. The per-hectare yield of grain has risen from 24.8 decitonnes in 1956–60 to 45.2 in 1981–5 (Hohmann, 1986, p. 60; *DIW Handbuch*, 1984, p. 374). However, crop and milk yields and animal production lag behind West German levels. Karl Hohmann calculates that for the years 1981–5 GDR per-hectare yields of grain, potatoes and sugar beet were 84 per cent, 67 per cent and 60 per cent below those obtained in the FRG (Hohmann, 1985b, p. 138). Labour productivity, or net production per full-time workers, presents a similar picture. Although labour productivity has increased since 1961–2, Western experts estimate that in the early 1980s it was only half that of the Federal Republic. The gap is attributed to inadequate management, poor motivation and overmanning. In 1982, there were twelve full-time equivalent workers per 100 hectares of agricultural land in the GDR, or twice the West German average (Merkel, in Zimmermann, 1985, p. 799; *DIW Handbuch*, 1984, pp. 192–4,

197–9). The 1986–90 Economic Plan aims to raise productivity through the more rapid exploitation of microelectronics and biotechnology, the more efficient application of humus to the soil, the large-scale cultivation of leguminous plants and the saving of between 40 and 45 million man hours. This will mean the redeployment of about 25,000 workers in the maintenance, manufacture and repair of agricultural machinery and equipment (Five-Year Plan Act, 1986, p. 62; Hohmann, 1986, pp. 57–8).

Services

In 1984, the GDR's railway network totalled 14,226 km. and the extensive roadwork system 1,850 km. of autobahns, 11,251 km. of trunk roads and 34,097 regional roads. The waterways, amounting to 2,315 km. in length, suffer from the absence of a direct link between the main system, the Saxon industrial region and the country's major port, Rostock.

The oil price explosion and the need to economize on resources led to a re-evaluation of the policy of conversion from steel to diesel on the railways and to a shift towards electrification. Between 1981 and 1986, 1,000 km. of track were electrified. Despite this recent expansion, the level of electrification at the end of 1984 (19.4 per cent) and of electrical traction (35 per cent) was low not only by Western but by East European standards (*DIW Handbuch*, 1984, pp. 205–6; Schneider, 1986, p. 62).

The general improvement in the standard of living has encouraged the growth in car ownership (from 15.6 passenger cars per 100 households in 1970 to 48.2 in 1985), despite the cost and long waiting period for the delivery of a new vehicle. Although the volume of public transport has contracted, the government continues to give it priority in the planning of urban transport. In 1983, state subvention of public enterprises amounted to about half their operating costs. A single journey on a tram or bus costs a mere 20 *Pfennig* (Hopf, in Zimmermann, 1985, p. 1428).

The transportation of goods is primarily undertaken by rail (72.5 per cent in 1984). The rapid increase in road transport's share during the 1970s was reversed in the 1980s because of the need for energy saving measures and the consequent shift in freight transport from road to rail and a reduction in works transport capacity. Between 1980 and 1985, an energy saving of about 25 per cent was achieved in the transport sector (Schneider, 1986, pp. 5–6). The 1986–90 Five-Year Plan proposes to continue along the same track as its predecessor. Efforts will be made to switch freight from road transport to energy-saving rail and inland waterway transport and at lower unit consumption figures for energy and materials, a decreasing number of man-hours and lower cost levels. Another 1,500 km. of railway track will be electrified, and by 1990 electric traction should account for 60 per cent of freight haulage.

Although the contribution of small private plots to agricultural production has received official blessing, the artisan trades are the only sector in which ownership of the means of production is mainly in private hands. In 1985, private enterprises accounted for 58.9 per cent of the performance of artisan trades as against 41.4 per cent by production cooperatives (the 1972 percentages were 65.8 and 34.2 respectively; see *StJB*, 1986, p. 174). Independent artisans had been subjected to heavy pressure throughout the 1950s to join production cooperatives. The vast majority of these cooperatives are of type II, in which machines, tools and other means of production are transferred to social ownership. In 1972, the government attempted to stem the drain of skilled workers from industry, attracted by good pay in the artisan trades, by restructuring existing production cooperatives. Pragmatic considerations—shortages of meat and bread, bottlenecks in services and repairs—subsequently caused the government to change its mind: an unpublished Council of Ministers decree in 1976 admitted past errors and encouraged the promotion of cooperatives and independent artisan trades by the extension of credits and the granting of business licences (Ruban & Schwartau, in Bethkenhagen *et al*., 1981, p. 83; Haendcke-Hoppe, in Zimmermann, 1985, pp. 591–4). This episode clearly illustrates that in a society bedevilled by frequent shortages of small everyday items and parts and by the vagaries of bureaucratic procedures, the small independent plumbers, electricians, joiners, mechanics, builders and tailors continue to fulfil a valuable (through restricted) role.

Domestic trade encompasses wholesale and retail trade, hotels and restaurants. Private enterprises, once dominant in this sector, have experienced a decline in their share of retail trade outlets, from 80 per cent in 1952 to 25 per cent thirty years later. Many of the remaining concerns are small shops, restaurants and boutiques, often run on a family basis. The socialist part of retail trade is represented by consumer cooperatives and the shops and restaurants of the State Trading Organization (*Handelsorganisation*), which together account for over 90 per cent of total turnover (*DIW Handbuch*, 1984, p. 223; Haendcke-Hoppe & Ruban, in Zimmermann, 1985, pp. 237, 241). Although small shops, whether private or public, still enjoy a significant share of retail turnover, the concentration process has enhanced the position of the large department stores (*Warenhäuser*, often trading under the name *Centrum*) and the self-service supermarkets (*Kaufhallen*).

Although the assortment of goods has improved in recent years, especially in the larger cities such as Leipzig and East Berlin, the quality of goods, even in the department stores, leaves much to be desired. GDR consumers with money in their pockets can purchase high-quality clothing and leather goods, often of Western origin, at the 300 or so *Exquisit* shops and, since 1976, foodstuffs and drink at the 550 *Delikat* shops (1982 figures). Goods are paid for in GDR Marks, and Western items are usually overpriced. Hard-currency Intershops, which opened in 1962, the same year as the *Exquisit* establishments, stock Western cosmetics, TV sets, clothing, drinks, foodstuffs and other items at lower prices than are usually charged in the West. GDR citizens have been able to venture into these treasure troves of Western consumerism since 1974, although five years later the government obliged them to make their purchases with special coupons which they obtain at state banks in exchange for their Western currency. Official GDR figures estimated Intershop turnover at DM700 million in 1978, a useful windfall for the regime. The consumer, too, obviously benefits from the availability of high-quality Japanese television sets or Scottish whisky, but this has to be balanced against the circulation of a capitalist currency in a socialist economy and the dissatisfaction of the 'have-nots', that is, those East Germans without Western relatives or contacts. The existence of Intershops can only serve to reinforce popular perceptions of the disparity in living standards between the two systems (Zimmermann, 1985, pp. 369, 672).

The *Delikat* and *Exquisit* outlets provide the government with one way of obtaining higher prices for a range of goods. In fact, the principle of constant prices for consumer goods was modified by the SED leadership in December 1979. While the prices of such basic necessities as bread and potatoes have remained stable, those of better-quality goods, including textiles, clothing and electrical equipment, have been raised. New products, too, have become relatively more expensive and price increases have been justified, sometimes speciously, on the grounds of an improvement in quality or a change in product assortment.

The early 1980s were relatively difficult years for the GDR consumer. Until 1983 the increase in retail trade turnover was less than planned and the position of the consumer probably deteriorated in real terms until 1984 (Cornelsen, 1985, pp. 54, 67). For reasons of political legitimacy and social stability, the SED cushioned the consumer from the full impact of the shock waves of a price explosion by massive subventions of consumer prices, amounting to 40.6 billion Marks in 1985 as opposed to 16.8 billion in 1982 (*StJB*, 1986, p. 261).

The 1986–90 Five-Year Plan envisages an average growth in retail trade turnover of slightly more than 4 per cent. The prices of basic necessities are to remain stable and the production of newly developed consumer goods in 1990 is expected to be 45–50 per cent higher than in 1985. But as the average 4 per cent annual retail trade growth rates includes 2.7 per cent for foodstuffs and semi-luxuries as well as 5.3 per cent for industrial consumer goods, which have experienced sharp price increases in recent years, no appreciable improvement in supplies can be anticipated. It is also known that some of the high-quality consumer goods are earmarked for export (Stinglwagner, 1986, p. 638).

Foreign Trade

Foreign trade occupied a relatively minor role in economic policy until the mid-1960s; it was essentially limited to plugging shortages of raw materials and commodities. Subsequently, foreign trade was accorded a growth-promoting function and turnover increased rapidly. In 1980, exports represented about 30 per cent of produced national income (*DIW Handbuch*, 1984, pp. 294–5).

The GDR usually achieved relatively modest trade surpluses throughout the 1960s; a cumulative trade surplus of 5.7 billion Valuta Marks was recorded between 1960 and 1973. After 1973, the GDR, which has limited supplies of raw materials, was adversely affected by the explosion in raw material and energy prices. Although

COMECON raw material prices lagged behind those on the world market, the GDR soon ran into serious balance-of-trade deficits and debts. Out of a total deficit of 29 billion Valuta Marks between 1976 and 1980, 25 billion were in trade with the capitalist industrial countries. Trade with the USSR, the main supplier of oil, soon showed substantial deficits but, unlike those with the West, these could be partly financed on the basis of favourable Soviet credits. The GDR's net external debt against the West rose from $6.6 billion in 1977 to a massive $11.66 billion in 1981 (Cornelsen, 1985, p. 69). The situation became critical when the deterioration in East–West relations consequent upon the conflict in Afghanistan, the political crisis in Poland and the necessity of rescheduling debt repayments for Poland, and then Rumania directly affected foreign banks' perception of the credit-worthiness of the GDR. Credits were curtailed and pressure was increased on the GDR to repay its debts. A further element in the crisis was spiralling Soviet oil prices which in 1982 rose by 48 per cent over the preceding year (Haendcke-Hoppe, 1986a, p. 22).

The events of 1982 required even more drastic countermeasures than had originally been envisaged. The 1981–5 Economic Plan had anticipated reductions in the use of energy and raw materials and only a modest rise in personal consumption in order to reduce the level of indebtedness. The SED leadership now made a concentrated effort to increase exports to the West and to reduce the external debt burden. Mineral oil and mineral oil products were targeted as the major earners of hard currency. To the surprise of many outside observers, the export drive soon began to pay dividends: between 1982 and 1985, a surplus of 26 billion Valuta Marks was achieved in trade with the West and net indebtedness was halved between the end of 1981 and the end of 1985 (see Table 4.3). West German credits and the special characteristics of inter-German trade (in statistical units, not in hard currencies) were vital to the GDR's eventual recovery. On the other hand, the GDR remained in the red in its trade with the USSR; a cumulative trade deficit of 3.3 billion transferable roubles, the equivalent of $3.9 billion, was recorded in 1985 (see Table 4.4). The cost at home for the primacy of foreign trade was a curtailment of private

Table 4.3 Hard currency indebtedness of the GDR, 1981–86 ($ billion)

OECD*	1981	1982	1983	1984	1985	1986 (June)
Bank credits	10.7	9.1	8.6	8.5	10.4	10.8
Suppliers' credits	1.6	1.6	1.6	1.7	1.6	1.6†
Gross indebtedness	12.3	10.7	10.2	10.3	12.0	12.4
Assets	−2.2	−2.0	−3.4	−4.5	−6.5	−6.9
Net indebtedness	10.1	8.7	6.8	5.8	5.5	5.5

* Excluding inter-German trade.

† Estimate.

Source: Haendcke-Hoppe, 1986b, p. 74.

Table 4.4 Cumulative trade deficits of the GDR, 1981–86

	1981	1982	1983	1984	1985	1986 (June)
Inter-German trade Cumulative deficit in billions of units of account	3.7	3.7	4.1	3.1	3.5	3.6
$US billions	(1.6)	(1.6)	(1.6)	(1.1)	(1.2)	(1.6)
Trade with the USSR Cumulative deficit in billions of transferable roubles	2.3	2.9	3.1	3.2	3.3	3.6
$US billions	(3.2)	(4.0)	(4.2)	(3.8)	(3.9)	(4.7)

Source: Haendcke-Hoppe, 1986, p. 74.

consumption, a stagnation of social services and a slight fall in investments (Haendcke-Hoppe, 1986a, pp. 22–3).

Looking ahead to 1990, the GDR plans to increase total trade with the Soviet Union by 26 per cent and its exports by a disproportionate growth rate of 30 per cent; the latter is indicative of the intention to reduce the trade deficit. Trade with non-socialist countries is to grow by 20 per cent. In its trading relations with capitalist countries, Willy Stoph declared 'that it is necessary to expand the scope for the pursuit of trade policies and to enhance further the GDR's economic invulnerability' (*Directives*, 1986, p. 14). It is intended to maintain the present regional patterns of the GDR's trade: about two-thirds of total turnover will be with the USSR and the other socialist countries; no further shift toward the West is anticipated (Haendcke-Hoppe, 1986b, pp. 57–8). Finally, the SED defines the 'main need' as the achievement of 'a considerable export surplus in the 1986–90 period through 'the production of state-of-the-art products, a better and faster response to day-to-day market requirements, reliable spare parts supplies and improved market research' (*Directives*, 1986, pp. 14–15). However, the goal of trade surpluses with the West is threatened by the fall in the price of mineral oil and mineral oil products and the room for manoeuvre in foreign trade will be limited by Moscow's plans to establish even closer economic relations and by commitments to supply capital and consumer goods to the Soviet Union. Early indications suggest that Soviet-GDR economic cooperation is not proceeding smoothly: in the first nine months of 1986 GDR imports exceeded exports to such a degree that if the trend continued an annual deficit of 4 billion Valuta Marks would be recorded (Cornelsen, 1987, p. 61)

The GDR's main trading partners are the Soviet Union, the East European members of COMECON, Austria and the Federal Republic (see Table 4.5). In 1985

Table 4.5 Regional structure of the GDR's foreign trade, 1960–85 (per cent)

	1960	1970	1980	1982	1985
Socialist countries	75	72	66	66	66
COMECON countries	68	67	63	63	64
of which:					
USSR	43	39	35	38	39
Czechoslovakia	9	10	8	7	7
Poland	7	7	6	5	5
Hungary	4	5	5	5	5
Western industrial countries	21	24	27	28	29
of which:					
FRG	10	10	8	9	8
Developing countries	4	4	6	6	5

Source: *StJB*, 1986, pp. 240–1.

The COMECON countries' share of GDR foreign trade amounted to 64 per cent; the Soviet Union alone accounted for 39 per cent (*StJB*, 1986, p. 240). GDR–Soviet trade is based on a series of trade agreements and various integration mechanisms. The joint Governmental Commission for Economic and Scientific–Technical Cooperation between the GDR and the USSR, founded in 1966, acts as the major body for scientific–technical cooperation. It meets at least twice per year and also coordinates the five-year economic plans. The pattern of trade is characterized by a heavy GDR dependence on Soviet industrial and agricultural raw materials and extensive Soviet imports of GDR capital goods. In the early 1980s, it is estimated that the Soviet Union supplied virtually all of the GDR's imports of cotton, natural gas, sawn timber and about 50 per cent of hard coal and coke. Soviet oil, as a proportion of GDR import requirements, fell from 88.6 per cent in 1976–80 to 73.6 per cent in 1984. About 25 per cent of Soviet machinery and equipment imports stem from the GDR (Diech, in Zimmermann, 1985, pp. 128–9; Meier, 1986, p. 19). Seventy per cent of the GDR's engineering goods exports are destined for the USSR and 40 per cent of patents granted to other countries go there, too (Boot, in Gerber, 1986, p. 20).

Whereas the GDR, between 1949 and 1973, enjoyed a cumulative trade surplus of .45 billion Valuta Marks in its trade with the USSR. a trade deficit was recorded from 1975 onward. By the end of 1979, the cumulative trade deficit stood at billion Valuta Marks. Exports had to be increased in order to pay for Soviet oil: the GDR required 33 per cent from its receipts from its exports to the Soviet Union in 970 as against only 8 per cent in 1970 (Haendcke-Hoppe, in Gutmann & Haendcke-Hoppe, 1981, pp. 72–3). Despite a reduction in the supply of Soviet oil from 19 million tonnes in 1981 to 17.7 million in 1982 and then 17.1 million in

subsequent years), the doubling of the price of Soviet oil from 92 to 183 transferabl
roubles per tonne between 1981 and 1984 ensured a continuation of the GDR defici
(Meier, 1986, p. 19). It remains to be seen whether, in view of the fall in world oi
prices, the Soviet Union will scale down its own charges for the benefit of the smalle
East European economies or whether it will prefer them to drop gradually on the
grounds that its smaller partners must now be prepared to accept some dis
advantages whereas formerly they had enjoyed the benefits of the intra
COMECON price formula (Bethkenhagen, 1986a, pp. 214–15). The favoured
solution seems to be to boost the physical quantity of GDR exports at a faster rat
than imports, thus reducing the GDR's trade deficit, providing the Soviet consume
with a wider variety of high quality consumer goods and helping to moderniz
Soviet industry. Exports of GDR consumer goods to the USSR are to increase b
40 per cent during the 1986–90 plan period. Robots, printing machines wit
electronic steering, more chemical products, natural gas service stations an
equipment for the energy and raw material sectors are to be supplied to the Sovie
(Meier, 1986, p. 33; *Mit qualitativ neuen Schritten*, 1986, p. 4).

Does the Soviet Union exploit the GDR's more advanced economy or is th
relationship one of mutual advantage? The question of dominance or inter
dependence is difficult to answer, partly because of the difficulty in obtainin
reliable information on the prices of machinery and consumer goods and on cred
transactions and loans. An evaluation of the cost–benefit ratio would suggest that th
GDR may have benefited from Soviet net price subsidies on imports of 'sof
manufactured goods and, though the Soviet Union has enjoyed a surplus on one o
the hardest commodity groups, fuels, the sharp difference between world mark
and intra-COMECON prices, at least until 1982, represented an 'implicit subsidy' t
the GDR. Between 1971 and 1978, according to Paul Marer's calculations, the Sovi
Union implicitly provided a net cumulative subsidy to the GDR of $4.8 billion o
trade in fuels, non-food raw materials, semi-manufactured goods and agricultur
goods combined. On a per capita basis, the GDR ranked second, behind Bulgari
among COMECON members (Marer, in Terry, 1984, p. 179). Marrese and Vano
have produced calculations of implicit subsidies, based on high as well as low dolla
transfer rouble conversion rates for manufactured goods. Their conclusion is th
between 1970 and 1984 the GDR was ranked first among COMECON states bo
on the cumulative dollar value of subsidies and on the per capita value of subsidi
Soviet subsidies, based on the low conversion rate, peaked in 1980 and 1981 wi
$4.4 billion and $4.6 billion respectively and then fell to $3.5 billion in 1984. T
high conversion rate produces lower subsidies in these three years of $3.24, $3.28 ar
$1.64 billion (Marrese, 1986, pp. 302, 319).

As a proportion of total turnover, the GDR's trade with the West, including t
FRG, fell from 34.7 per cent in 1949 to 17.4 per cent in 1962; the latter figu
indicates the sensitivity of trade to political events. However, in 1974, according
the West German expert, Maria Haendcke-Hoppe, it temporarily exceeded t
Soviet Union's share (30.9 per cent to 30.2 per cent), a consequence not only
Western inflation but also of the SED's strategy of seeking greater access to Weste

echnology and goods. Although GDR total imports from OECD countries lagged far behind the COMECON pacesetters Poland and Hungary, the SED leadership hoped to promote the modernization of the GDR's economic potential by an increase in technological imports during the first half of the 1970s. The credits needed to finance these imports would, it was intended, be repaid in the second half of the decade as a result of the anticipated expansion in exports. The GDR's policy was relatively cautious toward direct involvement in technological transfer, whether in the form of technology embodied in machines or in the transfer of know-how, mainly for organizational and political reasons. The GDR's relative inactivity in the various forms of East-West industrial cooperation, such as licence agreements and co-production, is illustrated by the fact that its share of COMECON participation in such projects in 1975 was 1.4 per cent, the lowest in the bloc and far behind the leaders Hungary and Poland (Haendcke-Hoppe, 1983, p. 378; Machowski, 1985, p. 6; Schoppe, in Gutmann, 1983, p. 347; Levcik & Stankovsky, in Freeman, 1985, p. 117).

Despite its caution, the GDR's policy of credit-subsidized imports had to be revised when stagnation in most Western economies after the price shocks of 1973– and 1979 adversely affected the GDR's trade with the West. The mounting net hard-currency debt and the credit crisis of 1981–2 finally persuaded the SED leaders to launch an export drive and squeeze imports. Between 1980 and 1984, GDR exports to the West, excluding the FRG, increased by 13.7 per cent and imports fell by 25 per cent. The most important customers during this period were Sweden, France and Great Britain (Plötz, 1985, pp. 59–62). Several changes took place in the commodity structure of this trade. The export of capital goods declined from 7.5 per cent between 1976 and 1980 to 15.9 per cent in 1983. Mineral oil products emerged as the main earner of hard currency: their share of exports to the West increased from 9 per cent to 30 per cent during the same period. The decline in the proportion of capital goods exports partly reflects Soviet demands for better quality goods but it also underlines the greater difficulties in penetrating the highly competitive Western markets (Plötz, 1985, pp. 64–5, 75–8).

The GDR's main trading partner in the West is, of course, the Federal Republic. Considerable benefits are derived by the GDR from normal inter-German trade. Quotas and tariffs of the European Economic Community do not apply to this trade. Other advantages include access to the West German market for GDR goods which may not be easily sold in other hard-currency markets and a permanent interest-free credit swing. The swing allows the GDR to delay repayment of its trade deficit until the annual settlement of balances. Payment is assessed in units of account (Verrechnungseinheiten or VEs), which correspond *de facto* to the Deutschmark (DM). The amount of the swing has been set at varying levels of VEs: 200 million in 1970, 850 million from 1976 to 1982 and 600 million in 1985. The GDR has never exceeded these credit limits. In addition to the swing the GDR was able to make use of two large West German bank loans of DM1 billion and DM950 million in 1983 and 1984 to facilitate its debt restructuring and the expansion of imports without a commensurate increase in exports. Among the many other benefits are road and other tolls, postal payments, visa charges, payments for the sewage disposal of West Berlin and purchases in hard currency at Intershops. Some of these payments can be calculated more precisely than others. In 1982, the GDR obtained, it is estimated DM2.18 billion from formal German–German agreements, including transit charges on traffic between the FRG and West Berlin (DM525 million), charges for the use of roads within the GDR (DM50 million), revenue from the minimum currency exchange requirements (DM200 million), payment to improve transportation links to and from West Berlin (DM410 million), and revenue from Intershops, Intertank and Genex (DM1,000 million) (Bethkenhagen, in Stent, 1985 p. 82). Whatever the final total, the West German 'subsidy' amounts to a massive support of the GDR's economic and social policies, and one which West German governments have employed to promote the 'humanization of separation'.

Although the FRG is the GDR's most important trading partner after the USSR (see Table 4.5), the GDR accounted for a mere 1.5 per cent of her Western neighbour's foreign trade in the early 1980s (*DIW Handbuch*, 1984, p. 321). As the German Institute for Economic Research has noted, the commodity structure of this trade does not reflect the two countries' highly industrialized structure. Basic materials and semi-manufactures enjoy a disproportionately high share, while capital goods, notably plant and machinery, are under-represented. Despite attempts to modernize its industry, capital goods accounted for only 10 per cent of GDR exports to the Federal Republic in 1982; in contrast, basic materials and produced goods, especially mineral oil products, totalled 55.8 per cent (*DIW Handbuch*, 1984, pp. 322, 410).

Inter-German trade played a crucial part in the SED's crisis-management strategy from 1982 onward. Whereas the SED leadership ruthlessly reduced imports from the other OECD countries, the gap was partly filled by imports from the FRG, some of which were re-exported to foreign customers in return for hard currencies. Although the GDR succeeded in converting its trade deficit with the OECD countries into a surplus in 1982 and 1983, it still faced serious problems. Net indebtedness to the FRG rose by over 1 million VEs between mid-1982 and mid-1983 and access to the capital markets remained closed. The two bank credits in 1983 and 1984, both guaranteed by the West German government, undoubtedly made a significant contribution to the restoration of the GDR's credit-worthiness and to a successful resolution of the general crisis. The fall in deliveries from the FRG, including services, by about 1 million VEs between 1983 and 1984 and the partial replacement from other OECD sources indicated that the worst was over (Groß, 1985, pp. 27–35). Although it would be a distortion to claim that inter-German trade alone was decisive in enabling the SED to overcome the crisis which broke out in 1982, the episode does illustrate the utility of the special relationship with the Federal Republic.

Economic Performance and the Outlook for the 1990s

A relatively successful economic performance is critical to regime legitimacy and to the continuation of the social compact established between the regime and populace since the late 1960s. Economic performance is judged by the SED elite in terms of economic growth. The SED's foremost economics functionary, Günter Mittag, articulated this view at a high-level economics conference in 1983: 'There is no alternative in the socialist economy to the continuous growth of production and national income. It is and remains the basis for social progress in all areas' (*Ökonomische Strategie*, 1983, p. 36). Measurement of economic performance is, however, extremely difficult, given the serious deficiencies in the details and quality of official statistics. Other problems concern the selection of appropriate indicators and the value of these indicators for comparing different systems. Indicators widely used to compute economic performance include produced national income, commodity production, labour and capital productivity and per capita income. Produced national income, like gross national product in the West, is the most important indicator of the national accounting system used by GDR economists. As produced national income covers only those economic activities concerned with the production or distribution of material goods and omits most of the non-material services sector where wages are relatively low, this indicator tends to have an upward bias. Several attempts have been made, notably by Thad Alton and his associates, to convert produced national income data into figures comparable to Western gross national product. Even though these calculations tend to arrive at a figure about 2 per cent lower than those arrived at for produced national income, the GDR record throughout the turbulent late 1970s and early 1980s is by no means discouraging (see Table 4.6).

Table 4.6 GDR macro-economic growth rates, 1961–84 (per cent)

	1961–65	1966–70	1971–75	1976–80	1981	1982	1983	1984
Produced national income	3.4	5.2	5.4	4.2	4.8	2.5	4.4	5.5
Gross national product	NA	3.2	3.5	2.4	2.4	.5	NA	NA

Source: Stahnke, in Gerber, 1986, p. 3.

This economic record is by no means uniformly positive, however. Planned growth rates in the second half of the 1970s and the first half of the 1980s were not achieved: the growth of national produced income failed by 0.8 per cent to achieve the 1976–80 Five-Year Plan target of 5 per cent. Secondly, Erich Honecker freely admitted in 1981 that the GDR's labour productivity was 30 per cent lower than that of the FRG and France. In a recent important West German study, *Materialien zum Bericht zur Lage der Nation im geteilten Deutschland 1987*, the gap between the two Germanies, based on a comparison between the producing sectors, was reckoned to be 50 per cent at the beginning of the 1970s, considerably higher than the 30 per cent mentioned by Honecker and the figure which is also usually accepted in the West. One consolation for the GDR from this report was that the disparity had not widened in the 1980s (see Bundesminister für innerdeutsche Beziehungen, 1987c, p. 36). Finally, as one form of adjustment to its economic problems since the late 1970s, the GDR has had to reduce the growth of domestic utilization, that is, private and public consumption plus investment. Investments tended to be cut back more sharply in the 1980s than the more politically and socially sensitive retail trade turnover indicator. Hans–Dieter Schulz's comparison of the rates of change between 1975 and 1980 reveal a slower growth rate of retail trade turnover (13 per cent) than for produced national income (24.4 per cent), but a decline of investments by -5.6 per cent (Schulz, 1986, p. 235). The danger here is that the protection of current consumption entails some sacrificing of economic modernization and hence future competitiveness and the growth potential of the economy.

The SED leadership, in addition to devising temporary solutions to its immediate economic problems, has attempted to devise a basic concept for the GDR's future economic development. The overall economic strategy of the SED is usually characterized by the term 'intensification', that is, the achievement of economic growth not through increased material inputs and an expansion of capital assets but through the intensive or more efficient utilization of existing productive assets and labour. The term 'intensification' was first employed in the early 1960s; it was propagated at the SED Eighth Party Congress in 1971 as the main way to higher productivity and efficiency. The growth and energy problems since the mid-1970s stimulated a more urgent search for an efficient use of resources; consequently, the 1981 Party Congress gave even greater prominence to what it called 'comprehensive intensification' as a key determinant of the socialist planned economy.

The essence of the comprehensive intensification strategy has been defined by Honecker as combining 'the advantages of socialism still more effectively with the achievements of the scientific and technological revolution' (*Report of the Central Committee*, 1986, p. 58). Given the dramatic shortening of the life-cycle of products, the flexibility and adaptability of key technologies, and the potential improvements in productivity, the GDR's political leaders and economists believe that the GDR cannot afford to ignore new developments in science and technology. Innovation is regarded as a *sine qua non* for maintaining the GDR's position as a leading industrial state and for creating the resources for financing social welfare and security goals. Honecker has portrayed the competition in a manner which conjures up the image of an Olympic race:

The rate at which the productive forces on an international scale are developing is increasing, and we are therefore unable to choose our own pace. We will have to succeed in this race against time, leading the field in key areas to achieve major economic and social changes. [*Report of the Central Committee*, 1986, p. 59]

The key technologies on which the SED elite is pinning so many hopes are microelectronics, identified by Mittag as 'the main source for the further acceleration of scientific–technical progress' (*Mit qualitativ neuen Schritten*, 1986, p. 27), robotics, electronic data processing, biotechnology, CAD/CAM, flexible automated manufacturing systems, laser technology and nuclear energy. The 1986–90 Economic Plan has assigned high priority to the following targets:

— the production of at least 170,000 office and personal computers, 1,950 minicomputers and 670 mainframes;
— 90,000 CAD/CAM work stations (28,000 had originally been planned), employing 500,000 workers;
— the manufacture of 80,000 industrial robots, including 10,000 to 12,000 of the flexible type;
— the completion of at least sixty large-scale automation projects in the metal-working industries and another thirty-five elsewhere in the economy;
— the tripling of production in biotechnology, the upgrading of indigenous raw materials, the development and manufacture of highly potent diagnostic and pharmaceutical preparations, the use of enzymes and flavouring substances to enhance production and quality in the food industry, and the application of genetic engineering and bioprocessing to increase crop and livestock yields (Five-Year Plan Act, 1986, pp. 51–2; *Directive Issued by the 11th Congress*, 1986, pp. 48–51).

The SED leadership is anticipating major economic benefits from these key technologies. First, it hopes to achieve 25 per cent of the planned increase in labour productivity between 1986 and 1990 by means of the more rapid deployment of industrial robots. Secondly, the manufacturing and construction sectors are expected to achieve productivity increases of up to 500 per cent in the pre-production stages and in the control of manufacturing operations as a result of the rapid expansion of CAD/CAM work stations. According to Mittag, 35 million man-hours were saved in 1985 when about 1,100 CAD/CAM work stations came into operation (Five-Year Plan Act, 1986, pp. 14, 51; *Mit qualitativ neuen Schritten*, 1986, p. 42). Thirdly, the more widespread application of microelectronics has already contributed significantly to the increase in the automation level of production equipment from 33 per cent in 1970 to 51 per cent in 1984 and opens up possibilities for the development of flexible automation (Krakat, 1986, p. 96). Flexible automation, which is still restricted to a handful of combines, such as the machine-tool combine 'Fritz-Heckert' in Karl-Marx-Stadt and the metal-forming combine 'Herbert Warnke' in Erfurt, enables auxiliary tasks to be combined with the main production processes in an integrated design and production system of CNC-machines, robots, and CAD/CAM. While single-purpose automation is restricted to mass production, flexible automation extends to the production of small and medium-sized batches. The expansion of flexible automation will be extremely beneficial in, for example, metal-working, where individual, small and medium-sized batch production accounts for 70 per cent of production time (Haustein & Maier, 1985, pp. 13–28). Finally, the annual production innovation rate, which rose from 20.9 per cent to 27.5 per cent between 1983 and 1985, is planned to increase until 1990 by an average annual rate of at least 30 per cent and by between 30 and 40 per cent in the consumer goods sector (*Directives*, 1986, p. 26).

The GDR has long possessed an impressive research base which makes the attainment of these scientific and technological goals a feasible proposition. Whereas in 1965 2.1 per cent of produced national income was expended on science and technology and R & D personnel accounted for 1.1 per cent of the total workforce, these percentages had increased to 4.2 and 2.0 respectively by 1980 (Kröber & Laitko, in Kröber & Maier, 1985, p. 180). Of the 182,000 R & D personnel in 1980, about 152,000 were to be found in industry, 10,000 in other producing sectors and 20,000 in the Academy of Sciences. The total had increased to 200,000 by 1986, accounting for about 5 per cent of produced national income (Lauterbach, 1982, p. 40; *Tribüne*, 25 July 1986, p. 11). Although the GDR figures, by including persons not providing R & D in a narrow sense, inflate R & D manpower and although the relation of scientific to non-scientific personnel at 1 : 1.1 in the late 1970s was lower than the international norm of 1.2 or 1.3 generally regarded as desirable, Western scholars readily acknowledge that the GDR's research effort is extremely high by international standards (Lauterbach, 1982, p. 41).

The major problem lies in the realization of this potential and the rapid diffusion of basic research. The GDR attempts to resolve the problem by a variety of organizational measures and financial and non-material incentives. Since 1982, priority projects, such as those involving microelectronics, have been designated as state commissions (*Staatsaufträge*) for science and technology. The commissions are centrally planned and cover all stages from research to the transfer into production. They are not restricted to the one- or five-year planning cycles but extend over the entire lifespan of a project. The duty booklets (*Pflichtenhefte*) have been utilized by enterprise managers since 1977 to determine the costs and benefits of an innovation. And since 1984, in another attempt to ensure the more rapid application of research, combines, enterprises and state organs have been obliged to purchase R & D projects from their own research institutions. Projects must be financed from the research institutions' own working capital and credits. If the results do not fulfil the stipulations in the contract agreed upon by the research institution and its customer various financial penalties are imposed. On the other hand, if a profit is achieved, the research institution may use it for the creation of risk, bonus and performance funds. As they are allowed to draw upon the risk fund to promote additional R & D activities, the research institutions have an additional incentive to pursue their own inventions. Another feature of the new regulations is that any surplus profit (*Extragewinn*) from an outstanding achievement is transferred to the bonus and performance funds (Bentley, 1986, p. 27; Lauterbach, 1984, pp. 42–5).

Combine formation has produced some improvement in the persistent problem of unnecessary delay in transferring new ideas into a marketable product or process. Transfer times at the Polygraph Combine were reduced from between five and six years in 1975 to between three and four years in 1980 (Koziolek, 1981, p. 123). Combines now have their own research centres, each employing several hundred R & D staff. In order to accelerate the development and application of microelectronics, the Carl-Zeiss Jena Combine and the Erfurt Microelectronics Combine are to be established as centres for state-of-the-art technology. Furthermore, cooperation agreements are concluded between combines and the research institutes of the Academy of Sciences of the GDR and the universities as part of a drive to establish a more effective linkage between basic and applied research. The Friedrich-Schiller-University in Jena has close contacts with the Carl-Zeiss Jena Combine, and the Microelectronics Combine Dresden cooperates in the field of electronics with the Technical University of Dresden and numerous scientific institutes of the Academy of Sciences. The research activities of the latter body, which is a major basic research centre, have been orientated more and more towards industry. In 1986, 47 per cent of the Academy's research potential was tied to cooperation agreements with combines, an increase of 12 per cent in one year; and higher education's research commitment to combines rose from 42 to 52 per cent (*Mit qualitative neuen Schritten*, 1986, pp. 48–50; Bundesminister für innerdeutsche Beziehungen, 1987a, p. 10).

These and other measures suggest that the GDR's 1986–90 Five-Year Plan goals are by no means unrealistic. The GDR should have little difficulty in increasing its stock of industrial robots by a further 80,000 during the current Five-Year Plan in view of the fact that in 1985 56,601 were already in operation (*StJB*, 1986, p. 108). The CAD/CAM target is on schedule: 13,600 CAD/CAM work stations and systems came on stream in 1986 (*Report by the Central Statistical Office*, 1987, p. 24). The output of personal computers rose by 148 per cent in the same year and the workers of the office machine enterprise in Sömmerda manufactured 10,318 personal computers in excess of the plan (*Report by the Central Statistical Office*, 1987, p. 7). Top international standards have been achieved, according to West German observers, in the isolation of monoclonal antibodies, production lines for the prefabrication of cement components for house construction, some types of integrated microelectronic circuits and certain optical instruments (Burrichter & Förtsch, 1985, p. 847).

However, these achievements should not be allowed to disguise the fact that the GDR still faces serious problems in raising the quality of its products and in closing the technological gap. Honecker's judgement in 1977 that only about 10 per cent of the GDR's scientific-technical output achieved top international standards is probably also true of the 1980s (Burrichter & Förtsch, 1985, p. 547; Buck in Gutmann, 1983, pp. 263–4). Honecker may have been acknowledging this at the Eleventh Party Congress when he declared that 'all products, and not just a few, should be of uniform high quality, whether produced for inland consumption or for export' (*Report of the Central Committee*, 1986, p. 61). Even in microelectronics, which was reinvigorated in 1977 and now seems to enjoy among SED leaders the status of a magic formula for resolving productivity and efficiency problems, GDR producers lag behind their Western counterparts both in terms of the quality and the quantity of output. While the GDR aims to produce 160,000 to 170,000 office and personal computers during the 1986–90 planning period, the Californian company Apple Computers produced about 1.2 million in 1985 alone. The deputy director of the Erfurt-based Microelectronics Combine estimated, according to a report in *The Economist*, that a gap of at least five years existed between the GDR's electronics industry and that of the West (*The Economist*, 22 February 1986, p. 60).

The gap can be illustrated by developments in microprocessors, memories, industrial robots and mechanical engineering products. While 8-bit microprocessors still represent the standard type in the GDR, they were replaced in the Federal Republic in 1982 by the 16-bit processors, a type which was first exhibited by the GDR at the 1985 Leipzig Fair. When the GDR announced the serial production of the 64-K-RAM in 1985, it was already six years behind the United States and Japan. The prospects for an economically profitable serial production of the 1-megabit memory by the close of the current Five-Year Plan appears unlikely; IBM, however, commenced production of this memory in 1986 (Klinger, 1987, pp. 9, 15; Krakat, 1986, pp. 46, 48).

This time-lag can have serious repercussions for the competitiveness and profitability of products. For example, the 64-K-memory cost DM150 when it appeared on Western markets in 1979; in 1985 it was worth only DM3 (Klinger, 1987, p. 15). The high-quality products of the mechanical engineering sector, notably machine tools, can usually be sold at a profit in Western markets only if they contain microelectronic elements. Honecker, in 1987, estimated that no more than 50 per cent of the GDR's mechanical engineering products incorporated microelectronic elements (*Neues Deutschland*, 7–8 February 1987, p. 6); another report indicated that 70 per cent of machine tools lack such elements. The absence of these components means that most of the products are exported to COMECON countries rather than to Western customers (Klinger, 1987, p. 16). Finally, official propaganda notwithstanding, most of the GDR's stock of industrial robots are little more than simple handling devices: in 1986, the GDR possessed about 4,500 relatively sophisticated robots, or approximately half the number in operation in the Federal Republic (Cornelsen, 1986b, p. 394). The major obstacles to overcoming the disparity in standards and the time-lag include: the slow transfer of basic research into the production of new products; the bureaucratic nature of the planning process; the reluctance of many managers to undertake risky innovations; the limited resources available for investment in new technologies; and the difficulty in expressing innovations in realistic industrial prices (Krakat, 1986, pp. 40–1; Klinger, 1987, pp 5–7; 13–15).

As the GDR looks ahead to the 1990s and beyond, it faces a number of difficult decisions. Should it, for example, seek to increase its imports of Western technology in order to accelerate the modernization of key economic sectors, increase foreign trade competitiveness and raise labour productivity? Energy and consumer goods are two sectors where the benefits would be extremely high. However,

COMECON's modernization and restructuring process in the 1970s, with the help of Western credits and technology, demonstrated that this strategy entailed many political as well as economic disadvantages. The SED leadership, which pursued a more cautious policy in respect of the average value of imported Western capital goods than Poland, Hungary and Bulgaria, is unlikely to become an enthusiastic proponent in the late 1980s—COCOM permitting—of a high level of technological imports. The GDR's limited supply of hard currencies, its experience of the West's credit squeeze in 1982-3, the balance of payments disequilibria and the political vulnerabilities of extensive trading with the West are all factors which seem to point to a limited degree of cooperation and trade with the OECD countries, whilst at the same time not neglecting the advantages of the West German connection.

While economic interchange will, indeed must, continue with the West, close ties will be maintained with the GDR's main trading partner, the Soviet Union, which is now demanding higher-quality GDR goods and even closer cooperation between economic and research bodies and production units (see Chapter 5). It is difficult, however, to envisage how socialist integration will provide the GDR with the necessary 'technological push'. The likelihood is that the GDR's technological gap with the major Western industrial powers will not be closed and may even widen, with the strong possibility of negative consequences for economic performance and consumer satisfaction.

Finally, the GDR will undoubtedly continue to strive for the more efficient use of domestic resources by improvements in the system of planning and combine organization; by offering additional material and non-material incentives to managers and the scientific–technical elite; and by the more intensive exploitation of the workforce. This does not, however, constitute fundamental reform of the economic system which, in the eyes of the SED leadership, has worked sufficiently well to have maintained, without jeopardizing the SED's political primacy, the GDR's position as the wealthiest and technically most advanced COMECON power. Honecker's reference at the Eleventh Party Congress, to the GDR's 'socialist economic planning' system as functioning well and as 'efficient, dynamic and flexible' (*Report of the Central Committee*, 1986, p. 52) hardly suggests that the SED leadership considers it necessary to implement a Gorbachëv-type restructuring of the economy. Perhaps some concessions may be made to *glasnost*, such as more autonomy in decision-making at combine level and allowing social scientists more room for critical pronouncements on the scientific–technical revolution. However, Kurt Hager's dismissal of the extension to the GDR of Gorbachëv's proposals for the election of factory managers (*Neues Deutschland*, 10 April 1987, p. 3) is a clear indication of the Politburo's continued commitment to a cautious 'perfecting of the system of management, planning and cost accountancy' (Mittag, in *Mit höchsten Leistungen den XI. Parteitag vorbereiten*, 1985, p. 73).

Industrial Relations

The GDR mass media invariably present a picture of harmony and cooperation between workforce, unions, party organizations and management. The 'complete harmony existing between the interests of the individual and society in socialism' (*Introducing the GDR*, 1987, p. 70) is supposedly based on the people's ownership of the means of production and finds expression in various forms of socialist democracy such as the emulation drive. This kind of 'democratic' involvement is also intended to improve the quality of work and to increase efficiency, thereby creating resources for the country's social welfare system. Socialist emulation or competition (*sozialistischer Wettbewerb*) comprises the activists' movement, socialist community work, the innovator's movement and so forth. Innovators or innovators' collectives advance new ideas or suggestions for the 'creative' solution of a technical, organizational or scientific problem. Ideas are usually submitted within the framework of an enterprise's plan. Renumeration for an invention varies from a minimum of 75 Marks to a maximum of 200,000 Marks. High participation rates are recorded and in 1984 the benefits from the utilization of innovations amounted to over 5.87 million Marks (*StJB*, 1986, p. 131).

The Labour Code, which came into effect in 1978, replacing the former Code of Labour of 1961, regulates and defines the legal rights and obligations of the workforce, the trade unions and management. It guarantees, among many others, the right to work and the right to codetermination (*Mitwirkung*) in management and planning. One difference between the 1961 and 1978 codes is the inclusion of the term co-determination in the Honecker legislation and its application to the workers' right of co-determination of wages, bonuses, the planning of working time and holidays and personal matters such as changes in contracts and dismissals. The Ulbricht code referred only to the right of cooperation; the present code, significantly, applies this more restricted right to two vital areas, the drafting of the enterprise plan and labour intensification. Where the workforce, or rather its union representatives, enjoys co-determination rights, the decision of the enterprise manager can only come into effect with the agreement of the enterprise's trade-union body. Cooperation rights may be overridden against the wish of the trade union by a decision of the manager.

Certain duties are expected of the worker: the fulfilment of work tasks and norms, the protection of socialist property and the strict observance of working hours. The emphasis here is on order and discipline. The right to strike was granted to the unions by the 1949 Constitution but it was omitted from the 1961 and 1978 Labour Codes. Although the only major manifestation of widespread strikes remains the June 1953 uprising, unconfirmed reports have circulated in the 1970s and 1980s of strikes against working and living conditions (Zimmermann, 1985, pl. 1346).

The workers' rights to participate in the decision-making processes are normally exercised through their trade-union organization (*Betriebsgewerkschaftsorganisation*), which may be formed in any enterprise or institution if at least ten members of the

FDGB are employed there. An elected executive presides over each organization; its size varies from three to twenty-five members and work is undertaken on an honorary basis. The executive creates special commissions, including those for agitation and propaganda, holidays, culture and education, to help it perform its duties. Since the decline in the importance and number of the permanent production councils, the commission for work and wages is the only one which deals directly with economic questions such as labour rationalization, plan discussions and the organization of socialist competition.

A central feature of trade-union work is the drafting and implementation of enterprise planning, especially the annual enterprise collective contract (*Betriebskollektivvertrag*). This contains agreements between the manager and the trade-union executive regarding the innovator's movement, wages, improvements in working conditions, social and educational measures, lowering costs and support for the women members of the labour force. The contract ensures extensive trade-union rights over workers' training, leisure activities, sickness pay and the allocation of holiday places in the trade-union hotels and hostels (Zimmermann, 1985, pp. 210–12, 379–81).

The trade-union organizations enjoy some opportunity for determining enterprise policy. The chairman of the executive has the right to attend works management meetings and to examine enterprise documents, including personal files. The FDGB also manages to mobilize a high proportion of workers in the numerous trade-union commissions and bodies. There were over 336,315 shop stewards, 324,048 cultural officials, 275,442 sports organizers and 79,465 members of women's commissions in 1985 (*StJB*, 1986, p. 403). However, significant limits are imposed on the trade-union organizations' participation and co-determination rights. The FDGB, as we have already seen, is constructed on the basis of democratic centralism. And the unions' and workers' rights of participation and consultation are circumscribed: by the principle of individual management, which entails the manager having the final say on economic conditions within the enterprise; by the need to integrate enterprise economic planning within the framework of the national and territorial plans; and by the control and inspection functions performed by the SED's enterprise party organization and executive.

The SED leadership was certainly alarmed at the popularity of Solidarity in Poland and sought to defuse the situation by depicting Walesa and his colleagues as counter-revolutionaries and the economic tribulations as typical Polish mismanagement. Although seven workers in Thuringia were supposedly arrested in the summer of 1981 for seeking the democratization of the FDGB, the GDR industrial workforce remained politically quiescent (McCauley, 1981a, p. 25). However, worker dissatisfaction has expressed itself in the seemingly timeless struggle against increases in work norms and in occasional strikes in Berlin, Karl-Marx-Stadt and elsewhere. Strikes have been triggered off by the non-payment of end-of-year premiums, poor-quality coffee in work canteens and demands for payment of a proportion of wages in hard currency (Bust-Bartels, 1980, pp. 134, 211–14). Labour turnover, absenteeism, down time and theft of materials and parts from factories and stores have been interpreted as other manifestations of workers' grievances against their working and living conditions. One GDR source reports down time as having attained an undesirably high level of 8.1 per cent in 1980. The same authors also criticized some workers for doing their shopping chores during working hours and for drinking an excessive amount of alcohol (Kroh, Schmollack & Thieme, 1984, pp. 76–8).

The annual rate of job turnover, in the late 1970s, has been estimated as ranging between 7 and 8 per cent, or over 500,000 workers. This figure refers essentially to unplanned job-switching as opposed to what has come to be defined as societally necessary mobility. The average cost of a change of job between enterprises and for workers in the same occupational group has been calculated as 10,000–15,000 Marks for skilled workers and up to 30,000 Marks for graduate engineers and economists. In 1978, unplanned labour turnover cost the national economy about 10 billion Marks, or about 6 per cent of produced national income (Schaefer, Schmidt & Wahse, 1982, pp. 26–9). Although the determinants of job-switching have primarily been related to personal matters (change of residence, marriage), other factors reveal the existence of social conflicts in the enterprises. Dissatisfaction with superiors and colleagues, deficiencies in work organization, limited opportunities for participation in decision-making processes, a monotonous job, the introduction of multi-shiftworking, the desire for higher pay, the under-utilization of qualifications have all been identified as the major material and non-material conditions for job-switching (Belwe, 1982, pp. 119–28).

The value attached by workers to human relations at work as a determinant of job turnover is a reflection of the rule of the workplace as a focus of the average citizen's life experiences. Irene Böhme, a former editor of the GDR cultural weekly *Sonntag*, has dubbed it the worker's 'second home' (1983, p. 26). Friendships are formed there, efforts are made to manipulate the economic plans to the workers' advantage, and the enterprise provides a range of educational and social amenities. This terrain has not gone uncontested, however. A joint Central Committee, FDGB and Council of Ministers resolution in 1976 aimed to relate wages more directly to work performance, and since 1974 scientific work organization methods have been applied to work study and work classification. The most serious intrusion upon the workers' niches is the labour rationalization programme, the Schwedt Initiative, launched in 1978 at the main enterprise of the Schwedt petro-chemical combine; the Initiative has subsequently been extended to other combines and enterprises. Under the slogan 'Fewer produce more', the Initiative aims at the release of workers from less productive jobs and their redeployment, without additional investments, in those sectors where they can be used to greater economic advantage. Key sectors for the redeployment of released workers include consumer goods production, the in-house manufacture of rationalization equipment, production for export markets, energy conversion and the costly labour processes in livestock farming (Hummel & Pietrzynski, in *Jahrbuch für Soziologie und Sozialpolitik*, 1985, pp. 44–5).

By means of rationalization programmes such as the Schwedt Initiative, it is hoped to avoid the kind of situation which occurred in 1976–8 when 30,000 new workplaces were created but only 7,700 were abolished. Empirical investigations revealed that by the end of 1981 the proportion of workplaces rationalized at Schwedt's main enterprise totalled 28.5 per cent over a four-year period. About 200,000 workers were released throughout the economy between 1981 and 1984. The rationalization quota at Schwedt and other combines such as the *Eisenhütten-kombinat Ost* represent above-average standards which were attained by only 5–10 per cent of all enterprises. The release of workers tends to proceed in a sporadic manner at 30–40 per cent of enterprises (Belwe, 1984a, p. 10; Hummel, in *Territorial-struktur und umfassende Intensivierung*, 1985, p. 70). Lothar Hummel of the GDR's Central Institute for Socialist Economic Management attributes these disappointing results to the absence of a clear concept in the enterprises and combines as to how to redeploy workers, the neglect of the rationalization of auxiliary and ancillary jobs and the lack of integrated planning between territorial organs and production units (Hummel, in *Zur weiteren Vervollkommnung der wissenschaftlichen Arbeitsorganisation*, 1983, pp. 61–3).

Despite the inadequacies of the labour rationalization programme, a change of workplace or enterprise can cause many problems for the workers affected. Administrative and management personnel may resent being transferred to production jobs. Secondly, workers who move willingly to workplaces utilizing modern technology may find their expectations of more interesting work disappointed. Shiftwork schedules, especially if they involve nightwork, create difficulties in the upringing of young children and the pursuit of time-related leisure activities. If both partners are on shifts, the family may rarely meet as a unit. Multi-shiftworking has been increasing in recent years as part of the drive to utilize more effectively expensive new machinery and equipment. Furthermore, workers who are well integrated into their work collectives are likely to be reluctant to leave familiar surroundings and colleagues unless the collective can be transferred virtually intact to the new workplace. Failure to accommodate workers' wishes and to anticipate problems can lead to what the authorities regard as societally undesirable or 'spontaneous' labour turnover. Finally, the importance of social relations at work may operate as a barrier to the social acceptance of the new technologies and new performance norms. GDR sociologists have discovered that even R & D collectives are not committed to 'management values' such as personal success and the absolute priority of work over leisure, hobbies and the family (Belwe, 1984b, pp. 502, 505–8; Klinger, 1985, pp. 26–8).

Workers enjoy considerable legal protection against violations of their employment contract by the enterprise management. In the case of job rationalization, an enterprise is obliged to conclude an alteration contract (*Änderungsvertrag*) with the worker and the trade-union representative; this should include the offer of a 'reasonable' alternative job. If a similar job is unavailable at the same enterprise or if the worker rejects the first offer, a transfer contract (*Überleitungsvertrag*), involving a change of enterprise, may be drawn up. A reasonable alternative must be offered once more. If the worker rejects the transfer contract, the enterprise has the right of dismissal. A worker's appeal against the terms of the new contract or dismissal is heard by the Chamber for Labour Law of the District Court or the enterprise conflict commission. However, the term 'reasonable' is sufficiently flexible to allow a judgement in favour of the enterprise management and cases have been discovered where workers have only agreed to accept an alteration contract because the enterprise has threatened them with dismissal (Klinger, 1985, pp. 29–30).

Although labour rationalization schemes have introduced a new element of conflict into industrial relations, it would certainly be premature to regard them as having induced a mass exodus of workers from their niches and as having created dynamic new work values. Some workers may in fact be without a job for a limited period of time after being dismissed without notice or after handing in their notice as a consequence of their dissatisfaction with the terms of an alteration contract. Workers' entitlemement to a monthly rent allowance and a daily payment of 8 Marks helps them to bridge the gap between jobs (Belwe, 1984a, p. 43). However, despite rumours in the West German press of tens of thousands of unemployed workers in the GDR, long-term unemployment does not yet threaten the GDR workforce, an important lever in labour's resistance to management and state economic goals.

5 The Regime's Policies

At the beginning of the 1980s a heavy hard-currency debt, the potential destabilizing effect of the crisis in Poland, a deterioration in the GDR's terms of trade, and a sharp increase in military expenditure consequent upon the new Cold War required the SED leadership to redefine its policy from a combination of several alternatives, all of them attended by serious political and social risks. Fundamental economic and political reform was eschewed; instead the regime combined a medium-term strategy to modernize key sectors of the economy with a series of short-term, often unpalatable, countermeasures: a reduction in imports, investments and domestic consumption; the launching of an export offensive; and stagnation in expenditures on education, health and research. It also took full advantage of the economic benefits which accrued from its West German connection. Conscious, however, of the need to maintain the social contract, the SED continued the heavy subvention of basic consumer items and the housing programme retained its position as a major feature of social policy (see Table 5.1).

Table 5.1 Selected budget expenditures of the GDR, 1980–85 (billions of Marks)

	1980	1982	1983	1985
Research, science and technology	2.6	2.9	2.9	3.4
Investments	5.8	8.1	8.1	6.7
Subsidies for national economy	7.1	7.2	7.6	15.0
Agricultural subsidies	8.5	9.6	11.4	6.2
Consumer prices subsidies	17.0	21.6	22.0	40.7
Housing	7.2	9.0	9.5	14.3
Education	9.8	11.0	11.1	12.4
Health and social welfare	9.5	11.0	11.2	12.4
Social insurance	29.4	30.5	30.5	32.5
Culture, sport and youth	3.4	3.9	4.1	4.6
Administration	3.7	3.8	3.7	4.1
Defence, internal security and border protection	13.2	15.1	16.0	18.2
Other	38.2	43.0	48.3	56.8
Total	160.3	182.1	191.7	234.4

Source: Vortmann & Weißenburger, 1986, p. 530.

At the Eleventh Congress of the SED in April 1986, party leaders, in the presence of Mikhail Gorbachëv, were unable to resist congratulating themselves on the relative success of their crisis-containment strategy. Nevertheless, the future of their economic modernization strategy remained uncertain, the military budget continued to spiral, and the Soviet Union, which two years before had publicly expressed its displeasure with Honecker's *rapprochement* with the Federal Republic, was pressing a somewhat reluctant SED leadership to assist in the modernization of the cumbersome Soviet economy. Despite serious problems and an uncertain international economic environment, sustained economic growth was still regarded by the political and economic elites as a *sine qua non* for providing the resources for priority areas such as defence, price subsidies, social security and housing.

Domestic Policies

Education

The educational system is lauded by GDR pedagogues and politicians as one of the showpieces of the socialist system. Western observers, too, acknowledge the positive aspects: the comprehensive reform of the pre-war system; the high proportion of young people with a vocational qualification; and the relatively open access to educational opportunities enjoyed by all strata.

In the immediate post-war period many teachers were dismissed from their posts because of their connections with the NSDAP. By January 1946, 20,000 teachers (about 50 per cent of the teaching profession) had been purged. Crash training programmes enabled about 40,000 new teachers to alleviate the shortage. The Democratization of the German School Law of 1946 replaced the previous system of elementary, intermediate and grammar schools by a compulsory eight-year schooling in coeducational, comprehensive *Grundschulen*. The new system was designed to remove the material and social barriers which had impeded the access of the working class and farmers to educational opportunities. In order to bring the educational system into line with subsequent economic, social and political developments, a third Education Act, the Law on the Integrated Socialist Educational System, was introduced in 1965. With the exception of the reform of higher education in 1967, the system entered the 1980s substantially unchanged.

The 1965 Law defines the general objective of the system as 'the education of universally and harmoniously developed socialist personalities who consciously shape social life, change nature, and lead a full and happy life worthy of human beings'. The Law proceeds to delineate the economic, political and social functions of the education sector. Citizens should be enabled

to shape the socialist society, to master the technological revolution, and to participate in the development of socialist democracy. It imparts an up-to-date general education and a high level of special training, and at the same time develops traits of character in accordance with the spirit and principles of socialism morality. [Act on the Integrated Socialist Educational System of the GDR, 1972, p. 16]

The realization of these aspirations should be a cooperative act between schools, parents, the FDJ and other organizations.

Crèches and kindergartens constitute the pre-school stage of the system. In 1985, 72.7 per cent of all children aged 0–3 attended a crèche and 89.9 per cent aged 3–6 a kindergarten. The degree of care in kindergartens has fallen gradually from a peak of 92.3 per cent in 1979, whereas provision has been increasing in the crèches, exceeding 70 per cent for the first time in 1985 (*StJB*, 1986, pp. 121, 143).

The ten-class general polytechnic school, established by the second Education Act of 1959, is the hub of the whole educational system. After the mandatory ten-year schooling, pupils have three options: either two years of vocational training, a three-year vocational course at a technical college which also leads to the *Abitur* (A-levels), or two years at an EOS (extended secondary school) preparing for *Abitur* and university or college entry. The EOS programme is pursued by about 10 per cent of those who complete their general schooling. The majority of school leavers, about 85 per cent, proceed to some form of vocational training as apprentices at the 963 enterprise or local government vocational schools. Theoretical lessons are combined with practical work, the average ratio being 30:70. Vocational training is free of charge and courses normally last for two years.

The curriculum of the ten-year polytechnic secondary school is determined by the Ministry of Education. No significant segregation takes place until the completion of the tenth grade. The major subjects on the curriculum are German and mathematics; Russian, history, geography and biology commence in the fifth grade; and music and sport are available throughout all ten grades. Pupils are provided with an insight into the work environment. In grades seven to ten, pupils receive four to five hours of polytechnic instruction; this is subdivided into an introduction to socialist production, productive work and technical drawing. As part of their instruction, pupils usually spend one day per week at a factory, a building site or a farm. Revised syllabuses, gradually being incorporated into the curriculum since 1982, aim to bring all subjects into line with the latest developments. Micro-electronics and the automation of production, for example, now occupy a more significant place in polytechnic instruction. Since 1985, pocket calculators have been used as part of the mathematics syllabus.

The educational attainment of pupils is impressive: 85 per cent of all school leavers attain the tenth grade certificate and a highly developed vocational guidance system helps them to find 'the right job' and to negotiate the difficult transition from work to school. Erich Honecker claims that 85 per cent of school leavers find an apprenticeship in the trade of their first choice. A caveat is needed, however: this figure is the outcome of a lengthy process of vocational guidance and reappraisal of pupils' original career intentions. The vast majority of young people obtain a qualification. In 1980, 69 per cent acquired a skilled worker qualification, 14 per cent a technical college certificate and 11 per cent a university degree. The

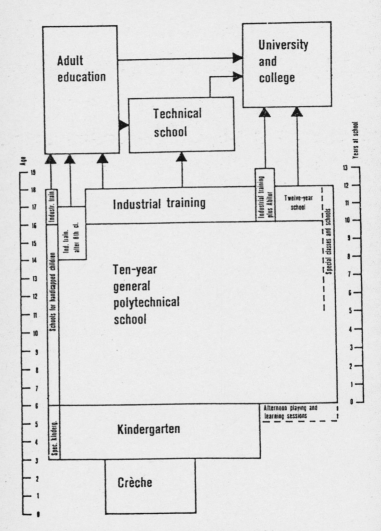

Figure 5.1 The integrated socialist education system of the GDR.
Source: Kohn & Postler, 1976, p. 16.

remaining 5–6 per cent were able to train for part of a normal trade qualification (Wolter, in Sydow, 1983, p. 125). By international standards, this represents a considerable achievement and provides the GDR with a well-trained and skilled labour force.

Set against these successes, however, are those young people who fail to achieve the tenth grade at school (about 15 per cent in 1980) and the pupils (some Western sources put the figure at 20–30 per cent) who do not manage to find a suitable apprenticeship or course by the time they leave school. The explanation for the mismatch between expectations and reality lies in a combination of factors: unrealistic career aspirations; limited opportunities in certain careers; the unpopularity of monotonous manual work; misguided parental advice; and the unsatisfactory vocational guidance at some schools which leaves young people inadequately informed about a range of possibilities. Moreover, as polytechnical education tends to neglect the preparation of pupils for jobs in the non-producing sectors, school leavers are usually ill equipped for a career in services, communications and commerce (Hille, 1981, p. 339).

Parallel to the general polytechnical schools are special schools and other pedagogical institutions for the education and training of children, young people and adults suffering from some significant physical or mental handicap. The principle of the uniformity (*Einheitlichkeit*) of the curriculum is qualified by the special schools and special classes for talented pupils. They represent the structural differentiation of the educational system which has been openly admitted by the authorities since the early 1960s. Special classes exist in the normal schools, mainly in the EOS, and provide intensive instruction in languages, Russian in particular, music, art, mathematics, physics, biology and engineering. Special schools were recognized in the 1965 Education Act as serving 'the special needs of developing talented cadres for the economy, for science, sports and culture'. These institutions are usually boarding schools. Only about 3 per cent of pupils in any one age group find places in the special classes and special schools. State, party, economic and academic functionaries, it is generally believed, enjoy considerable success in placing their children in such classes and schools (Vogt, in Zimmermann, 1985, pp. 328–9).

Higher education comprises fifty-four universities and colleges of higher education (*Hochschulen*), of which twenty-nine are directly controlled by the Ministry of Higher and Technical Education. In 1985, 129,885 students were enrolled at institutions of higher learning; women accounted for 50.1 per cent of the student population (*StJB*, 1986, p. 123). Most students pursue their studies on a full-time basis (70 per cent in 1970, 83.9 per cent thirteen years later). Correspondence study has declined in significance (from 25.3 per cent in 1970 to 9.5 per cent in 1983) and the evening mode has virtually disappeared. The basic qualification to enter a university is normally acquired by matriculation at the EOS or technical college but it can also be gained by attending institutions for the further training of working people, an engineering or technical college and special courses designed by universities and colleges. Potential students are expected to be politically active and the social structure of the student population should correspond, at least in theory, to that of the whole of society. Some GDR sources report that in recent years the proportion of applicants who succeed in obtaining a place in the subject of their first choice has increased from 85 to 90 per cent. The Minister of Higher Education, Böhme, has indicated, however, that in the 1982–3 academic year, a lower figure (about 75 per cent) realized their first choice (Günther, 1983, pp. 161, 164; Husner, 1985, p. 26).

Although every effort is made to harmonize the availability of places in higher education with manpower requirements, subjects such as mathematics, mechanical engineering, energetics, socialist enterprise management and the teaching of Marxism–Leninism are undersubscribed. Some other subjects, including medicine, psychology, pharmacy and biology, have a surplus of applicants. In addition to specialized training (about 73 per cent of the curriculum), obligatory instruction is provided in sport, Russian and a second foreign language, and Marxism–Leninism.

A highly developed system of further education and training for adults is designed to improve the professional and political expertise of cadres and to raise the vocational knowledge and skills of other workers. Opportunities are afforded to enable workers without a full vocational training to complete their qualification for their job. Many women acquired a skilled worker's certificate via the further education route. At a time of rapid economic and technological change, the further education sector is instrumental in preparing workers and staff for new vocations and in familiarizing them with the new techniques. The most important further education institutions are the enterprise and cooperative academies, the adult education institutions and higher education and technical colleges.

Although the state's absolute expenditure on education has tended to increase throughout the 1980s (except for the stagnation in 1982–3), education's share of the total state budget actually fell from 8.6 per cent to 6.7 per cent between 1978 and 1983. One of the major tasks now confronting pedagogues and educational planners is how to improve the quality of education and how to make more effective use of existing resources. Economic restrictions are expressed in the decline, since 1971, in opportunities for acquiring higher qualifications outside the 'normal' channels at adult education institutions. Entrance to higher and technical education was also curtailed in the early 1970s, partly as a result of the increasing proportion of cadres and workers whose qualifications were being under-utilized. Economic pressures for cutbacks sharpened later in the decade (see Table 5.2).

The educational expansion of the 1960s had been based on the optimistic assumption that the scientific–technical revolution would lead not only to a general improvement in educational standards but also to an effective use of higher qualifications. By the 1970s, it had become apparent that a level of qualification had been attained which exceeded requirements in many parts of the economic sector. In 1981, Erich Honecker informed the Central Committee that about 12 per cent of cadres with a university degree and about 22 per cent of all foremen (*Meister*) were employed in jobs which did not match their level of qualification; 18 per cent of all skilled workers were engaged as semi-skilled or unskilled labour. Reasons advanced for this disparity include the lack of clear job specifications and the downgrading of

Table 5.2 The number and proportion of newly enrolled students at universities, colleges of higher education and technical colleges, 1970–80

	No of students 18–22	Newly enrolled students at technical colleges	of which: correspondence courses	Newly enrolled students at universities and colleges of higher education	of which: correspondence courses
1970	1,181,000	56,500	19,400	44,000	9,950
1975	1,316,000	52,300	15,100	34,400	4,300
1980	1,393,000	52,100	14,200	31,900	2,900
Percentage change 1970–80	+18	−8	−27	−27.5	−71

Source: Waterkamp, in Wehling, 1983, p. 127.

certain tasks at higher technological stages, especially in the stage of partial automation. A large-scale sociological investigation in the early 1970s established that, whereas about 70 per cent of production workers in the stage of partial automation were skilled workers, only about 55 per cent of the workforce was required to have a skilled worker's certificate (Dennis, in Gerber, 1986, p. 62–3).

The GDR no longer envisages any further fundamental change in the proportions between the various qualification groups. Semi-skilled jobs, for example, will continue to be reproduced and, as two GDR sociologists, Ingrid and Manfred Lötsch, argue, their performance by semi-skilled workers will be 'functional' but 'dysfunctional' in the case of skilled workers (Lötsch & Lötsch, in *Jahrbuch für Soziologie und Sozialpolitik 1985*, 1985, p. 171). Moreover, as attempts to enrich and enlarge work contents, in order to combat dequalification tendencies, have not been adopted on a comprehensive scale and as a sharp cutback in the proportion of skilled workers is not envisaged, partly for reasons of political legitimation, disproportions will continue between the requirements of the economy and the workers' level of qualification. The reaction pattern of skilled workers to the resulting dequalification tendencies and job monotony has been characterized by GDR authors as job dissatisfaction, high labour turnover and poor job motivation (see Pietsch, in Anweiler & Kuebart, 1984, pp. 217–21).

Another challenge to the educational system is how to reconcile the uniformity principle with increasing structural differentiation. The uniformity principle, as represented by the emphasis on the desirability of a general education and by 'a socially just and politically desirable distribution of educational opportunities' (Glaessner, in von Beyme & Zimmermann, 1984, p. 204) through the polytechnical school system, has had to be reconciled in the past with the promotion of talented individuals in the special classes and the special schools. In the 1980s, however, the encouragement of and the search for creative and gifted individuals, especially in the natural sciences and engineering, has been intensified in order to stimulate innovation and increase efficiency in key sectors of the economy. This is part of the general strategy to master the economic, scientific and technical challenges of the 1980s and 1990s. As the policy of advancing talented individuals is intended to permeate all sectors of the educational system, it has had to be justified on the grounds that it serves the geneal needs of society: by their contribution to economic growth talented individuals are said to be strengthening socialism and improving cultural and living standards. Adroit political management of this process will be required in view of education's legitimation function (equality of opportunities) for the political system as a whole. Some members of the GDR's teaching profession are already complaining that the furtherance of talented pupils is an expression of bourgeois ideology (Schreier, 1986, pp. 244, 253).

Teachers are now being exhorted to devote more attention to problem-solving exercises as part of the school curriculum, to promote a creative atmosphere at school and to encourage pupils to take full advantage of extra-curricular activities such as optional courses and special seminar groups. The higher-educational sector is required to create the conditions necessary for top performance by the most highly gifted students by making provision for independent study, by incorporating gifted students into research teams and by ensuring the earlier completion of study programmes. According to Erich Honecker, top performances are achieved by individuals who 'excel by virtue of their creativeness, urge for knowledge, critical imagination, extraordinary diligence and cooperativeness' (*Report of the Central Committee*, 1986, pp. 68-9). It will, however, be an extremely difficult task, many Western observers would say an impossible one, to release the creative potential of pupils and students on the scale envisaged. Even GDR educational experts concede that the system has tended, in most areas, to set greater store by memorization, diligence and the solution of well-defined problems and has neglected 'creative impatience', flexibility and independent thinking (Neuner, 1986, p. 71). Dieter Voigt, formerly of the German College of Physical Culture in Leipzig and now a professor of sociology in the Federal Republic, and Sabine Meek are highly sceptical. In their view, top performance and creativity are hindered by systemic obstacles: the requirement of allegiance and absolute loyalty to the party leadership; the lack of communication with Western scientists; inadequate material and psychological incentives; and the relatively high proportion of valuable study time wasted on Marxism-Leninism (Voigt & Meek, in Voigt, 1984, pp. 21-7).

Cultural Policy

Cultural policy is subsumed under the overall political strategy of the SED. Culture and the arts, according to an official text, 'play an essential part in developing the personality and instilling a socialist lifestyle, in releasing people's creative talents and contributing to the general well-being' (*Cultural Life in the GDR*, 1982, p. 7). By propagating socialist values, cultural policy seeks to integrate citizens into the socio-political system and by fostering and disseminating the legacy of German history and the achievements of the workers' and farmers' state it contributes to the cultural legitimation of the GDR.

Cultural policy was characterized during the anti-fascist, democratic period by the revival of the humanistic traditions in the arts, the privileged treatment of the bourgeois intelligentsia, the occupation of key positions by communists such as Johannes Becher and by a campaign against fascist influences. Among the distinguished authors and writers who returned from exile were Erich Weinert, Anna Seghers, Willi Bredel, Bodo Uhse and, after careful deliberation, Bertolt Brecht. Under the influence of the Soviet campaign against formalism, the SED, in 1951, tightened up its control over literature and the arts. A primitive socialist realism, which eschewed a critical appraisal of contemporary society and idealized the heroic builders of socialism, was imposed on the cultural intelligentsia.

Writers and artists sought to shake off the bureaucratic shackles both in the aftermath of the June uprising of 1953 and during the brief de-Stalinization thaw after the Twentieth Congress of the CPSU in 1956. The suppression of the Hungarian uprising and Ulbricht's victory over the Schirdewann-Wollweber group enabled the SED leadership to rein in its dissident intellectuals and reimpose its authority in 1957. Two years later the SED launched the overambitious 'Bitterfeld Path'; writers were to cooperate with factory workers, farmers and construction workers in overcoming the separation between the arts and life.

The construction of the Berlin Wall and the gradual consolidation of the GDR created more favourable conditions for writers such as Stefan Heym, Stefan Hermlin and Christa Wolf to protest against the provincialism of GDR culture and to plead for the representation of conflicts in literature. Wolf's *Divided Heaven* (1963) and Erwin Strittmatter's *Ole Biedenkopp* (1964) both exemplify a critical appraisal of sensitive issues. The Eleventh Plenum of the Central Committee in December 1965 terminated this debate. Writers were castigated for undermining public morale by popularizing difficulties and for abetting imperialism's encouragement of immorality in the GDR. Immorality was associated with poor labour discipline, sexual promiscuity and a love of beat music.

Ironically, a liberalization in cultural policy was initiated in 1971 by the writers' severest critic at the Eleventh Plenum. In December 1971, Erich Honecker declared that 'If one proceeds from the social premises of socialism, there can be no taboos in the realm of art and literature. This applies both to content and style—in short, to the concept of artistic mastery'. The SED's Central Committee secretary for science and culture, Kurt Hager, provided further encouragement in July 1972 when he broadened socialist realism to encompass 'scope for a wealth of forms, variations of presentation of style, and individual refinements' (in *Cultural Life in the GDR*, 1982, p. 73). The 'thaw' released works such as Stefan Heym's critique of Stalinism (*The King David Report*), Plenzdorf's realistic depiction of youthful subculture (*The New Sorrows of the Young W*) and Brigitte Reimann's observations on the clash between an idealistic young woman architect and an inflexible bureaucracy (*Franziska Linkerhand*).

The limits on the autonomy of the writers and artists were exposed by the Biermann affair of 1976. In order to nip opposition in the bud, the party reacted fiercely against its critical intellectuals who had opposed Biermann's expatriation. Controls were tightened up in 1979 when a reform of the penal law made it more difficult for authors to publish in the West. At the Eleventh Party Congress in 1986 Honecker seemed to confirm this harder line when he called for a clear stance by the cultural intelligentsia: 'Given the responsibilities of the arts community in a socialist society, the only valid position is that of a fellow-fighter, or a fervent protagonist who, with her/his own particular tools, spreads the ideas of peace and socialism among the masses' (*Report of the Central Committee*, 1986, p. 85).

Despite the reinstatement of taboos, the situation is by no means bleak. Although limits have been set by party and cultural functionaries suspicious of individual interpretations of the meaning of socialism, some GDR writers and artists have continued to question established opinions and works of lasting literary and artistic quality have been produced. These characteristics have been combined in the works of better-known writers such as Christa Wolf (*Cassandra*), Volker Braun (*Hinze-Kunze-Roman*), Irmgard Morgner (*Amanda*) and Christoph Hein (*Ah Q*). Moreover the concrete aspects of the burdens of women's emancipation have been brought to the forefront since the mid-1970s. As Margy Gerber has shown, alcoholism, suicide, physical and mental illness, a lack of self-confidence and loneliness are frequent themes in the novels of Brigitte Martin, Christa Müller, Monika Helmecke, Dorothea Kleine and others (Gerber, 1986/87, pp. 55–83).

The concern with everyday issues is a major characteristic of the works of the post-1945 generation. Some of these authors have utilized documentaries or semi-documentaries to explore social relationships. Gabriele Eckart, for example, compiled a series of remarkably frank interviews with people living in a fruit-growing area in the vicinity of Potsdam. She revealed a diversity of opinions with regard to management, the lack of opportunities for travel, and environmental pollution. The book, *So sehe ick die Sache*, was banned in the GDR. Other young writers have also experienced difficulties in obtaining permission for the publication of their works in the GDR. This has been the fate of the poet Sascha Anderson, now resident in West Berlin, and the more politically provocative Lutz Rathenow. Rathenow was imprisoned for a few days in 1980 for the publication of one of his works in the Federal Republic.

The sensitive nature of the issues explored by many GDR writers explains why there is often a large public demand for many of their works and why social scientists such as Jürgen Kuczynski regard literature as a most important source for the exploration of critical issues in GDR society. On the other hand, the extent of the public's interest in literature must not be exaggerated. One representative GDR survey of free-time pursuits ranked the reading of books, whether *belles-lettres* or specialist texts, in sixth place behind reading newspapers, watching TV, listening to music, gardening and keeping pets. A sociological survey of 989 workers at the 'Walter Ulbricht Works' in Halle found that 47 per cent read *belles-lettres* but their favourite author proved to be Alexander Dumas. Although well-established GDR authors such as Erik Neutsch, Anna Seghers and Erwin Strittmatter were popular, the appearance of names like Jules Verne, Jack London, D. H. Lawrence and the Polish science-fiction writer Lem indicates a desire for entertainment and fantasy and for escape from the everyday problems of GDR society (Albrecht, 1986, pp. 134–5, 138–9). The American political scientist Anita Mallinckrodt has drawn attention to the widespread popularity of 'dime novels' with their tales of adventure, crime and war; these cheap pamphlets and booklets enjoy a wider readership than the luminaries of GDR literature. For example, 200,000 copies of the criminal series *Blaulicht* are usually sold within two or three days of appearing on the bookstalls.

The SED, too, has no desire to confine culture to a small minority of intellectuals. However, its encouragement of a widespread enjoyment of all cultural forms also serves a political function. It is believed that the arts can influence people's feelings and actions and 'assist in bringing home to them the ideals and values of socialism' (*Cultural Life in the GDR*, 1982, p. 7). Political education and ideological socialization alone could not achieve these goals. Cultural opportunities have expanded since 1970 but not always in linear progression: book production declined in 1981 and theatre attendance has fallen sharply since the late 1950s (see Table 5.3). The regime's greater sensitivity in the Honecker era to the cultural needs of the populace,

Table 5.3 Cultural opportunities in the GDR, 1970–84

	1970	1984
Newly published books	5,324	6,395
Number of books borrowed from libraries per 100 readers	1,627	2,109
Number of places at houses of culture and clubs	344,102	505,309
Theatre performances	25,918	27,070
Theatre attendance ('000)	12,258.6	9,847.2
Cinema attendance ('000)	91,355.4	73,419.4
Visits to museums ('000)	19,830.8	33,685.4

Source: *StJB*, 1986, pp. 310–19.

especially those of young people, has led to the acceptance of rock and beat music, the expansion of discos and youth clubs and the development of a diversity of jazz forms. Ulbricht, in contrast, once condemned jazz as 'monkey culture'.

Thus under Honecker cultural policy, by responding in a more flexible manner to people's needs, has grown in significance as an integral component of the regime's policy to integrate diverse social groups into the political system. Cultural facilities have been expanded in many areas, officialdom has shown a more relaxed attitude towards light entertainment, and both painters and writers have usually enjoyed a greater latitude for the expression of critical opinion than under Ulbricht. The concept of the GDR's cultural heritage, as noted in Chapter 1, has been widened to embrace traditions from the whole of German history. However, a separate GDR national identity has not been established and the regime continues to live uneasily with its critical authors and the 'alternative' cultural scene in what Henry Krisch has called 'a floating world of communal apartments and friendship networks, of makeshift jobs and ephemeral cultural events' (1985, p. 52).

Religion

The division of Germany left the Soviet Union in occupation of a predominantly Protestant area: 81.9 per cent of the zone's population was Protestant and 11.9 per cent Catholic in 1946. The churches could anticipate a bitter struggle with the socialist state whose ideological forebears had insisted upon the abolition of religion as a necessary precondition of people's real happiness and freedom from oppression. Yet, as John Sandford observes, 'the death of religion—like the "withering away of the state"—is postponed for the communist future and is not expected of the socialist present' (1986/87, p. 29). The churches' survival lay in a combination of factors: the reluctance of the political authorities to provoke unnecessary conflict whilst creating a new social order in the anti-fascist, democratic period; the numerical strength of the evangelical community; the churches' vital contribution to the relief of destitution in the war-ravaged zone; and the humanistic values of justice, peace and solidarity which underpin both Marxism and Christianity (Dähn, 1982, p. 21; Smith, in Childs, 1985, pp. 66, 69).

Although the Soviet authorities and the SED were not intent on the destruction of the churches, a fierce struggle broke out, especially in the 1950s, between church and state. The members of the Evangelical Church's organization for young people (*Junge Gemeinde*) suffered discrimination at school and university and religious instruction was banned in schools. The conflict eventually centred around the introduction in 1955 of the atheist youth consecration ceremony (*Jugendweihe*) for 14-year-olds. The Evangelical Church objected to the pseudo-religious character of the ceremony and declared it irreconcilable with confirmation. However, faced by the participation of over 87 per cent of pupils in the eighth grade in the *Jugendweihe*, the church authorities withdrew their ban in 1960. Not only was communion being denied to these young people, but the church was depriving itself of potential followers.

The church-state struggle abated in the 1960s. Ulbricht's statement to the People's Chamber in 1960 that 'Christianity and the humanist goals of socialism are not irreconcilable' heralded a change in the regime's strategy: the churches were to be gradually coopted or incorporated into the socialist order. The regime took issue, however, with the Evangelical Church's links with its Western brethren. Not until 1969 did the church finally establish its own separate League of Evangelical Churches in the GDR, thus withdrawing from the all-German umbrella organization, the Evangelical Church of Germany. Two years later, the state acknowledged the League as the official representative of the eight provincial churches of the GDR. Paul Verner, the influential Politburo member and Central Committee secretary for security and church questions, confirmed the drawing-together of state and church when he explicitly denied that the SED aspired to the socialization of the Christian doctrine. Cooperation, though somewhat uneasy, rather than incorporation became the keynote of SED policy under its new leader.

Honecker's meeting in March 1978 with the executive of the League of Evangelical Churches and its chairman Bishop Schönherr bore witness to the more harmonious relationship. Schönherr himself had made a significant personal contribution to laying the groundwork for the compromise. His famous statement in 1971 was a clear indication of the church's new attitude: 'We do not want to be a church against or alongside but we wish to be a church within socialism'. Honecker reaffirmed the permission, first granted in 1976, for the construction of church buildings in new towns and new suburbs; he granted the League a modest amount of TV time and additional access to the state radio; and he accepted the import of church literature from the West. These and other concessions were not enshrined in a formal agreement, but they did represent the state's acknowledgement of the church's position within socialism. Honecker designated the church as 'an autonomous organization of social relevance' (Henkys, in Henkys, 1982, pp. 19–22).

The SED leadership's willingness to conclude this informal pact with the Evangelical Church may have been accelerated by its wish to defuse the crisis triggered off by Pastor Brüsewitz's self-immolation in 1976 in what has been interpreted as a protest against the state's treatment of the church. The 1978 accord should, however, be primarily understood as the outcome of the greater willingness on both sides, since the early 1970s, to establish a working relationship. From the standpoint of the SED leaders, church policy was yet one more aspect of their general policy to integrate diverse social and political groups into the socialist system. Furthermore, the church, due to its links with the West, was probably regarded as a useful ally in the SED's efforts to influence Western political leaders and peace movements.

A second high-level meeting was held in February 1985 between the heads of state and church. Honecker expressed his 'warm thanks' to the Evangelical Church for its past work and commended its social services, its witness for peace and its attitude to the celebrations of the fortieth anniversary of the liberation from fascism. The new chairman of the League of Evangelical Churches, Bishop Hempel, also acknowledged that relations had developed constructively since 1978 but he added the rider that 'Trust between us (church and state) will grow only to the extent that such trust is felt by ordinary believers' (*Neues Deutschland*, 12 February 1985, p. 1). The *modus vivendi* has therefore survived into the 1980s, albeit subject to certain restraints. These limits were clearly drawn by the secretary of state for church affairs, Klaus Gysi, in 1981: cooperation, he averred, is desirable where state and church agree but the church should respect the state's decisions in the event of disagreement (Henkys, in Henkys, 1982, p. 25).

The major issues now in dispute between state and church concern the discrimination against young Christians in education and employment and, from time to time, the Evangelical Church's involvement in autonomous peace activities. Nevertheless, the church is firmly embedded in society: it enjoys the right to levy church taxes; it has the right of free assembly; and its many homes and hospitals care for the aged, the physically and mentally handicapped, and social outcasts. The church's 'open' youth work enables it to reach beyond the official membership: many young people take part in excursions, Bible study groups, social activities and weekend retreats.

Despite its higher social profile, the internal situation of the church gives cause for concern. First, the church leadership finds itself performing a difficult balancing act between the state and the peace activists, many of whom are not members of the church. Tension also surfaces over the severe constraints on the church's freedom to articulate in public the political, philosophical and ethical ideas discussed within its walls. Secondly, young people, whether involved in the activities of the *Junge Gemeinde* or the church's 'open' youth work, are frustrated by bureaucratic tendencies within the church and by what they perceive as a senescent leadership. And finally, the church's membership has been eroded by the secularization and urbanization of GDR society. The most recent reliable data, from 1977, show a church membership of 7,895,000 or 47.13 per cent of the country's total population (as against 55.6 per cent in 1971). Membership has most probably continued to decline in the 1980s: the state secretary for church affairs estimated church membership at between 4 and 5 million in 1986 and a leading Evangelical official, Manfred Stolpe, has predicted that by the end of the century only 10 per cent of the population will belong to a church (Büscher, in Henkys, 1982, p. 426; Mechtenberg, 1986, p. 166).

The Roman Catholic Church has traditionally played a less active role in GDR society than its evangelical counterpart, partly because it lacks the latter's numerical strength (1.2 million members in 1977). It has, however, always been intimately concerned with pastoral and charitable work and, more recently, it has adopted a more outspoken line on political matters. In January 1983, the Berlin Bishops' Conference, the executive committee of the Catholic Church in the GDR, released a pastoral letter on peace. The arms race between East and West was condemned as 'an intolerable vexation' and a war with modern weapons of destruction as 'immoral'. The bishops reiterated their 'serious misgivings' about military instruction in schools and confirmed their support for unarmed service for conscripts. In the past, the Catholic Church and state have frequently clashed over the *Jugendweihe* and the administrative links between the GDR and West German dioceses. The bishop of Berlin, as a result of his jurisdictional rights in West Berlin, is a member of the German Bishops' Conference under the chairmanship of the Archbishop of Cologne. The Berlin bishopric is divided into three parts—East Berlin, Berlin and the GDR—and about 270,000 of its 435,000 members live in West Berlin.

The GDR's Jewish community is represented by a tiny group of about 350 registered members, over half of whom reside in East Berlin, and several thousand people of Jewish origin. The regime appears to be making a conscious effort to accommodate Jewish interests: the rebuilding of the New Synagogue in the Oranienburger Straße in East Berlin is under planning consideration; a projected road through the large Jewish cemetery in the Weißensee district of the capital has been cancelled; and the magnitude of the murder of the Jews during the Third Reich is receiving a more explicit recognition rather than, as hitherto, being partially obscured by a concentration on the fate of national groups (Henkys, 1986b, pp. 237–8). Anti-semitism is virtually unknown in the GDR but anti-semitic tendencies occasionally surface. In December 1985, the SED newspaper *Berliner Zeitung* printed a cartoon showing a Jew with a hooked nose as an Israeli aggressor against the Lebanon. And on the fortieth anniversary of Crystal Night the Evangelical Church alluded to 'a hidden hostility' towards the Jews (Urban, 1986, pp. 54–5).

Environmental policy

Environmental concern is reflected in the Constitution, innumerable legal provisions, the creation of state organs for the protection of the environment and popular ecological initiatives. Article 15 of the 1968 Constitution made state and society responsible for 'the protection of nature in the interests of the well-being of the citizens'. On the basis of this constitutional article the 1970 Environmental Protection Act provided for pollution control, the rational use of resources and the conservation and improvement of residential and recreational areas. The Ministry of Environmental Protection and Water Management, created in 1971, is responsible for the coordination and elaboration of environmental protection measures and about fifty academic establishments are engaged in environmental research. Among the state organs with responsibilities for environmental protection are the State Office of Nuclear Safety and Radiation Protection and the Ministries of Health and Transport. Finally, in 1980, the Society for Nature and the Environment was founded within the League of Culture. Its 50,000 members and 1,500 circles and interest groups are actively involved in the supervision of nature reserves and in the maintenance of parks and recreational and residential areas. The interest groups take part in seminars on various aspects of nature conservation and some contact has been established with autonomous eco-groups. The Society represents an interesting attempt by the state to mobilize popular initiatives in a politically sensitive area; however, it is restricted to propagating the official view that ecological problems can only be resolved under socialism (Wensierski, in Redaktion Deutschland Archiv, 1985, pp. 151–65).

The official line serves a legitimizing function: capitalism is depicted as the fundamental cause of environmental deterioration, whereas socialism is represented not only as a social necessity but also as a necessity of nature. The antagonism between society and nature cannot be abolished in capitalism as the primary economic interest of capitalist corporations and firms remains the realization of maximum profits. In contrast, economic growth in socialism benefits the owners of production, not private capital; therefore, socialism is better equipped to plan the rational utilization of resources and the gradual reduction in environmental damage. The GDR firmly rejects the view that economic growth is incompatible with environmental protection. The official view was put succinctly by the influential political economist, Harry Nick: 'Communism without growth would not be a different communism, but none at all' (quoted in DeBardeleben, 1985, p. 180; see also Kosing, 1984, pp. 1020–3).

Despite this optimistic assessment of socialism's intrinsic advantages over capitalism, it is openly acknowledged that socialism faces a long and complex task in overcoming environmental damage. The GDR's capitalist heritage is usually blamed for many of the country's environmental problems. The forces of production of capitalism are, it is claimed, necessarily inherited by the successor formation, socialism. This initial and fundamental problem is then exacerbated by deficiencies and problems connected with the development of socialist society itself: the unsatisfactory state of existing scientific knowledge about the environment; the failure to make environmental protection an integral component of long-term economic planning; and the diversion of resources to meet the military and economic challenge of capitalism. Enterprises, it is confessed, frequently fail to implement effective environmental policies: material incentives are often inadequate; fines for the infringement of regulations are insufficiently punitive; and some enterprise managers and cadres lack a responsible and proper attitude towards environmental issues (Timm, in Redaktion Deutschland Archiv, 1985, pp. 125–8; Paucke & Bauer, 1979, pp. 61–70; Motek, in Lohs & Döring, 1975, pp. 7–12).

Like other industrialized nations, the GDR suffers from innumerable environmental problems but these are aggravated by its geographical location and its tight resource situation. It has a relatively lower water endowment than other countries: 880 cubic metres per capita compared to 1,710 in Europe as a whole and a world average of 11,200. An unusually high proportion of water resources (about 66 per cent) is used by industry; in the early 1980s the requirements of industry, agriculture and private households amounted to 10 billion cubic metres out of a total annual capacity of 15 billion cubic metres. The heavy dependence on domestic lignite has serious environmental consequences as lignite contains a high level of powerful sulphur pollutants. The increase in the emissions of sulphur dioxide from lignite are traced in Table 5.4. The GDR's annual emission density (40 tonnes of sulphur dioxide per square kilometre) puts it well ahead of all other European countries (von Berg, 1984, p 37).

Table 5.4 Sulphur dioxide emissions from lignite in the GDR, 1970–90 ('000 tonnes)

	1970	1975	1980	1985*	1990*
Lignite of which:	3,874	3,354	3,528	4,000	4,300
Lusatia	800	858	888	1,120	1,200
Halle/Leipzig	3,074	2,496	2,640	2,880	3,100

* Estimate.
Source: Schwartau, in Redaktion Deutschland Archiv, 1985, p. 19.

Environmental deterioration is most acute in the industrial conurbations of the south where the chemical and lignite mining industries are concentrated. About 70 per cent of the GDR's total emissions of sulphur dioxide occur in the Halle/Leipzig and Lusatian regions alone (Schwartau, in Redaktion Deutschland Archiv, 1985, p. 33). GDR calculations suggest that a 50 per cent reduction in sulphur dioxide emissions, ashes and dust in the most severely affected regions, essentially those in the south, would lower the general mortality rate by about 4.5 per cent and heart and circulatory diseases by 10 to 15 per cent. Average life expectancy would increase by four years. Rivers and forests are under threat, too. The United Nations Commission for Europe claims that damage to forests is more advanced in the GDR than anywhere else in the world. About 12 per cent of forests are damaged in the vicinity of the Czech border and near the industrial centres of Leipzig, Halle, Bitterfeld, Cottbus and Karl-Marx Stadt. The dumping of chemicals such as potassium salt into the rivers, inadequate purification plants and increases in water temperature as a result of industrial usage have produced high levels of pollution in sections of the rivers Werra, Elbe and Saale.

The intensive use of chemicals in agriculture is linked to a deterioration in the quality of the soil. Furthermore, about 10,000 hectares of useful agricultural land are lost each year; this includes considerable good-quality land in the lignite mining areas. Restoration schemes, though well publicized, have not reversed this process: only 13,000 acres, destroyed as a result of opencast lignite mining, have been reclaimed, according to a 1985 West German source (Kurjo, in Redaktion Deutschland Archiv, 1985, p. 56). Given the GDR's limited natural resources and the continuing primacy of economic growth, the environmental protection measures—recycling raw materials, reafforestation, cooperation with capitalist and socialist countries and improvements in the water supply—are unlikely to bring about any fundamental improvement in the overall situation. A low-waste and closed cycle technology represents an ideal, but long-term solution.

The degradation of the environment has given rise, especially since the late 1970s, to a critical debate within religious circles and the small ecological groups which are invariably attached to the Evangelical Church. The three most prominent ecological centres are the Church Research Centre run by Peter Gensichen in Wittenberg, the Theological Study Department of the League of Evangelical Churches in East Berlin and the Church and Society Committee under the chairmanship of Dr Heino Falcke. Criticism is directed at the SED leadership's pursuit of economic growth without due care for environmental protection, its emphasis on the performance principle, its misplaced faith in the benefits of science and technology, and the lack of popular participation in decision-making processes. The Wittenberg Research Centre advocates a broader definition of social wealth to encompass spiritual-cultural as well as material wealth. Such a concept would, it is hoped, encourage a new attitude towards consumption and lower economic growth would no longer be viewed in a negative light. The way would thus be opened, in the opinion of Heino Falcke, to an equitable relationship between the highly developed industrial countries, including the GDR, and the developing countries of the Third World. A church study group in Greifswald also argues that the prioritization of material over spiritual–cultural needs should be redressed: free time would not then be reduced to a means for the reproduction of labour power and the emancipation of women would not be judged primarily in accordance with economic criteria (see the documents in Wensierski & Büscher, 1981, pp. 72, 131, 209).

The performance principle, a basic tenet of SED policy, is frequently a target of the church intellectuals. The designation of political office, sexual prowess, self-discipline and achievement at work as the main criteria for assessing 'performance' and the high status attached to material possessions such as furniture, fashionable clothes and a motor car deprive people of a sense of security and belonging. They always feel under pressure of time; pleasurable activities like singing are dismissed as 'unproductive'; and aspects of human existence, including the beauty of nature and a partner's mood, are not appreciated as they cannot be 'measured'. Moreover, at work, mechanization, specialization and the division of labour have reduced human beings to 'things' expressed only through their labour (Wensierski & Büscher, 1981, pp. 60–1, 142, 156).

Heino Falcke warns of another danger: society is becoming more complex and more dependent upon experts and technocrats. In order to combat 'technocracy' or 'expertocracy', a problem common to both socialist and capitalist societies, he urges a comprehensive programme of mass education which will enable every individual to participate effectively in democratic decision-making. Citizens should not be written off as lacking the necessary maturity for participation in this process and they should all have the right to be involved in those decisions which affect science and technology (Wensierski & Büscher, 1981, pp. 213–14). Although Protestant intellectuals such as Falcke have articulated a fundamental critique of official environmental policy, these and other church activists share certain attitudes and values with Marxists. The Wittenberg Research Centre, for example, contends that the social ownership of the means of production offers a more promising basis for a fundamental change in production than does capitalism. Elsewhere the possibility of mastering nature is not precluded and a dialogue is sought between Marxists and Christians (Wensierski & Büscher, 1981, pp. 72, 202).

The main activities of the small autonomous ecological groups include bicycle demonstrations against the noise and air pollution caused by cars, the planting of trees ('not only dogs need trees'), exhibitions and the distribution of postcards and literature with ecological themes. Concern has been voiced about the safety of the GDR's nuclear power stations. In the aftermath of the Chernobyl disaster a petition organized by Martin Böttger and Ralf Hirsch for the People's Chamber to hold a referendum on the use of nuclear power was signed by well over 10,000 citizens (see Ball, 1986, p. 35). Although ecological activities normally attract only a small minority, autonomous ecological groups have been identified in a dozen or so GDR towns. Discussions take place, albeit in small circles about alternative lifestyles and abstaining from the consumption of meat, coffee and alcohol. While opportunities for an alternative lifestyle are limited and the state authorities occasionally suppress some of the more public expressions of ecological concern such as bicycle demonstrations, the ecological movement has established itself, during the 1980s, as part of the 'alternative' political culture. However, it is not entirely divorced from the official culture: considerable overlap exists between 'official' debates in party and state circles and those in the ecological groups on the basic questions of social and economic progress. The church has been allowed more space for operation, the Society for Nature and the Environment facilitates citizen participation and 'messages' on ecological issues are transmitted in cultural journals and the writings of Christa Wolf and Hans Cibulka (see the latter's book, *Swantow*).

Defence Policy

At the SED Congress in 1986, Erich Honecker, who in addition to his high party office holds the post of chairman of the National Defence Council, sang the praises of the socialist soldier for safeguarding peace and preventing recourse to 'the language of weapons'. The GDR's military and defensive forces, he reminded his audience, were 'steadfastly fulfilling their class mission to protect the socialist order and the peaceful life of the community against any enemy'. He also highlighted their contribution to safeguarding 'peace and the military security of the socialist countries' in conjunction with 'their brothers-in-arms of the glorious Soviet army and the other armed forces of the Warsaw Treaty member countries' (*Report of the Central Committee*, 1986, p. 96). His emphasis on the essentially defensive mission of the GDR's armed forces should not, however, obscure the NVA's (National People's Army) increasing activity in the cause of the 'victory of socialism round the globe' and the militarization of life in the GDR. Moreover, the NVA performs an important domestic role as one of the regime's major instruments of social control and indoctrination.

Although the GDR did not possess its own army until 1956, SMAD authorized, in 1946, the formation of garrisoned alert squads or, as they soon came to be known, Garrisoned People's Police (KVP), which served as the basis for the later NVA. The decision to create the NVA was determined by the entry of the FRG into NATO and the GDR into the Warsaw Pact in 1956. Military service did not become compulsory until 1962, after the building of the Berlin Wall made it politically less risky for the regime to introduce such a controversial measure. An additional consideration was Warsaw Pact pressure on the GDR to increase its armed forces.

The numerical strength of the NVA in 1986 stood at 179,000 (as against 85,000 in 1962), of which 123,000 troops were in the army, 16,000 in the navy and 40,000 in the air force. NVA conscripts serve for a period of eighteen months but every effort is made to encourage them to extend their military service. Reservists are obliged to perform active duties until the age of 50, or 60 in the event of a declaration of a state of emergency. The defence forces are by no means limited to the NVA. They included in 1986: 49,000 border troops, 13,000 people's police alert units, 6,000–7,000 members of the Friedrich Dzierzynski guard regiment, 8,500 transport police, 500,000 men in the working-class combat groups (*Kampfgruppen der Arbeiterklasse*) and, in 1983, 5,000 civil defence volunteers (International Institute for Strategic Studies, 1986, pp. 51–2).

The border troops played a vital role in the sealing-off measures in 1952 and 1961. Although not part of the NVA, their commander is a deputy of the Minister of Defence. Their basic function, the security of the borders, is lauded as an arduous but vital contribution to preserving peace and a reminder to imperialism of the limits of its power in the heart of Europe (Hillebrenner, 1986, p. 83). The SED's working-class combat groups, originally called factory combat groups, were formed after the 1953 uprising as a countermeasure against so-called 'fascist provocations'. They subsequently assumed the character of a territorial army. Training is usually conducted after work and at weekends.

The defence sector incorporates numerous other institutions—GST, FDGB, FDJ, Red Cross—which are involved in pre-military training, military propaganda and civil defence work. The GST, for example, prepares 16–18-year-olds for military service by providing them with opportunities for rowing, driving,sailing, parachuting and other para-military sports. The Society, which had a membership of 600,000 in 1982, is acclaimed for its part in the development of socialist personalities who 'recognize the defence of socialism as the most important consequence of socialist patriotism and proletarian internationalism' (Hillebrenner, 1986, p. 43).

The strongest strike force on GDR territory is not the NVA but the Group of Soviet Forces in Germany with its HQ at Wünsdorf-Zossen, south of Berlin. With a numerical strength of about 380,000, it constitutes the largest build-up of Soviet military power outside the USSR. In 1986, twenty out of the Soviet Union's thirty-one military divisions in Central and Eastern Europe were stationed in the GDR. The vital role of the GDR in Soviet military strategy is revealed by the exceptionally close ties between the two defence systems: the NVA is the only East European military establishment under the direct command of the Warsaw Pact Supreme Command in peacetime; the commander-in-chief of the Soviet forces in Germany can in theory declare a state of emergency in the GDR; the navy is under the operational command of the fleets of the Warsaw Pact; and Soviet officers are believed to be more frequently involved in the work of GDR military bodies than anywhere else in Eastern Europe. Despite the GDR's heavy dependence on the Soviet military establishment, it has been argued by one Western authority, Dale Herspring, that the regime has enhanced its bargaining position thanks to the quality and efficiency of the GDR's armed forces, the willingness of the GDR to support the USSR in Africa and its relatively heavy commitment of resources to defence (Herspring, in Childs, 1985, pp. 135, 145).

Expenditure on defence, in so far as the published data can be regarded as a reliable guide, rose throughout the 1980s both in absolute and relative terms. The London-based International Institute for Strategic Studies has calculated that GDR defence expenditure grew from $385 per capita in 1981 to $457 in 1984; the latter figure was higher than in any other NATO and Warsaw Pact country with the exception of the two superpowers (1986, p. 212). The social costs of a high level of military spending have been criticized by the GDR's leading economic historian Jürgen Kuczynski. An end to expenditure on armaments in the late 1970s would, he estimated, have enabled the government to provide free gas and electricity and to introduce a 35-hour working week (see Neugebauer, in von Beyme & Zimmermann, 1984, p. 189).

The onset of *détente* and the agreements between the two Germanies in the early 1970s increased rather than diminished military propaganda, a consequence of the SED's demarcation (*Abgrenzung*) policy. The head of the Central Committee's security department warned:

In the implementation of our policy of peaceful co-existence, the class fronts and the class enemy are not always immediately recognizable for young Party members and especially for young army members. It is sometimes difficult for these young people to recognize the connection between the struggle for peaceful co-existence, strengthening of the military power of socialism and the struggle against the imperialist system and to draw conclusions for their own work. [quoted in Johnson, Dean & Alexiev, 1982, p. 97]

The militarization of life in the GDR manifests itself in propaganda against the class enemy, pre-military education in schools, the partial mobilization of women, the frequent use of military symbols and traditions and the high level of participation in military and paramilitary organizations. Ideological education aims 'to give all servicemen a clear picture of the aggressive nature of imperialism and a vivid impression of the enemy, and enhance their capacity for offensive ideological training' (from a 1977 article in *Militärwesen*, quoted in Forster, 1980, p. 230). Hatred of the enemy is also encouraged in the schools. A 1974 textbook on socialist military education for schoolchildren advised: 'Training pupils to love the working class and its Party ... must be accompanied by training in hatred toward every form of exploitation and aggression' (quoted in Forster, 1980, p. 48). And in 1981, a *Militärverlag* publication insisted on the justice of a war in defence of the socialist fatherland against an imperialist war of aggression (Scheler & Kießling, 1981, pp. 10, 136).

Despite the many indications of the greater militarization of life and the growing importance of the military as an agent of socialization, the GDR should not be classed as a militarized society (see Neugebauer, in Gerber, 1985). First, the GDR has the largest autonomous peace movement in Eastern Europe; not only do peace activists attempt to counter the influence of military propaganda but the movement has also managed to secure its own niche in society. Secondly, it remains possible for young men to serve in a construction unit, and among conscripts the tedium of life in the barracks partly accounts for the failure of political indoctrination to produce the desired enthusiasm and commitment. Thirdly, the regime itself unceasingly propagates its devotion to the cause of peace and security. Honecker has identified 'Averting the threat of a nuclear inferno and making peace secure and durable ... as the overriding priority of the present time' (Honecker, 1984, p. 6). In a nuclear war, argues Herbert Krolikowski, the secretary of state in the Foreign Ministry, 'there would be neither victors nor vanquished' (Krolikowski, 1986, p. 791).

Several important conclusions have recently been drawn from this concern about a nuclear inferno. Indeed, the concept of a just war has been abandoned by some GDR philosophers and military theoreticians. Ernst Woit of the University of Dresden regards peaceful coexistence between socialism and imperialism as the only possible alternative to a common destruction. Peaceful coexistence is characterized, in his view, by economic, cultural and political relations to the mutual advantage of both sides and by cooperation in the solution of other social problems (Woit, 1986, pp. 1081-2). Whether this new perspective will ultimately become the standard doctrine remains to be seen, but it is indicative of a new criticality which is producing a reassessment of other orthodoxies such as the class struggle and the need for the Warsaw Pact to enjoy a military superiority over NATO rather than establish a balance of power (Rehm, 1985, pp. 1198-1208; Kuppe, 1986, pp. 691-2).

A final objection to the thesis of the GDR as a militarized society is the SED's tight control over the military. The party is firmly entrenched within the NVA: virtually all the officers and over one-third of the warrant officers and NCOs are party members and thus subject to party discipline. Major military questions are controlled by the top SED organs and functionaries and a network of political organs and party organizations within the NVA reinforces the party's authority and ensures the implementation of policy.

The Main Political Administration (*Politische Hauptverwaltung*), which probably has the status of a Central Committee department, directs political work within the armed forces; the SED basic organizations, the FDJ organizations and the political organs in the NVA are all subordinate to it. Political work includes the political and ideological training of troops, the coordination of military and political tasks and the implementation and supervision of party directives and policies. A political organ is located within the NVA down to regimental level; below this, political work is discharged by a political representative, not a political apparatus. The key member of the staff of a political organ is the political deputy who is his commander's second-in-command as well as the first secretary of the basic SED party organization. The political deputy and his staff monitor the work and decisions of the military commander. Potential conflict is defused, to a considerable extent, by the fact that as a military professional himself a political deputy, like his commander, has an inherent interest in the efficiency of the military unit which is their formal co-responsibility.

The major military and security matters are dealt with, at civilian level, by the SED Politburo and the security apparat of the Central Committee. Egon Krenz, the Central Committee secretary for security affairs, heads this section of the national apparat and oversees the Central Committee department of security questions. The decisions of the SED's central organs are implemented by the National Defence Council whose chairman, Honecker, is also SED general secretary. The Ministry of National Defence, created in 1956, is enjoined to implement SED and state decisions relating to military affairs. Willy Stoph, the first Minister of Defence, relinquished this post in 1960 to Heinz Hoffmann. A loyal supporter of Honecker, Hoffmann was regarded in the West as a hardliner. He advocated the military superiority of socialism and did not rule out a just nuclear war (Fricke, 1986a, p. 11). After Hoffmann's death, in December 1985, he was succeeded by the head of the Main Political Administration, Heinz Keßler. As members of the Politburo, Hoffmann (1973–85) and Keßler (since 1985) have been in a favourable position to represent military interests in the SED's highest political body. Several top military functionaries also sit on the Central Committee. However, among this group, the military professionals are less prominent than those officers with responsibility for coordinating military and political questions. In short, as Henry Krisch has observed: 'As an instrument of statecraft . . . the armed forces of the GDR remain strong and firmly in the party's hands' (1985, p. 49).

Foreign Policy

The GDR's foreign policy is determined by the interplay of several key variables: its limited power capacity; its exceptionally vulnerable position on the frontline between the socialist and capitalist systems; the vital and close connection with the Soviet Union; the ambivalent relationship with the Federal Republic; and the tenets of Marxist–Leninist ideology.

The limited demographic, economic and military potential of the GDR restricts it to the role of a medium-sized political actor with, especially until the 1970s, essentially regional interests. A comparison with the resource potential of the USSR highlights the vast disparity between the nuclear superpower and its junior ally. Whereas the Soviet Union's population in 1985 was 271,203,000, that of the GDR was a mere 16,698,555. The total strength of the two countries' armed forces in July 1985 stood at 5,300,000 and 174,000 respectively. Although they are each other's major trading partner, the GDR's trade with the Soviet Union in 1984 accounted for 38.4 per cent of its total foreign trade turnover as against the GDR's 10.6 per cent stake in Soviet foreign trade (Meier, 1986, p. 10). However, the GDR's general economic performance, its relatively advanced technological development and its vital strategic and geopolitical position guarantee it a voice in the shaping of policy in the major organizations of the socialist bloc, COMECON and the Warsaw Pact.

A second fundamental determinant of foreign policy is Marxism–Leninism. One should distinguish here between two levels: the doctrine or official ideology and the action programme or operating ideology. The doctrine embraces the philosophical assumptions and the historical laws of Marxism–Leninism as well as ultimate ends. The action programme, which is more flexible and pragmatic in its orientation than the doctrine with which it is intertwined, encompasses the pursuit of the key goals derived from doctrinal principles.

The major doctrinal aim of foreign policy is the creation of conditions favourable for the ultimate establishment of socialism and communism on a worldwide scale in association with the Soviet Union and the other socialist states. Related to this major aim are the two core foreign policy principles: proletarian internationalism and peaceful coexistence between states with different social orders (*Kleines politisches Wörterbuch*, 1978, pp. 96–7). These core principles shape perceptions of friends and adversaries and serve to legitimize the actions of the regime. The legitimacy of historical continuity is also provided by the attempt to sustain the appearance of doctrinal rigour through frequent quotations from the scriptures of Marxism–Leninism. However, as we shall see, the content of the core principles has undergone modification and ideology has never precluded tactical shifts in policy in response to changes and new opportunities in the domestic and international environment.

The GDR's relations with the Soviet Union and the other socialist countries are conducted on the basis of socialist internationalism, a higher form of proletarian internationalism which 'represents the fundamental principle of the ideology and the policy of the working class and its Marxist–Leninist party in the field of international relations'. Socialist internationalism, according to the authoritative *Kleines politisches Wörterbuch* (1978, p. 728), makes it possible, for the first time in history, for relations between states to be conducted on the basis of the strict observance of equal rights, independence, sovereignty and non-interference in each other's internal affairs. The close relationship of all communist parties with the CPSU and the USSR is identified as 'a cardinal question' of proletarian internationalism. Indeed, the 1974 Constitution ties the GDR 'forever and irreversibly' to its fraternal alliance with the Soviet Union. Professions of brotherly love are strengthened, as we have seen, by close military and economic ties. The 1975 Friendship Treaty obliges the partners to render, without geographical restriction, military assistance to each other in the event of attack.

Yet even fraternal bonds can fray, as they did in the late 1960s when the Soviet Union refused to allow Ulbricht to impede its *rapprochement* with the West. Ironically, the roles were reversed in the mid-1980s when the GDR leadership, conscious of the economic benefits of closer contacts with the Federal Republic and perhaps more confident of its ability to control the domestic impact of its opening to the West, sought to insulate inter-German *détente* from the adversarial East–West relations. Honecker also made it known that he was less than enthusiastic about the installation of Soviet missiles in the GDR. Despite the postponement, in September 1984, of the General Secretary's eagerly awaited visit to the FRG, Honecker's policy survived Soviet displeasure and has remained intact since Gorbachëv took office in March 1985.

What are likely to be the main developments in GDR–Soviet relations now that the Soviet Union has a more vigorous and sophisticated leader? Although agreement will most probably prevail on all fundamental issues, the complexity of the agenda will no doubt foster stress and sharp debate. The most problematic areas are expected to be the price and level of Soviet energy and raw materials, the trade balance, the GDR's 'rediscovery of the German past', its dialogue with the FRG within the general framework of East–West relations, defence funding and the improvement in the quality of the GDR's export of capital and consumer goods to the Soviet Union. And another major problem concerns the repercussions in the GDR of Gorbachëv's reformist course in the Soviet Union, as symbolized by such concepts as *glasnost* and *perestroika*.

Gorbachëv's aspirations to tighten scientific, economic, military and political cooperation and coordination in the Soviet bloc were spelled out in his address to the 1986 SED Party Congress:

> All of us, I think, are aware that the socialist countries are entering a period in which their mutual collaboration must be raised to a higher level. It must be raised not just by a few degrees, but—to borrow a term from mathematics—by a whole order of magnitude. [Mikhail Gorbachëv, 1986, p. 12]

That the GDR is expected to play an important role in this integration process can be judged by his praise of the GDR's system of management. Perhaps he was also expressing his respect for the GDR's combine structure, a model which he might like to see adopted in the Soviet Union:

> You have a rich store of experience in coordinating science and production, rationally utilizing material resources, efficiently deploying your labour force and systematically adopting the results of scientific and technological progress. [Mikhail Gorbachëv, 1986, p. 6]

Gratifying though this praise must have been for Honecker's team of political and economic managers, the early signs indicate a certain coolness toward Gorbachëv's aspirations for closer cooperation between Soviet and GDR institutions, enterprises and organizations in order to apply a 'modernization push' to the Soviet economy. Direct cooperation threatens to disturb GDR economic and technical planning without any significant scientific and technological benefits accruing to the GDR (Kupper, 1987, pp. 56–7).

Relations with the socialist countries of Eastern Europe are of less importance to the GDR than its links with the Soviet Union. The combined trade of the five East European members of COMECON accounted for 25 per cent of the GDR's total foreign trade turnover in 1985 as against 39 per cent with the Soviet Union (*StJB*, 1986, p. 240). The GDR is, of course, highly sensitive to political developments in Eastern Europe which might affect its own internal stability and offend its concept of fraternal relations. When Romania broke ranks and established diplomatic relations with Bonn in 1967, the GDR accused it of having harmed the cause of peace and the struggle against militarism and neo-Nazism in the FRG. A further source of GDR displeasure was Romania's public disapproval of the Warsaw Pact suppression of the Prague Spring. GDR–Polish relations experienced a marked improvement in the 1970s, signified by an upsurge in tourism and the 1973 declaration on consolidating friendship between the two countries. The rise of Solidarity set the alarm bells ringing in East Berlin because of the possible ideological and political impact on the GDR workforce. The visa-free travel, introduced in 1972, was virtually terminated by administrative restrictions in 1980. The SED leadership supported the establishment of Jaruzelski's military regime in December 1981, although its preference lay in the restoration of the authority of the Polish United Workers' Party.

Not until the early 1970s did the GDR succeed in breaking out of the confines of its own regional sphere of interest. It had been relatively inactive in the Third World where its major preoccupation throughout the 1960s had been the modest one of securing diplomatic recognition. Despite a series of long-term trade agreements with Egypt, Iraq, Syria and others, the first ripple of recognition did not occur until 1969 when those three countries plus Cambodia and South Yemen finally established diplomatic relations with the GDR. By 1972–3 the GDR was fully recognized by most states.

The dramatic improvement in the GDR's international status and the onset of *détente* in Europe encouraged the SED to undertake a more energetic economic and political role in the Third World. The GDR presented itself as the natural ally of all peoples and states fighting for national liberation, self-determination and social progress against imperialist exploitation and coercion. The basic goals of SED policy were to alter the status quo in the Third World to the detriment of imperialism and, though a more distant target, to create a new world economic order out of the joint struggle against imperialism. Positive assistance in the form of material aid and contractual agreements replaced verbal expressions of sympathy for revolutionary movements in Southern Africa, including MPLA, ZAPO, FRELIMO and ANC. Policy-makers concentrated on countries with a 'socialist orientation', that is, those who had already undergone fundamental socio-economic change and who were opposed to imperialism and colonialism. Eight countries belonged to this category in 1970; they included Syria, Egypt, Algeria and the Congo. At the beginning of the next decade, their number had swollen to about twenty: Libya, Iraq, Afghanistan and Angola were among the new members, though Egypt was excluded (Spanger, 1984a, pp. 36–41).

Whilst it favours socialist states and those with a socialist orientation, the GDR has no alternative but to pursue a flexible policy in the Third World. Economic, military and political considerations require it to be able to adapt to changing circumstances and even to develop contacts with authoritarian regimes.

India's influence in the non-aligned movement and its geographical position and size make it an important element in the GDR's Third World policy. Foreign trade turnover with India rose from 276.7 million Valuta Marks in 1970 to 640.1 million in 1985; this makes India the GDR's eighth most important trading partner among Third World countries and slightly ahead of the United States (*StJB*, 1986, p. 241). Relations with another major Asian power, China, have fluctuated between open enmity and socialist friendship in the slipstream of Moscow's Chinese policy. After the Moscow–Peking rupture at the beginning of the 1960s, contacts were reduced to a bare minimum. A process of normalization commenced in 1982, culminating in October 1986 with Honecker's visit to China and his meetings with Deng Xiaoping and Hu Yaobang. Whereas Honecker, in the 1960s, had attacked Chinese leaders for destroying the foundations of China's democratic order and for creating a bureaucratic dictatorship, he found time at the Eleventh Party Congress to praise China as 'that vast socialist country'. Despite attempts to reactivate trade between the two countries, trade with China is expected to remain below 1 per cent of the GDR's total trade turnover in 1990 (Haendcke-Hoppe, 1986b, p. 60).

Trade has been an important consideration in determining relations with the Iranian monarchy and Khomeini's theocracy. Attitudes toward the hitherto much-abused Shah were modified in 1973 as part of a campaign to foster trade with the oil-rich monarchy. Even the revolutionary events in Iran were virtually ignored by the GDR press until mid-1978 (von Plate, in Jacobsen, Leptin, Scheuner and Schultz, 1980, p. 68). The search for markets and raw materials, especially oil, became more urgent in the 1980s. Iran and Iraq helped, in 1982, to make up deficits arising from the cutback in Soviet oil supplies. Trade with Iran represented 10.9 per cent of the GDR's trade with so-called developing countries in 1981. In fact, Iran is now the

GDR's third largest trading partner in the Third World after Cuba and Iraq (1,181.5 million Valuta Marks in 1985; see *StJB*, 1986, p. 241).

Trade is also pursued with countries in South and Central America—Brazil, Argentina and Mexico—whose regimes clearly do not possess a socialist orientation. Brazil is by far the most important of these states (926.9 million Valuta Marks foreign trade turnover in 1984 and 793.1 million in the following year).

As a proportion of the GDR's total trade turnover, trade with developing countries has not experienced any dramatic change: it amounted to 4 per cent in 1970 as against 6 per cent in 1982. One favourable development has been the conversion of a deficit of 0.21 billion Valuta Marks in 1975 into a surplus of 2.56 billion Valuta Marks in 1984 (Haendcke-Hoppe, 1984, pp. 1061–2, 1066; Cornelsen, 1986a, p. 13).

Economic aid to the developing countries is by no means exorbitant and is concentrated in a few countries, especially those with a socialist orientation and with whom friendship treaties have been concluded. Favoured recipients include Angola, Ethiopia, Mozambique, South Yemen, Afghanistan, Campuchea, Vietnam and Cuba. GDR net capital aid of 0.14 per cent of gross national product falls, according to Western data, well below the UNO recommendation of 0.7 per cent. The GDR's own estimate of aid to developing countries and liberation movements in 1981 is 0.78 per cent; however, this figure is based on national income, a category which has an inflationary impact on the contribution (Spanger, 1984b, p. 151).

A notable feature of GDR–Third World contacts is the training of civilian personnel, a potentially invaluable long-term investment for the GDR. During the 1970s, about 40,000 people from Third World countries participated in training or further education courses at GDR educational establishments. In 1981, as many as 12,827 were involved in training schemes. In the developing countries themselves, GDR advisers focus on the organization and administration, the education sector, the creation of a central economic planning system, agriculture, mining and industry. South Yemen, in particular, has been highly penetrated by the GDR's development experts (Spanger, 1984b, pp. 152–3). More controversially, military advice, equipment and training are provided to a few African and Near Eastern countries. The International Institute for Strategic Studies estimates that 2,270 military personnel were active in nine countries.

While GDR and Soviet policies are obviously closely coordinated in certain regions, such as the strategically important region of Southern Africa, the GDR should not be written off as a passive adjunct to the superpower's global aspirations. The GDR has its own economic interests to pursue in the Third World and since the mid-1970s it has expanded its capital and personnel investment in certain key areas. Its present activity in the Third World may also be regarded as a continuation of its long-standing strategy to enhance its legitimacy and its status as a political actor on the international stage.

Peaceful coexistence, the second core foreign policy principle, underpins relations between countries with different social systems in the period of transition from capitalism to socialism. Marxist–Leninists have usually regarded the principle as an

Table 5.5 GDR military personnel in Third World countries, 1981–86

	1981	1986
Algeria	nd	250
Angola	800	500
Ethiopia	nd	550
Guinea	nd	125
Iraq	nd	160
Libya	1,600	400
Mozambique	nd	100
South Yemen	100	75
Syria	nd	210
	2,500	2,370

Source: International Institute for Strategic Studies, 1981, p. 19 and 1986, p. 51.

important form of the class struggle and as precluding ideological coexistence and the preservation of the socio-economic status quo. The principle is frequently utilized to present the socialists in a favourable light as the defenders of global peace. In his hard-hitting speech at Gera in October 1980, Honecker contrasted the Warsaw Pact's commitment to international agreements for the maintenance of peaceful coexistence with the efforts of the most reactionary imperialist circles, notably those in the United States and the FRG, together with 'the Peking hegemonists', to inflame the international situation. A policy of peaceful coexistence, argued Honecker, runs contrary to the interests of monopoly capitalists who are intent on increasing profits and interfering in the affairs of other states (Honecker, 1982, pp. 425–8).

Honecker's vitriol notwithstanding (and it can be interpreted in the context of his alarm at the effect of the Polish crisis on the GDR and the threatened installation of missiles in the FRG), the concept of peaceful coexistence has been undergoing a modest but potentially important revision in the mid-1980s. Alarm at the real danger of omnicide has prompted some GDR philosophers and social scientists to call for a new way of thinking in the nuclear age; the cooperative aspect of peaceful existence is assuming greater significance at the expense of the class struggle component. Max Schmidt, the director of the influential Institute for International Politics and Economics, has argued that it is no longer sufficient for peaceful coexistence in the nuclear age to involve only the absence of war and states with different social systems living alongside each other; it requires the development and fostering of many different forms of peaceful collaboration between peoples and states (Schmidt, 1986, p. 730; see also Kuppe, 1986, pp. 691–2).

Whilst still in its embryonic stage (the new thinking has not yet, for example, affected political–ideological training in the armed forces), these considerations provide a theoretical underpinning for political dialogue with capitalist states, whether members of NATO or not, and for what Honecker is fond of calling 'a worldwide coalition of common sense and realism'. Sweden, Finland, Austria, Greece and, more recently, Belgium and The Netherlands, rank high among the Western states wooed by the GDR head of state for his coalition of peace and security and for the enhancement of the GDR's standing as a diplomatic partner.

But it is the FRG which remains the fulcrum of Honecker's Western policy. The GDR has many political and economic incentives for wishing to maintain the 'network of relationships' with West Germany. As we have seen, it derives innumerable economic advantages: the swing, the bank loans of 1983 and 1984, exemption from EEC import tariffs, road tolls, and so forth. Economic relations have been buttressed by a plethora of agreements on postal and telephone communications, environmental protection, personal visits and cultural and scientific exchanges (a cultural agreement was finally signed in May 1986). Secondly, both states have a common interest in the maintenance of peace and security in what Honecker has called 'this neuralgic spot of world politics'. The SED continually propagates the view that both German states have a special moral responsibility for ensuring that 'only peace should ever emanate from German soil'. Finally, the GDR's current rehabilitation of Luther and the positive re-evaluation of aspects of Prussian history are a reminder of the common though ambivalent historical links between Germans in East and West.

Although the GDR's dialogue with its Western neighbour and its reprocessing of German history aroused some apprehension in the Kremlin (however, inter-German *détente* no longer seems to be such a controversial issue under Gorbachëv), the country is still firmly ensconced in the political, military and economic institutions of the Soviet system. Moreover, even if the two German republics manage nowadays to cooperate on many issues, they are not yet cohabiting. The SED leadership continues its search for a separate GDR identity and it is allergic to the claim that the German question is still open. Hence it is fond of quoting the joint statement by Honecker and Chancellor Kohl of 12 March 1985 that the inviolability of the frontiers and respect for the territorial integrity of all states in Europe is a fundamental precondition for peace. Another bone of contention is the Federal Republic's involvement in the American Strategic Defence Initiative which is condemned as a threat to peace and as an escalation of the arms race. GDR criticisms dovetail here with the recent Soviet 'peace offensive'. Finally, and most obviously, the SED leadership must always be wary of Western penetration of their country, whether by the electronic media or personal visits, as it still provokes fundamental questions about the GDR's identity and the legitimacy of SED rule. Thus while present circumstances favour political dialogue, the balance of interests could well lead to a more adversarial relationship.

Japan arouses a lively interest nowadays among SED leaders impressed by its innovative capacity and its sophisticated technology. This has not always been the case: until the early 1970s, Japan was depicted in traditional stereotyped formulae. Although trading relations had opened in 1954, Japan did not rank among the GDR's twenty major trading partners by the mid-1970s. A significant impetus to political and trading relations was given by Japan's diplomatic recognition of the GDR in 1973. Four years later a delegation led by Günter Mittag negotiated agreements on bilateral trade and scientific–technical cooperation. Trade expanded rapidly in the early 1980s, reaching a peak of $356.8 million in 1983, or 1.5 per cent of the GDR's foreign trade. The GDR imported mainly high-quality mechanical engineering products as well as electronic goods and chemical products. Entry into the Japanese market has proved extremely difficult for the GDR as it is unable to produce high-quality goods for sale in Japan. The unfavourable balance of trade (in 1983, the GDR exported goods worth $30 million but imports cost $326 million) and the GDR's limited supply of hard currency for the purchase in dollars of Japanese goods have led to a decline in trade since 1983 (Kuppe, 1981, pp. 673–6; Bundesminister für innerdeutsche Beziehungen, 1987b, p. 16; Glaubitz, in Jacobsen, Leptin, Scheuner & Schultz, 1980, pp. 731–3).

Membership of International Organizations

The GDR's political weakness and its legitimacy deficit were reflected in the difficulties which it experienced before its final acceptance as a member of several international bodies. Its application for membership of the United Nations was rejected in 1966; final acceptance, in 1973, was delayed until the conclusion of the Basic Treaty between the two German republics. When the GDR signed the Warsaw Pact Treaty in May 1955 it did not formally enjoy full sovereignty in foreign and security affairs. As the NVA, which was formally created and incorporated into the Pact in 1956, was probably not regarded as a highly reliable force, it was only accorded auxiliary tasks in the event of war. Not until 1963 did the NVA become part of the Pact's first strategic echelon. Bilateral defence treaties between member states complement the security provisions of the Pact. Unlike the other members, the GDR had to wait until the 1960s before concluding a bilateral treaty with the Soviet Union.

With regard to the Soviet bloc's other major organization, COMECON, the GDR did not join until September 1950, that is, twenty months after its formation in response to the American Marshall Aid Plan. Although the agreement has never been published, special provision was made for the GDR to maintain its trading relations with West Germany. The organization remained virtually moribund until the late 1950s and attempts to create an integrated, supra-national community, notably in 1962, have foundered on the diverging economic and political interests and the uneven level of economic development of the member states. However, forms of cooperation such as the coordination of national economic plans and the development of organizational and legal mechanisms have increased since the agreement in 1971 on a complex programme on economic integration. At the close of 1985 a 'Complex Programme for the Scientific–Technical Progress of the

Member Countries of COMECON until the Year 2000' was accepted; it envisages cooperation in five areas: the complex automation of production; the introduction of electronics into all economic areas; an acceleration in the use of nuclear energy; the introduction of new technologies and materials; and the more rapid development of biotechnology. It remains to be seen whether this programme can overcome the usual cooperation problems in the production stage and it is doubtful whether the GDR, the most advanced technological power in COMECON, will derive any decisive qualitative benefits from the proposed integration (Haendcke-Hoppe, 1986b, p. 65).

The GDR occupies a leading position within COMECON. Although its gross national product is less than that of the USSR and Poland, it enjoys the highest standard of living among member states and occupies first place in terms of gross national product per head of population. Its share of intra-COMECON trade (about 16 per cent) is second only to that of the USSR and it is usually involved in all the major investment projects. As a highly developed industrial and technological power, it is heavily committed to production specialization agreements. In 1980, it had 379 bilateral and 102 multilateral specialization agreements with its COMECON partners. Specialized products as a proportion of GDR exports to the other COMECON states are higher than the community average: 35 per cent as against 17.5 per cent in 1982 (Machowski, in Zimmermann, 1985, p. 1084).

The SED leaders, like their counterparts in the other East European countries, are keen to protect what they perceive to be the interests of their own state. For example, the GDR, as the major COMECON power outside the USSR, scrutinizes the feasibility of new projects and community initiatives which might require the investment of scarce resources. The GDR's objection in 1981 to Mozambique's application to join COMECON was conditioned by its realization that membership would entail considerable GDR aid to this relatively underdeveloped African state (Seiffert, 1983, pp. 177–9). As the member country with the most advanced technological base, the GDR is usually the foremost advocate of integration measures in the scientific and technical area. However, many COMECON specialization agreements are disappointing from the GDR's point of view: they do not enable the GDR to concentrate on those lines which have the greatest potential for economic growth. In general terms, the GDR regards its own economic development as being held back by its less sophisticated partners (Autorenkollektiv Morgenstern, 1984, pp. 15–17, 58).

Conclusion

Like the Soviet Union, the GDR has come a long way—but in a shorter time (on the Soviet Union, see Hill, 1985, pp. 207–8). In 1945, the Soviet zone's economy was in ruins; political apathy was widespread. Anti-bolshevism, inflamed by Nazi propaganda and compounded by stories of brutal behaviour by Soviet troops in the wake of the invasion of Germany, alienated many East Germans from their occupying power. And when the GDR was founded four years later, it was frequently derided as the artificial construct of the totalitarian dictator in the Kremlin. Deprived of the benefits of Marshall Aid enjoyed by its Western neighbour, the new republic seemed to lack the necessary economic and political preconditions for survival. In stark contrast, the GDR of today appears to be a politically stable, relatively prosperous and increasingly self-assured state. It is often upheld as a model for its particular brand of socialism.

The stability of the GDR is attributable to the capacity of its economy to provide an adequate supply of material goods; to the efforts of its highly skilled and relatively well-disciplined workforce; to the incorporation of key sections of the intelligentsia into the system; to the economic advantages derived from the special relationship with West Germany; and, whatever the doubts harboured in private, to the public consensus on the GDR's integration into the Soviet bloc. International recognition now underpins domestic stability. Indeed, Honecker's role as an elder statesman on the world stage represents the fruit of the hard-fought struggle for his country's diplomatic credentials. The SED leader's official visit to the Federal Republic in September 1987 further underlined the enhanced status both of the 'other' Germany and its *Landesvater*.

The greater pragmatism of the Honecker era, too, has undoubtedly contributed to the country's stability. More attention is paid by the regime to the diverse wishes and needs of the populace. Social policy, notably the housing policy, exemplifies the regime's overall strategy of attaining a *modus vivendi* with the majority of the population. And in fact the regime does appear to have been successful in purchasing the functional loyalty of a high proportion of East Germans. Outright opposition is confined to small groups of relatively isolated individuals; conveniently for the SED leadership, its critics can be exported to the West. However, firm commitment to the substance of the Marxist–Leninist *Weltanschauung* is confined to a small minority. One final though crucial aspect of the social compact is the Honecker regime's tolerance of the retreat of many citizens into the private sphere, the so-called *Nischengesellschaft*. Away from the external pressures of party, mass organizations and the other manifestations of the public sphere, people seek the company of friends and relatives in their home or dacha. Whilst the regime continues to prioritize the collective, it has come to terms with this discrete atomization of socialist society. People might grumble in private; they do not rebel.

If, then, 'real existing socialism' in the GDR gives the outward impression of stability and of a more flexible system of rule than in the days of the autocratic Ulbricht, what are the forces, both internal and external, which might engender instability and perhaps undermine the legitimacy of SED rule? Three major problem areas will be highlighted: the 'revitalization' of that conglomerate of issues known as the 'German Question'; a renewed economic crisis; and the political shock waves of Soviet-style reform.

The 'German Question', including the issue of German reunification, has resurfaced in the 1980s as an object of lively debate in academic and political circles in the Federal Republic. This debate is inextricably interwoven with the broader questioning of the European post-war settlement. The whole situation has become more fluid as governments, grass-roots movements and political parties attempt to devise solutions to the internal and external strains arising from the differential impact of economic crisis and a nuclear Armageddon. The resolution of the division of Germany is seen by some commentators in West Germany as not only a crucial step toward overcoming the Cold War but also, by decoupling both German states from their respective blocs, as creating necessary conditions for mutual security and stable peace.

The diverse hopes in the FRG for progress on the 'German Question' have been kindled by the emergence of an innovative leader in the Soviet Union who has publicly appealed for 'new thinking' in the nuclear age. This has given substance to one scenario: namely, that the Kremlin, reassured by an accommodation with the United States, might be prepared to upgrade the present complementary inter-German relationship into a confederation of the two republics. Such an arrangement could be expected to involve the withdrawal of the two German states from their respective military alliances and would offer the Soviet Union not only a lightening of its defence burden but also the tempting bait of greater access to West German technology to help modernize the Soviet economy. Ultimately, the argument runs, the two superpowers and their allies might countenance a gradual convergence of the two states into a neutral and reunited Germany.

Gorbachëv, however, has dampened such hopes. He made it clear to the President of the Federal Republic, on the occasion of von Weizsäcker's official visit to Moscow in July 1987, that he was unwilling to 'theorize' about the question of the German nation (*Der Spiegel*, 13 July 1987, pp. 21–2). It is highly improbable at this juncture that Gorbachëv would wish to jeopardize his reform strategy at home and the delicate superpower armaments reduction negotiations by opening the Pandora's box of German reunification. And given the economic and military strength of the Federal Republic—never mind the combined might of the two German states—the prevention of German reunification seems likely to prevail as one of the over-whelming priorities of Soviet foreign policy. Economic aid to foster the development of the Soviet economy would be inadequate compensation for the emergence of an economic colossus and the loss of a more or less reliable SED-controlled GDR.

For the SED leadership, any talk of a reopening of the 'German Question', in whatever form, is anathema. The Politburo has firmly rejected as 'unsuitable' the proposal emanating from the CDU Bundestag deputy Bernhard Friedmann that negotiations on the reduction of nuclear missiles should be linked to a debate on German reunification. This kind of talk is condemned as harmful to further progress in inter-German relations (*Junge Welt*, 19 June 1987, p. 3). The GDR rulers' preference is to seek further advantage from the accords of the early 1970s which more or less secured their Western frontier and delivered significant economic advantages.

If the concept of German reunification or even a confederation based on closer economic cooperation is still too much of a chimera to pose a real threat to the GDR as a separate and autonomous political entity, the whole question does, however, highlight some of the 'flaws' in the GDR edifice. First, the problem of national identity renders it far more difficult for the SED leaders than for their East European counterparts to play the card of nationalism to engender the populace's emotional loyalty to the GDR. Even the more sophisticated analysis in recent years of the place and role of the GDR within the whole of German history cannot resolve the dilemma of a past shared with a more prosperous and to many East Germans a politically more open and less coercive Western neighbour. Secondly, if the Western debates percolate into receptive channels in the GDR, this might conceivably create a dynamic which could yet destabilize the social and political order. Some indicators exist as to the receptivity of the GDR to this possibility. The League of German Communists aspired in their 1977 Manifesto to a reunited Germany. And a limited dialogue has been established between Western peace groups and autonomous peace activists in the GDR, a dialogue which extends beyond the question of peace to the interrelated issues of human rights and, in some circles, to a rethinking of the division of Germany. The 1982 Berlin Appeal thematized the 'German Question' by calling for the withdrawal of the former Allied occupation troops from 'Germany'. Furthermore, Robert Havemann, one of the inspirations behind the Appeal, came to advocate a reunited Germany even if it meant launching it with a form of multi-party bourgeois democracy such as the Weimar Republic (Sandford, 1983, p. 63).

Havemann's approach, it should be stressed, runs counter to the general tone of the debate within the GDR peace movement; its participants are inclined to search for a solution on the basis of the inviolability of the frontiers between the two republics. But improbable though German reunification is, its very discussion raises sensitive questions about the SED's methods of political control and the desirability of domestic reform. And if the rethinking about the 'German Question' stirs up widespread doubts among GDR citizens about the seeming immutability of their country's place within the Soviet bloc, this could lead to a severe test for the legitimation and even the continuation of communist rule.

However, given the fact that the GDR's relative economic success has probably been the major factor in sustaining the social compact in the Honecker era, a renewed threat to living standards and the system of social welfare is, in the short to medium term, much more likely to have a destabilizing effect than notions of German unity. A deterioration in the international economy, as in the late 1970s and early 1980s, must obviously have serious repercussions as the GDR has become increasingly dependent on foreign trade since the mid–1960s. A flagging economy could still destabilize the social order, particularly if Bonn shortened its 'credit line'. The attitude of the Soviet Union would be a critical factor, too.

Another threat to the economic growth strategy of the SED, in particular to the modernization push, is discernible within the GDR itself. The 'rationality' of the SED's pursuit of economic growth is challenged by environmental groups and critics. Given the consumerist mentality of a large section of the population this remains a less potent threat to economic modernization than the forces of inertia. The intensive exploitation of assets requires dislodging workers from their niches at work and the creation of new work values. Yet rationalization and automation projects fail to achieve their full impact because of systemic obstacles. But some of these obstacles, ironically, are vital ingredients in the social compact. They encompass the protective cloak of job security, a generous system of social welfare and a remuneration system which is not fully geared to payment by results. And despite Honecker's exhortations to managers and scientists, the command and administrative forms of the economy are not conducive to risk-taking.

Gorbachëv's campaign to restructure the Soviet economy demonstrates that the above are salient criticisms of the system of central planning, even though it must be conceded that the GDR does not suffer from some of the more chronic problems of the Soviet economy. It is apparent from the CPSU Central Committee plenum in June 1987 that the individual factory or farm rather than the central planner is emerging as the focus of economic activity in the Soviet Union. Annual plans are to be abolished and a sweeping shift to wholesale trade is envisaged. Gorbachëv's reformist policies have been welcomed in the GDR by well-known critical socialists like Stefan Heym, Stephan Hermlin, Günter de Bruyn and Jürgen Kucyznski. Furthermore the chants of '*glasnost*' and 'Gorbachëv' by protestors during clashes between young GDR rock fans and police on Unter den Linden in East Berlin are another indicator of the potential appeal in the GDR of the Soviet leader's twin-track policy of democratization and economic revitalization.

The Honecker team, on the other hand, would clearly prefer to cling to established routine and to introduce change in a gradual manner. Hitherto, it has been allergic to Soviet-style reconstruction. Some of Gorbachëv's speeches have been censored and leaders such as Honecker, Hager and Axen have pointedly kept their distance from *glasnost* and *perestroika*. This conservative approach is reflected in Honecker's description of the present economic and planning system as functioning well and as 'efficient, dynamic and flexible' (*Report of the Central Committee*, 1986 p. 52). In short, Honecker and his colleagues are intent on making the existing system work and on preserving a tight control over the main levers of political power. However, as the GDR approaches its fortieth anniversary it is becoming increasingly doubtful whether this is an adequate response to the qualitatively new and major challenges posed by economic and social modernization and by the reformist impulses generated by Gorbachëv.

Bibliography

Act on the Integrated Socialist Educational System of the German Democratic Republic 1972. Berlin (East), Staatsverlag der Deutschen Demokratischen Republik.

Adomeit, Hannes 1982. *Soviet Risk-Taking and Crisis Behaviour: A Theoretical and Empirical Analysis*. London, George Allen & Unwin.

Akademie für Staats- und Rechtswissenschaft in der DDR (ed.) 1979. *Einführung in die marxistisch-leninistische Staats- und Rechtslehre*. Berlin (East), Dietz Verlag.

Albrecht, Richard 1986. 'Literaturgesellschaft' DDR—oder das Bedürfnis nach 'echten Geschichten'. *Deutsche Studien*, vol. XXIV, no. 94, pp. 133–42.

Ammer, Thomas 1985. Menschenrechtsverletzungen in der DDR. *Deutschland Archiv*, vol. 18, no. 9, pp. 949–59.

— 1986. Mitglieder und Funktionäre in der SED. *DDR Report*, vol. 19, no. 9, pp. 497–500.

Ammer, Thomas & Kuppe, Johannes 1986. XI. Parteitag der SED. *Deutschland Archiv*, vol. 19, no. 6, pp. 615–32.

Anweiler, Oskar & Kuebart, Friedrich (eds) 1984. *Bildungssysteme in Osteuropa. Reform oder Krise?* Berlin (West), Berlin Verlag.

Arato, Andrew & Vajda, Mihaly 1980. The limits of the Leninist opposition: reply to David Bathrick. *New German Critique*, vol. 7, no. 19, pp. 167–75.

Ardagh, John 1987. *Germany and the Germans: An Anatomy of Society Today*. London, Hamish Hamilton.

Ash, Tim Garton 1983. Swords into ploughshares: the unofficial 'Peace Movement' and the churches in East Germany. *Religion in Communist Lands*, vol. 11, no. 3, Winter 1983, pp. 244–50.

Asmus, Ronald 1984a. The GDR and Martin Luther. *Survey*, vol. 28, no. 3, pp. 124–56.

— 1984b. The GDR and the German nation: sole heir or socialist sibling? *International Affairs*, vol. 60, no.3, pp. 403–18.

— 1985. The dialectics of detente and discord: the Moscow–East Berlin–Bonn Triangle. *Orbis*, vol. 28, no. 4, pp. 743–74.

— 1986. The GDR and the German past. *German Studies Newsletter*, no. 7, pp. 19–24.

Aßmann, Georg *et al*. 1977. *Wörterbuch der marxistisch-leninistischen Soziologie*. Berlin (East), Dietz Verlag.

Autorenkollektiv 1980. *Die Intelligenz in der sozialistischen Gesellschaft*. Berlin (East), Dietz Verlag.

Autorenkollektiv unter Leitung von Rolf Badstübner 1981. *Geschichte der Deutschen Demokratischen Republik*, 2nd edn. Berlin (East), Deutscher Verlag der Wissenschaften.

Autorenkollektiv unter Leitung von Günter Manz 1983. *Lebensniveau im Sozialismus*. Berlin (East), Verlag Die Wirtschaft.

Autorenkollektiv unter Leitung von Karl Morgenstern 1984. *Spezialisierung und*

Kooperation zwischen den RGW-Ländern: Neue Bedingungen und Aufgaben. Berlin (East), Verlag Die Wirtschaft.

Autorenkollektiv unter der Leitung von Kurt Krambach 1985. *Wie lebt man auf dem Dorf? Soziologische Aspekte der Entwicklung des Dorfes in der DDR*. Berlin (East), Dietz Verlag.

Badstübner, Rolf 1978. *Restaurationsapologie und Fortschrittsverteufelung. Das entspannungsfeindliche bürgerliche Nachkriegsgeschichtsbild in der BRD*. Frankfurt/Main, Verlag Marxistische Blätter.

Bahro, Rudolf 1978. *The Alternative in Eastern Europe*, tr. David Fernbach. London, New Left Books.

Ball, Kevin 1986. New voices from East Berlin. *Labour Focus on Eastern Europe*, vol. 8, no. 3, pp. 35–6.

Baring, Arnulf 1972. *Uprising in East Germany: June 17, 1953*. Ithaca and London, Cornell University Press.

Barthel, Alexander 1986. Der 'Beitrag für gesellschaftliche Fonds': eine Lohnsummensteuer? *Deutschland Archiv*, vol. 19, no. 4, pp. 381–8.

Barthel, Horst 1979. *Die wirtschaftlichen Ausgangsbedingungen der DDR*. Berlin (East), Akademie-Verlag.

Barthel, Horst, Mittenzwei, Ingrid & Schmidt, Walter 1979. Preußen und die deutsche Geschichte. *Einheit*, vol. 34, no. 6, pp. 637–46.

Bartholmai, Bernd & Melzer, Manfred 1987. Zur Entwicklung des Wohnungsbaus in der DDR und in der Bundesrepublik Deutschland. *Deutschland Archiv*, vol. 20, no. 2, pp. 180–7.

Baylis, Thomas 1986. Explaining the GDR's economic strategy. *International Organization*, vol. 40, no. 2, pp. 381–420.

Belwe, Katharina 1982. *Die Fluktuation Werktätiger als Ausdruck sozialer Konflikte in der DDR*. Bonn, Gesamtdeutsches Institut, Bundesanstalt für gesamtdeutsche Aufgaben.

— 1984a. *Probleme der Arbeitskräftefreisetzung*. Bonn, Gesamtdeutsches Institut, Bundesanstalt für gesamtdeutsche Aufgaben.

— 1984b. 'Weniger produzieren mehr': Probleme der Freisetzung von Arbeitskräften in der DDR. *Deutschland Archiv*, vol. 17, no. 5, pp. 496–509.

— 1987. Migration in der DDR; Landflucht und Verstädterung. *Deutschland Archiv*, vol. 20, no. 5, pp. 515–30.

Benser, Günter 1978. Antifa-Ausschüsse–Staatsorgane–Parteiorganisation. *Zeitschrift für Geschichtswissenschaft*, vol. 26, no. 9, pp. 785–802.

Bentley, Raymond 1986. Technologischer Wandel in der Industrie der DDR 1945–1985. *Aus Politik und Zeitgeschichte*, no. 4, pp. 16–27.

Berg, Michael von 1984. Zum Umweltschutz in Deutschland. *Deutschland Archiv*, vol. 17, no. 4, pp. 374–83.

Bethkenhagen, Jochen 1985. Der Primärenergievergleich in der DDR und seine Struktur. *DIW Wochenbericht*, vol. 52, no. 51–2, pp. 575–82.

— 1986a. Auswirkungen des Ölpreisverfalls auf die UdSSR. *DIW Wochenbericht*, vol. 53, no. 17, pp. 212–15.

—— 1986b. Die Kernenergiepolitik der RGW-Länder. *DIW Wochenbericht*, vol. 53, no. 25, pp. 305–12.

Bethkenhagen, Jochen *et al.* 1981. *DDR und Osteuropa: Wirtschaftssystem, Wirtschaftspolitik, Lebensstandard: Ein Handbuch*, Opladen, Leske.

Beyme, Klaus von & Zimmermann, Hartmut (eds) 1984. *Policymaking in the German Democratic Republic*, tr. Eileen Martin. Aldershot, Gower.

Biermann, Wolfgang 1978. *Demokratisierung in der DDR? Ökonomische Notwendigkeiten, Herrschaftsstrukturen, Rolle der Gewerkschaften 1961–1977*. Cologne, Verlag Wissenschaft und Politik.

Bierstedt, Heidi 1986. Die Teilnahme am Sporttreiben in Abhängigkeit von sozialdemographischen Merkmalen (Alter, Geschlecht). *Informationen zur soziologischen Forschung in der Deutschen Demokratischen Republik*, vol. 22, no. 1, 1986, pp. 26–31.

Böhme, Irene 1983. *Die da drüben: Sieben Kapitel DDR*. Berlin (West), Rotbuch Verlag.

Boot, Pieter 1983. Continuity and change in the planning system of the German Democratic Republic. *Soviet Studies*, vol. XXXV, no. 3, pp. 331–42.

Bracher, Karl Dietrich, Funke, Manfred & Jacobsen, Hans-Adolf (eds) 1983. *Nationalsozialistische Diktatur 1933–45. Eine Bilanz*. Düsseldorf, Droste Verlag.

Brandt, Heinz 1970. *The Search for a Third Way: My Path Between East and West*, tr. Salvator Attanasio. New York, Doubleday.

Brandt, Willy 1978. *People and Politics: The Years 1960–1975*, tr. J. Maxwell Brownjohn. London, Collins.

Brendler, Gerhard 1983. Martin Luther. *Prisma*, no. 3, pp. 102–5.

Bröll, Werner, 1974. *Die Wirtschaft der DDR: Lage und Aussichten*, 3rd edn. Munich, Olzog.

Brux, Arnim 1980. *Sportlehrer und Sportunterricht in der DDR*. Berlin (West), Verlag Bartels & Wernitz.

Bryson, Phillip 1984. *The Consumer Under Socialist Planning: The East German Case*. New York, Praeger.

Buch, Günther 1982. *Namen und Daten wichtiger Personen der DDR*, 3rd edn. Berlin (West) and Bonn, Verlage J. H. W. Dietz.

Büchner-Uhder, Willi, Hieblinger, Rudolf & Poppe, Eberhard 1986. Zur Erhöhung der Wirksamkeit der örtlichen Volksvertretungen und der Autorität der Abgeordneten. *Staat uind Recht*, vol. 35, no. 1, pp. 3–11.

Bundesminister für innerdeutsche Beziehungen (ed) 1986a. Zwei Drittel aller Mitglieder des neuen SED-Zentralkomitees sind hauptamtliche Parteifunktionäre oder hohe Staatsfunktionäre. *Informationen*, no. 11, 23 May 1986, pp. 9–12.

—— 1986b. 13. Parteitag der NDPD. *Informationen*, no. 10, 29 May 1986, pp. 9–10.

—— 1986c. Die 500 neuen Volkskammerabgeordneten standen bereits vor dem Wahltermin fest. *Informationen*, no. 11, 6 June 1986, pp. 9–12.

—— 1987a. Die Entwicklung der DDR-Wirtschaft im Jahre 1986. *Informationen*, no. 2, pp. 9–12.

—— 1987b. DDR und Japan wollen Beziehungen verbessern. *Informationen*, no. 2, pp. 15–16.

—— 1987c. Materialien zum Bericht zur Lage der Nation im geteilten Deutschland 1987 vorgestellt. *Informationen*, no. 9, pp. 22–38.

Burrichter, Clemens & Förtsch, Eckart 1985. Förderung von Spitzenforschung in der DDR. *Deutschland Archiv*, vol. 18, no. 8, pp. 846–8.

Büscher, Wolfgang & Wensierski, Peter 1984. *Null Bock auf DDR: Aussteigerjugend im anderen Deutschland*. Reinbek bei Hamburg, Spiegel-Verlag.

Bust-Bartels, Axel 1980. *Herrschaft und Widerstand in den DDR-Betrieben*. Frankfurt/Main, Campus.

Childs, David 1983. *The GDR: Moscow's German Ally*. London, Boston, Sydney, George Allen & Unwin.

—— (ed.) 1985. *Honecker's Germany*. London, Boston, Sydney, Allen & Unwin.

Chronik: 4 bis 8. April 1986, 1986. *Kirche im Sozialismus*, vol. 12, no. 3, pp. 135–6.

Cornelsen, Doris 1985. Bilanz des Fünfjahrplans 1981 bis 1985. *FS-Analysen*, vol. 12, no. 4, pp. 39–69.

—— 1986a. Die Wirtschaft der DDR 1981–1985: Bilanz des Fünfjahrplans. *Aus Politik und Zeitgeschichte*, no. 4, pp. 3–15.

—— 1986b. DDR-Wirtschaft 1986 bis 1990. *DIW Wochenbericht*, vol. 53, no. 31, pp. 391–6.

—— 1987. Zur Lage der DDR-Wirtschaft an der Jahreswende 1986/87. *DIW Wochenbericht*, vol. 54, no. 5, pp. 57–63.

Cornelsen, Doris, Melzer, Manfred & Scherzinger, Angela 1984. DDR-Wirtschaftssystem: Reform in kleinen Schritten. Deutsches Institut für Wirtschaftsforschung. *Vierteljahrsheft*, no. 2, pp. 200–23.

Cultural Life in the GDR: Review and Current Trends 1982. Berlin (East), Panorama.

Curry, Jane Leftwich (ed.) 1983. *Dissent in Eastern Europe*. New York, Praeger.

Dähn, Horst, 1982. *Konfrontation oder Kooperation? Das Verhältnis von Staat und Kirche in der SBZ/DDR 1945–1980*. Opladen, Westdeutscher Verlag.

Damus, Renate 1973. *Entscheidungsstrukturen und Funktionsprobleme in der DDR-Wirtschaft*. Frankfurt/Main, Suhrkamp.

DeBardeleben, Joan 1985. *The Environment and Marxism–Leninism. The Soviet and East German Experience*. Boulder and London, Westview Press.

Dennis, Michael 1982. Sports Participation in the GDR. *GDR Monitor*, no. 7, pp. 10–22.

Deuerlein, Ernst (ed.) 1971. *DDR 1945–1970: Geschichte und Bestandsaufnahme*, 3rd edn. Munich, Deutscher Taschenbuch Verlag.

Deutsches Institut für Wirtschaftsforschung Berlin (ed.) 1984. *Handbuch DDR-Wirtschaft*, 4th edn. Reinbek bei Hamburg, Rowohlt Taschenbuch Verlag.

Die Berlin–Regelung 1980. Seminarmaterial des Gesamtdeutschen Instituts, Bonn.

Directives Issued by the 11th Congress of the SED for the Five-Year Plan for the GDR's National Economic Development 1986–1990 1986. Dresden, Verlag Zeit im Bild.

Dölling, Irene 1986. *Individuum und Kultur: Ein Beitrag zur Diskussion*. Berlin (East), Dietz Verlag.

Eichholtz, Dietrich & Gossweiler, Kurt 1980. *Faschismus Forschung: Positionem, Probleme, Polemik*. Berlin (East), Akademie-Verlag.

Engelberg, Ernst 1985. *Bismarck: Urpreusse und Reichsgründer*. Berlin (West), Siedler Verlag.

Erbe, Günter *et al*. 1979. *Politik, Wirtschaft und Gesellschaft in der DDR*. Opladen, Westdeutscher Verlag.

Erdmann, Kurt 1985. Entwicklungslinien im DDR-Kombinat: Rückblick und Ausblick in der Mitte der 80er Jahre. *FS-Analysen*, vol. 12, no. 4, pp. 71–125.

—— 1986. Ökonomische Strategie und Wirtschaftssystem auf dem XI. Parteitag der SED. *FS-Analysen*, vol. 13, no. 2, pp. 1–19.

The Europa Yearbook 1987. London, Europa Publications Ltd.

Fehervary, Helen & Lennox, Sara 1978. Introduction to Self-Experiment: Appendix to a Report, by Christa Wolf. *New German Critique*, vol. 5, no. 13, pp. 109–12.

Forster, Thomas M. 1980. *The East German Army: The Second Power in the Warsaw Pact*, tr. Deryck Viney, 5th edn. London, Boston, Sydney, George Allen & Unwin.

Fowkes, Ben 1984. *Communism in Germany under the Weimar Republic*. London, Macmillan.

Freedom, Democracy, Human Rights: For Whom and for What? The GDR Presents its Views 1976. Berlin (East), Panorama.

Freeman, Christopher, T. (ed.) 1985. *East-West Trade and Finance in the World Economy: A New Look for the 1980s*. London, Macmillan.

Freiburg, Arnold 1981. *Kriminalität in der DDR*. Opladen, Westdeutscher Verlag.

—— 1985. Die DDR-Kriminologie auf dem Wege zum Realismus. *Deutschland Archiv*, vol. 18, no. 1, pp. 68–74.

Freiburg, Arnold & Mahrad, Christa 1982. *FDJ: Der sozialistische Jugendverband der DDR*. Opladen, Westdeutscher Verlag.

Fricke, Karl Wilhelm 1976. *Programm und Statut der SED*. Cologne, Verlag Wissenschaft und Politik.

—— 1984a. *Die DDR-Staatssicherheit: Entwicklung, Strukturen, Aktionsfelder*. Cologne, Verlag Wissenschaft und Politik.

—— 1984b. *Opposition und Widerstand in der DDR*. Cologne, Verlag Wissenschaft und Politik.

—— 1985. Naumanns Sturz: ein Sieg für Krenz, *Deutschland Archiv*, vol. 18, no. 12, pp. 1251–3.

—— 1986a. Hoffmanns Nachfolger: Armeegeneral Heinz Keßler. *Deutschland Archiv*, vol. 19, no. 1, pp. 10–13.

—— 1986b. Kaderpolitik der Kontinuität. *Deutschland Archiv*, vol. 19, no. 6, pp. 629–32.

—— 1987. Weder Konzentrationslager noch politische Gefangene in der DDR? *Deutschland Archiv*, vol. 20, no. 2, pp. 160–8.

Friedrich, Walter & Hoffmann, Achim (eds) 1986. *Persönlichkeit und Leistung*. Berlin (East), Deutscher Verlag der Wissenschaften.

Friedrich, Walter & Müller, Harry (eds) 1983. *Soziale Psychologie älterer Schüler*. Berlin (East), Volk und Wissen Volkseigener Verlag.

Gaus, Günter 1983. *Wo Deutschland liegt: Eine Ortsbestimmung*. Hamburg, Hoffmann & Campe.

Gelb, Norman 1986. *The Berlin Wall*. London, Michael Joseph.

Gerber, Margy (ed.) 1981. *Studies in GDR Culture and Society*. Washington, DC, University Press of America.

—— 1985. *Studies in GDR Culture and Society*, 5. Lanham, New York, London, University Press of America.

—— 1986. *Studies in GDR Culture and Society*, 6. Lanham, New York, London, University Press of America.

—— 1986/87. 'Wie hoch ist eigentlich der Preis der Emanzipation?' Social issues in recent GDR women's writing. *GDR Monitor*, no. 16, pp. 55–83.

Geschichte der sozialistischen Einheitspartei Deutschlands: Abriß 1978. Berlin (East), Dietz Verlag.

Gitter, Wolfgang & Wilk, Berhard 1974. *Fun–Health–Fitness*. Berlin (East), Panorama.

Gorbachëv Addresses Party on Change, III 1987. *The Current Digest of the Soviet Press*, vol. XXXIX, no. 6, pp. 8–14.

Groß, Karl–Heinz 1985. Die innerdeutschen Wirtschaftsbeziehungen. *FS–Analysen*, vol. 12, no. 5, pp. 27–48.

Grundmann, Siegried 1985. Territoriale Bedingungen und Faktoren zur Enfaltung der sozialistischen Lebensweise. *Informationen zur soziologischen Forschung in der Deutschen Demokratischen Republik*, vol. 21, no. 5, pp. 6–19.

Günther, Karl–Heinz (ed.) 1983. *Das Bildungswesen der DDR*, Berlin (East), Volk und Wissen Volkseigener Verlag.

Gutmann, Gernot (ed.) 1983. *Das Wirtschaftssystem der DDR: Wirtschaftpolitische Gestaltungsprobleme*. Stuttgart and New York, Gustav Fischer Verlag.

Gutmann, Gernot & Haendcke-Hoppe, Maria (eds) 1981. *Die Außenbeziehungen der DDR*. Heidelberg, Edition Meyn.

Gutmann, Gernot (ed.) 1983. *Das Wirtschaftssystem der DDR*. Stuttgart, Gustav Fischer Verlag.

Haendcke-Hoppe, Maria 1983. DDR–Außenwirtschaft unter neuen Vorzeichen. *Deutschland Archiv*, vol. 16, no. 4, pp. 378–85.

—— 1984. Konsolidierung in der DDR–außenwirtschaft: die Entwicklung 1983/ 1984. *Deutschland Archiv*, vol. 17, no. 10, pp. 1060–8.

—— 1986a. Die Außenwirtschaftlichen Perspektiven. *FS–Analysen*, vol. 13, no. 2, pp. 21–32.

—— 1986b. Startschwierigkeiten in der Außenwirtschaft. *FS–Analysen*, vol. 13, no. 4, pp. 49–74.

Hahn, Toni & Niederländer, Loni 1982. Zur großstädtischen Lebensweise: Theoretisch–methodologische Probleme ihrer Forschung. *Deutsche Zeitschrift für Philosophie*, vol. 30, no. 6, pp. 754–67.

Hamilton, Richard F. 1982. *Who Voted for Hitler?* Princeton, Princeton University Press.

Hartmann, Matthias & Urban, Detlef 1985. Gruppen im Abseits? *Kirche im Sozialismus*, vol. 11, no. 4, pp. 143–5.

Hanke, Irma 1986. Rural life under Socialism, seen from within: Gabriele Eckart's 'So sehe ick die Sache. Protokolle aus der DDR. Leben im Havelländischen Obstanbaugebiet'. *GDR Monitor*, no. 15, pp. 17–36.

Haustein, Heinz–Dieter & Maier, Harry 1985. *Flexible Automatisierung: Aufbruch einer Schlüsseltechnologie der Zukunft.* Berlin (East), Akademie-Verlag.

Havemann, Robert 1973. *An Alienated Man*, tr. Derek Masters. London, Davis-Poynter.

Heitzer, Heinz 1981. *GDR: An Historical Outline.* Dresden, Verlag Zeit im Bild.

Henkys, Reinhard (ed.) 1982. *Die evangelischen Kirchen in der DDR. Beiträge zu einer Bestandsaufnahme.* Munich, Chr. Kaiser Verlag.

— 1986a. Honecker's Signal. *Kirche im Sozialismus*, vol. 12, no. 1, p. 30.

— 1986b. Neue Perspektiven für die jüdischen Gemeinden. *Kirche im Sozialismus*, vol. 12, no. 6, pp. 237–8.

Herzig, Martin 1977. *Youth at Work, at Leisure and in Politics.* Berlin (East), Panorama.

Heuer, Uwe-Jens & Mollnar, Karl A. 1983. Sozialistische Demokratie: Errungenschaft und Anspruch. *Einheit*, vol. 38, no. 6, pp. 545–50.

Heym, Stefan 1974. *The Queen Against Defoe and Other Stories.* New York, Lawrence Hill & Co.

Hill, Ronald J. 1985. *The Soviet Union.* London, Frances Pinter.

Hille, Barbara 1981. Zum aktuellen Forschungsstand über die Jugendlichen in der DDR. *Deutsche Studien*, vol. 19, no. 76, pp. 332–45.

Hillebrenner, Dieter (ed.) 1986. *Sozialistische Landesverteidigung im Friedenskampf.* Berlin (East), Militärverlag der DDR.

Hohmann, Karl 1985a. Bereitstellung und Vertwendung von Getreide in der DDR nach 1970. *FS-Analysen*, vol. 12, no. 2, pp. 3–48.

— 1985b. Vorläufige Bilanz des Fünfjahrplans 1981 bis 1985 im Agrarsektor der DDR. *FS-Analysen*, vol. 12, no. 4, pp. 127–42.

— 1986. Zielsetzungen des XI. Parteitags im Agrarsektor. *FS-Analysen*, vol. 13, no. 2, pp. 55–60.

Honecker, Erich 1981. *From My Life.* Oxford, New York, Toronto, Sydney, Paris, Frankfurt, Pergamon Press.

— 1982. *Reden und Aufsätze*, vol. 7. Berlin (East), Dietz Verlag.

— 1984. The GDR: a state of peace and socialism. *Prisma*, no. 4, 1984, pp. 2–7.

Hundreds of Women Make Pacifist Protest 1982–83. *Labour Focus on Eastern Europe*, vol. 5, nos. 5–6, pp. 39–40.

Husner, Gabriele 1985. *Studenten und Studium in der DDR.* Cologne, Verlag Wissenschaft und Politik.

Implementing the Resolutions Adopted at the 11th Congress of the Socialist Unity Party of Germany. Erich Honecker, General Secretary of the SED Central Committee and Chairman of the Council of State Addressing a Conference of the First Secretaries of SED District Committees on 6 February 1987 1987. Dresden, Verlag Zeit im Bild.

International Institute for Strategic Studies 1981. *The Military Balance 1981–1982*. London, International Institute for Strategic Studies.

—— 1986. *The Military Balance 1986–1987*. London, International Institute for Strategic Studies.

Interview with Robert Havemann 1978. *New German Critique*, vol. 5, no. 15, pp. 37–46.

Introducing the GDR 1976. 5th edn. Berlin (East), Panorama.

Jäckel, Hartmut (ed.) 1980. *Ein Marxist in der DDR: Für Robert Havemann*. Munich and Zurich, R. Piper.

Jacobsen, Hans-Adolf, Leptin, Gert, Scheuner, Ulrich & Schulz, Eberhard (eds) 1980. *Drei Jahrzehnte Außenpolitik der DDR*. Munich and Vienna, Oldenbourg.

Jäger, Manfred 1982. *Kultur und Politik in der DDR: Ein historischer Abriß*. Cologne, Verlag Wissenschaft und Politik.

Jahrbuch für Soziologie und Sozialpolitik 1981 1981. Berlin (East), Akademie-Verlag.

Jahrbuch für Soziologie und Sozialpolitik 1984 1984. Berlin (East), Akademie-Verlag.

Jahrbuch für Soziologie und Sozialpolitik 1985 1985. Berlin (East), Akademie-Verlag.

Jeffries, Ian (ed.) 1981. *The Industrial Enterprise in Eastern Europe*. Eastbourne and New York, Praeger.

Johnson, A. Ross, Dean, Robert, W. & Alexiev, Alexander 1982. *East European Military Establishments: The Warsaw Pact Northern Tier*. New York, Crane Russak.

Joint Economic Committee, Congress of the United States 1985. *East European Economies: Slow growth in the 1980s*. Washington, DC, US Government Printing Office.

Kahl, Alice 1982. Ergebnisse und Probleme der soziologischen Erforschung des Wohnverhaltens in städtischen Neubaugebieten. *Informationen zur soziologischen Forschung in der Deutschen Demokratischen Republik*, vol. 18, no. 1, pp. 4–15.

Keiderling, Gerhard 1982. *Die Berliner Krise 1948/49*. Berlin (West), Verlag das europäische Buch.

Kershaw, Ian 1985. *The Nazi Dictatorship: Problems and Perspectives of Interpretation*. London, Edward Arnold.

Klein, Helmut & Zückert, Ulrich 1979. *Learning for Living: Education in the GDR*. Berlin (East), Panorama.

Kleines politisches Wörterbuch 1978. 3rd edn. Berlin (East), Dietz Verlag.

Klinger, Fred 1985. Soziale Statik und Dynamik in der DDR: zum Leistungsverhalten von Industriearbeiterschaft und wissenschaftlich–technischer Intelligenz. *Aus Politik und Zeitgeschichte*, nos. 46–7, pp. 19–35.

—— 1987. Die Krise des Fortschritts in der DDR: Innovationsprobleme und Mikroelektronik. *Aus Politik und Zeitgeschichte*, no. 3, pp. 3–19.

Köhler, Anne & Ronge, Volker 1984. 'Einmal BRD—einfach': die DDR-Ausreisewelle im Frühjahr 1984. *Deutschland Archiv*, vol. 17, no. 12, pp. 1280–6.

Kohn, Erwin & Postler, Fred 1976. *Polytechnical Education in the German Democratic Republic*. Dresden, Verlag Zeit im Bild.

Kolinsky, Eva (ed.) 1985. Youth in East and West Germany. *Modern German Studies*, no. 1. Aston University, Birmingham, Association for Modern German Studies.

Kolloquium des Instituts für Zeitgeschichte 1980. *Der Weg nach Pankow: Zur Gründungsgeschichte der DDR*. Munich, R. Oldenbourg.

Kosing, Alfred 1984. Natur und Gesellschaft. *Einheit*, vol. 39, no. 11, pp. 1018–23.

Koziolek, Helmut 1981. *Wissenschaft, Technik und Reproduktion*. Berlin (East), Verlag Die Wirtschaft.

Krakat, Klaus 1984. Technologiefortschritt durch Elektrotechnik und Elektronik. *FS-Analysen*, vol. 11, no. 6, pp. 63–106.

—— 1986. Elektronisierungs- und Automatisierungsplanungen der DDR. *FS-Analysen*, vol. 13, no. 2, pp. 39–54.

Kräupl, Günter 1980. Familiäre Fehlerziehung und Jugendkriminalität. *Neue Justiz*, vol. 34, no. 7, pp. 303–6.

Krisch, Henry 1974. *German Politics under Soviet Occupation*. New York, Columbia University Press.

—— 1985. *The German Democratic Republic: The Search for Identity*. Boulder and London, Westview Press.

Kröber, Günter & Maier, Harry (eds) 1985. *Innovation und Wissenschaft*. Berlin (East), Akademie-Verlag.

Kroh, Peter, Schmollack, Jürgen & Thieme, Karl-Heinz 1984. *Wie steht es um die Arbeitsdisziplin?* Berlin (East), Dietz Verlag.

Krolikowski, Herbert 1986. Die Friedensstrategie der sozialistischen Gemeinschaft: den Erfordernissen der Zeit entsprechend. *Einheit*, vol. 41, no. 9, pp. 791–7.

Krusche, Günter & Passauer, Martin-Michael 1985. Evangelische Friedensarbeit und Blockfreiheit. *Kirche im Sozialismus*, vol. 11, no. 4, pp. 159–61.

Kuhn, Rolf 1985. Soziologische Ergebnisse für die Realisierung des Wohnungs- und Städtebaus der 80er und 90er Jahre. *Informationen zur soziologischen Forschung in der Deutschen Demokratischen Republik*, vol. 21, no. 5, pp. 19–24.

Kuppe, Johannes 1981. Honeckers Staatsbesuch in Japan. *Deutschland Archiv*, vol. 14, no. 7, pp. 673–9.

—— 1985. Die Geschichtsschreibung der SED im Umbruch. *Deutschland Archiv*, vol. 18, no. 3, pp. 278–94.

—— 1986. 'Neues politisches Denken' auch in der DDR? *DDR Report*, vol. 19, no. 12, pp. 689–92.

Kupper, Siegfried 1987. Wachsender Druck—Unterschiedliche Interessen: zu den Wirtschaftsbeziehungen DDR–UdSSR und den Konferenzen des RGW. *Deutschland Archiv*, vol. 20, no. 1, pp. 56–61.

Kurjo, Andreas 1986. Zur Entwicklung der Land- und Ernährungswirtschaft der DDR. *FS-Analysen*, vol. 13, no. 4, pp. 75–108.

Laatz, Horst 1984. Soziologische Forschung und Gesellschaft in der DDR. *Aus Politik und Zeitgeschichte*, nos. 16–17, pp. 18–30.

Lane, Christel 1983. Women in socialist society with special reference to the German Democratic Republic. *Sociology*, vol. 17, no. 4, pp. 489–505.

Lapp, Peter Joachim 1984. *Wahlen in der DDR.* Berlin (West), Verlag Gebr. Holzapfel.

—— 1986. Zur Konstituierung der Volkskammer. 9. Wahlperiode 1986/91. *Deutschland Archiv*, vol. 19, no. 7, pp. 680–2.

Lapp, Peter Joachim & Löwis of Menar, Henning von 1987. Blockparteien im Aufwind? *Deutschland Archiv*, vol. 20, no. 7, pp. 728–32.

Lauterbach, Günter 1982. *Technischer Fortschritt und Innovation*. Erlangen, Verlag Deutsche Gesellschaft für zeitgeschichtliche Fragen.

——1984. Veränderungen in der Leitung, Planung und Kontrolle von Wissenschaft und Technik zur Jahreswende 1983/84. *FS-Analysen*, vol. 11, no. 6, pp. 51–62.

Leonhard, Wolfgang 1979. *Child of the Revolution*, tr. C. M. Woodhouse. London, Ink Links.

Leptin, Gert & Melzer, Manfred 1978. *Economic Reform in East German Industry*. Oxford, Oxford University Press.

Letgers, Lyman Howard (ed.) 1978. *The German Democratic Republic: a Developed Socialist Society*. Boulder, Westview Press.

Lippmann, Heinz 1973. *Honecker and the New Politics of Europe*, tr. Helen Sebba. London, Angus & Robertson.

Lohs, Karlheinz & Döring, Sonnhild (eds) 1975. *Im Mittelpunkt der Mensch: Umweltgestaltung–Umweltschutz*. Berlin (East), Akademie-Verlag.

Lötsch, Manfred 1984. Sozialstruktur und Triebkräfte. *Informationen zur soziologischen Forschung in der Deutschen Demokratischen Republik*, vol. 20, no. 3, pp. 3–16.

Lötsch, Manfred & Meyer, Hansgünter (eds) 1974. *Zur Sozialstruktur der sozialistischen Gesellschaft*. Berlin (East), Dietz Verlag.

Ludz, Peter Christian 1980. *Die DDR zwischen Ost und West: Politische Anlaysen 1961 bis 1976*. Munich, Verlag C. H. Beck.

McAdams, A. James 1985. *East Germany and Detente: Building Authority after the Wall*. Cambridge, Cambridge University Press.

McCauley, Martin 1981a. Power and authority in East Gemany: The Socialist Unity Party (SED). *Conflict Studies*, no. 132, pp. 1–28.

—— 1981b. Official and unofficial nationalism in the GDR. *GDR Monitor*, no. 5, pp. 13–20.

—— 1979. *Marxism–Leninism in The German Democratic Republic: The Socialist Unity Party (SED)*. London, Macmillan.

—— 1986. Moscow and the GDR: subtle distinctions. *Soviet Analyst*, vol. 15, no. 22, pp. 7–8.

Machowski, Heinz 1985. Ost–West Handel: Entwicklung, Interessenlagen, Aussichten. *Aus Politik und Zeitgeschichte*, no. 5, pp. 5–18.

Mallinckrodt, Anita 1986/87. Environmental dialogue in the GDR: The literary challenge to the sanctity of 'progress'. *GDR Monitor*, no. 16, pp. 1–26.

Mammach, Klaus 1984. *Widerstand 1933-1939: Geschichte der deutschen antifaschistischen Widerstandsbewegung im Inland und in der Emigration*. Cologne, Pahl-Rugenstein.

Marrese, Michael 1986. CMEA: effective but cumbersome political economy. *International Organization*, vol. 40, no. 2, pp. 287-327.

Martin, Ernst 1986. *Zwischenbilanz: Deutschlandpolitik der 80er Jahre*. Stuttgart, Verlag Bonn Aktuell.

Mechtenburg, Theo 1986. Evangelische Kirche in der DDR: 'Kirche im Sozialismus'. *Deutsche Studien*, vol. XXIV, no. 94, pp. 165-73.

Meier, Christian 1986. Die Wirtschaftsbeziehungen der DDR und der UdSSR am Ende der Fünfjahrplanperiode 1981-1985. *FS-Analysen*, vol. 13, no. 1, pp. 1-37.

Melzer, Manfred 1984. The GDR Housing Construction Program: problems and successes. *East Central Europe*, vol. 11, nos 1-2, pp. 78-96.

Melzer, Manfred & Vortmann, Heinz 1986. Das Kaufkraftverhältnis zwischen D-Mark und Mark der DDR 1985. *DIW Wochenbericht*, vol. 53, no. 21, pp. 259-68.

Merson, Allan 1985. *Communist Resistance in Nazi Gemany*. London, Lawrence & Wishart.

Mielke, Erich 1980. Verantwortungsbewußt für die Gewährleistung der staatlichen Sicherheit. *Einheit*, vol. 35, no. 2, pp. 151-8.

Mikhail Gorbachev 1986: Address to the 11th Congress of the SED 1986. Dresden, Verlag Zeit im Bild.

Ministerrat der Deutschen Demokratischen Republik. Staatliche Zentralverwaltung für Statistik, Zentrale Zahlbüro (ed.) 1975. *Ausgewählte Ergebnisse der Zeitbudgeterhebungen 1974 in Haushalten von Arbeitern und Angestellten*. Berlin (East), unpublished report.

Mitchell, I. R. 1983. The changing image of Prussia in the German Democratic Republic. *German Life and Letters*, vol. XXXVII, no. 1, pp. 57-70.

Mit höchsten Leistungen den XI. Parteitag vorbereiten. Seminar des Zentralkomitees der SED mit den Generaldirektoren der Kombinate und den Parteiorganisatoren des ZK am 7. März 1985 in Leipzig 1985. Berlin (East), Dietz Verlag.

Mit qualitativ neuen Schritten zu höchsten Leistungen. Seminar des Zentralkomitees der SED mit den Generaldirektoren der Kombinate und den Parteiorganisatoren des ZK 1986. Berlin (East), Dietz Verlag.

Moreton, Edwina 1978. *East Germany and the Warsaw Alliance: The Politics of Detente*. Boulder, Colorado, Westview Press.

Mushaben, Joyce Marie 1984. Swords to Ploughshares: the church, the state and the East German peace movement. *Studies in Comparative Communism*, vol. 17, no. 2, pp. 123-35.

Neubert, Ehrhart, 1986. Megapolis DDR und die Religion: Konsequenzen aus der Urbanisierung. *Kirche im Sozialismus*, vol. 12, no. 94, pp. 155-64.

Neuner, Gerhart (ed.) 1986. *Leistungsreserve, Schöpfertum: Forschungsergebnisse zur Kreativät in Schule, Ausbildung und Wissenschaft*. Berlin (East), Dietz Verlag.

Niederländer, Loni 1984. *Arbeiten und Wohnen in der Stadt*. Berlin (East), Dietz Verlag.

Nove, Alex, Höhmann, Hans-Hermann & Seidenstecher, Gertraud (eds) 1982. *The East European Economies in the 1970s*. London, Butterworths.

Ökonomische Strategie der Partei: klares Konzept für weiteres Wachstum 1983. Berlin (East), Dietz Verlag.

Paucke, Horst & Bauer, Adolf 1979. *Umweltprobleme: Herausforderung der Menschheit*. Berlin (East), Dietz Verlag.

Petzold, Joachim 1983. Die deutsche Großbourgeoisie und die Errichtung der faschistischen Diktatur. *Zeitschrift für Geschichtswissenschaft*, vol. 31, no. 3, pp. 214–32.

—— 1984. *Faschismus: Regime des Verbrechens*, 2nd edn. Berlin (East), Staatsverlag der Deutschen Demokratischen Republik.

Plötz, Peter 1985. Wirtschaftsbeziehungen der DDR zu den westlichen Ländern. *FS-Analysen*, vol. 12, no., 5, pp. 49–95.

Pohl, Reinhard (ed.) 1979. *Handbook of the Economy of the German Democratic Republic*, tr. Lux Furtmüller. Westmead, Saxon House.

Pratsch, Kristina & Ronge, Volker 1985. Arbeit finden sie leichter als Freunde: DDR–Übersiedler der 84er Welle nach einem Jahr im Westen. *Deutschland Archiv*, vol. 18, no. 7, pp. 716–25.

Pravda, Alex & Ruble, Blair A. (eds) 1986. *Trade Unions in Communist States*. Boston, Allen & Unwin.

Press and Information Office of the Government of the Federal Republic of Germany 1985. *Facts and Figures: A Comparative Survey of the Federal Republic of Germany and the German Democratic Republic*. Cassel.

Probst, Peter 1985. SED verspricht der Bevölkerung mehr Bürgernähe. *Deutschland Archiv*, vol. 18, no. 8, pp. 788–90.

Programm der Sozialistischen Einheitspartei Deutschlands 1976. Berlin (East), Dietz Verlag.

Prokop, Siegfried 1986. *Übergang zum Sozialismus in der DDR*. Berlin (East), Dietz Verlag.

Protokoll des IX. Parteitages der Sozialistischen Einheitspartei Deutschlands 1976. 2 vols. Berlin (East), Dietz Verlag.

Protokoll des X. Parteitages der Sozialistischen Einheitspartei Deutschlands 1981. 2 vols. Berlin (East), Dietz Verlag.

Quießer, Werner 1983. *Jugendstreiche oder Rowdytum?* Berlin (East), Verlag Neues Leben.

Questions and Answers. Life in the GDR 1981. Berlin (East), Panorama.

Redaktion Deutschland Archiv (ed.) 1985. *Umweltprobleme und Umweltbewußtsein in der DDR*. Cologne, Verlag Wissenschaft und Politik.

Rehm, Walter 1985. Wandlungen der kommunistischen Militärdoktrin. *Deutschland Archiv*, vol. 18, no. 11, pp. 1198–1208.

Reichelt, Hans 1984. Die natürliche Welt rationell nutzen, gestalten, schützen. *Einheit*, vol. 39, no. 11, pp. 1010–7.

Report by the Central Statistical Office of the GDR on the Fulfilment of the 1986 National

Economic Plan 1987. *Documents on the Policy of the German Democratic Republic*, no. 1.

Report of the Central Committee of the Socialist Unity Party of Germany to the 11th Congress of the SED 1986. Rapporteur, Erich Honecker. Dresden, Verlag Zeit im Bild.

Röder, Hans-Jürgen 1986. 'Weil es eben typisch ist, die Klappe zu halten!' *Kirche im Sozialismus*, vol. 12, no. 3, p. 106.

Rühle, Jürgen & Holzweißig, Gunter 1981. *13. August 1961: Die Mauer von Berlin*. Cologne, Verlag Wissenschaft und Politik.

Rundtischgespräch. Weltanschauliche Fragen der Durchsetzung des wissenschaftlich-technischen Fortschritts 1983. *Deutsche Zeitschrift für Philosophie*, vol. 31, no. 3, pp. 316–32.

Sandford, John 1983. *The Sword and the Ploughshare: Autonomous Peace Initiatives in East Germany*. London, Merlin Press/European Nuclear Disarmament.

—— 1986/87. The church, the state, and the peace movement in the GDR. *GDR Monitor*, no. 16, pp. 27–54.

Schaefer, Reinhard, Schmidt, Carol & Wahse, Jürgen 1982. *Disponibilität-Mobilität-Fluktuation*. Berlin (East), Akademie-Verlag.

Scheler, Wolfgang & Kießling, Gottfried 1981. *Gerechte und ungerechte Kriege in unserer Zeit*. Berlin (East), Militärverlag der DDR.

Schering, H. 1977. Alkoholabusus von jugendlichen und heranwachsenden Straftätern: eine wesentliche Dispositon zum kriminellen Verhalten? *Kriminalistik und forensische Wissenschaften*, no. 30, pp. 97–100.

Schmidt, Ines 1983. Migration und Wohnortbindung: ihre demographischen und sozialstrukturellen Aspekte. *Informationen zur soziologischen Forschung in der Deutschen Demokratischen Republik*, vol. 19, no. 1, pp. 34–48.

Schmidt, Max 1986. Forschung im Dienste des Friedens und des Fortschritts. *Einheit*, vol. 41, no. 8, pp. 728–33.

Schneider, Eberhard 1978. *The GDR: The History, Politics, Economy and Society of East Germany*, tr. Hannes Adomeit & Roger Clarke. London, C. Hurst.

Schneider, Gernot 1986. Die Lösung der Wohnungsfrage als soziales Problem in der DDR: eine Zwischenbilanz. *Deutschland Archiv*, vol. 19, no. 7, pp. 735–45.

Schneider, Rosemarie 1985. Eisenbahngüterverkehr: Realisierung der Aufgabenstellung nach dem X. Parteitag der SED. *FS-Analysen*, vol. 12, no. 3, pp. 3–84.

—— 1986. Zur Verkehrspolitik der DDR. *FS-Analysen*, vol. 13, no. 2, pp. 61–9.

Schreier, Gerhard 1986. Begabtenförderung in beiden deutschen Staaten: Möglichkeiten eines Vergleichs. *Deutsche Studien*, vol. XXIV, no. 95, pp. 242–54.

Schulz, Hans-Dieter 1986. Die DDR braucht 'ein kräftiges Wirtschaftswachstum'. *Deutschland Archiv*, vol. 19, no. 3, pp. 233–6.

Schwartau, Cord 1987. Modernisierung und Umweltschutz in der DDR. *DDR Report*, vol. 20, no. 5, pp. 257–60.

Schweigler, Gerhard Ludwig 1975. *National Consciousness in Divided Germany*. London, Sage.

Seiffert, Wolfgang 1983. *Kann der Ostblock überleben? Der Comecon und die Krise des sozialistischen Wirtschaftssystems*. Bergisch Gladbach, Gustav Lübbe Verlag.

Shaffer, Harry Q. 1981. *Women in the Two Germanies: A Comparative Study of a Socialist and a Non-Socialist Society*. New York, Oxford, Toronto, Pergamon.

Sontheimer, Kurt & Bleek, Wilhelm 1975. *The Government and Politics of East Germany*, tr. Ursula Price. London, Hutchinson.

Spanger, Hans-Joachim 1984a. Die beiden deutschen Staaten in der Dritten Welt I. *Deutschland Archiv*, vol. 17, no. 1, pp. 30–50.

—1984b. Die beiden deutschen Staaten in der Dritten Welt II. *Deutschland Archiv*, vol. 17, no. 2, pp. 150–65.

Spittmann, Ilse 1984. *Der 17. Juni im Wandel der Legenden*. Sonderdruck aus *Mut zur Einheit*, Festschrift für Johann Baptist Gradl. Cologne, Verlag Wissenschaft und Politik.

Spittmann, Ilse & Fricke, Karl Wilhelm (eds) 1982. *17. Juni 1953: Arbeiteraufstand in der DDR*. Cologne, Verlag Wissenschaft und Politik.

Spittman-Rühle, Ilse & Helwig, Gisela (eds) 1983. *Die DDR vor den Herausforderungen der achtziger Jahre: Sechzehnte Tagung zum Stand der DDR-Forschung in der Bundesrepublik Deutschland 24. bis 27. Mai 1983*. Cologne, Verlag Wissenschaft und Politik.

— (eds) 1984. *Lebensbedingungen in der DDR: Siebzehnte Tagung zum Stand der DDR-Forschung in der Bundesrepublik Deutschland 12. bis 15. Juni 1984*. Cologne, Verlag Wissenschaft und Politik.

— (eds) 1986. *Tradition und Fortschritt: Neunzehnte Tagung zum Stand der DDR-Forschung in der Bundesrepublik Deutschland 20. bis 23. Mai 1986*. Cologne, Verlag Wissenschaft und Politik.

Staritz, Dietrich 1984. *Die Gründung der DDR: Von der sowjetischen Besatzungsherrschaft zum sozialistischen Staat*. Munich, Deutsches Taschenbuch Verlag.

— 1985. *Geschichte der DDR 1949–1985*. Frankfurt/Main, Suhrkamp.

Starke, Kurt 1980. *Junge Partner*. Leipzig, Jena and Berlin (East), Urania-Verlag.

Starke, Kurt & Friedrich, Walter (eds) 1984. *Liebe und Sexualität bis 30*. Berlin (East), Deutscher Verlag der Wissenschaften.

Starrels, John M. & Mallinckrodt, Anita M. 1975. *Politics in the German Democratic Republic*. New York, Washington, London, Praeger.

Statistical Pocket Book of the German Democratic Republic 1985 1985. Berlin (East), Staatsverlag der Deutschen Demokratischen Republik.

Statistisches Bundesamt (ed.) 1986. *Statistisches Jahrbuch 1986 für die Bundesrepublik Deutschland*. Stuttgart and Mainz, W. Kohlhammer.

Statistisches Jahrbuch der Deutschen Demokratischen Republik 1986. Berlin (East), Staatsverlag der Deutschen Demokratischen Republik.

Statistisches Taschenbuch der Deutschen Demokratischen Republik 1986 1986. Berlin (East), Staatsverlag der Deutschen Demokratischen Republik.

Staufenbiel, Fred 1982. Zu theoretischen und methodischen Erfahrungen soziologischer Untersuchungen für die städtebauliche Planung. *Informationen zur soziologischen Forschung in der Deutschen Demokratischen Republik*, vol. 18, no. 1, pp. 15–27.

Steele, Jonathan 1977. *Socialism with a German Face: The State that came in from the Cold*. London, Jonathan Cape.

Stent, Angela E. (ed.) 1985. *Economic Relations with the Soviet Union. American and West German Perspectives*. Boulder and London, Westview Press.

Stern, Carola 1965. *Ulbricht: A Political Biography*, tr. Abe Farnstein. London, Pall Mall Press.

Stinglwagner, Wolfgang 1985. *Die Energiewirtschaft der DDR: Unter Berücksichtigung internationaler Effizienzvergleiche*. Bonn, Gesamtdeutsches Institut, Bundesanstalt für gesamtdeutsche Aufgaben.

— 1986. Modell mit Schönheitsfehlern. *Deutschland Archiv*, vol. 19, no. 6, pp. 633–40.

Supranowitz, Stephan 1986. FRG turned deaf ear to justified warnings. *Foreign Affairs Bulletin*, vol. 26, no. 15, pp. 119–20.

Sydow, Werner (ed.) 1983. *In die Zukunft gedacht*. Berlin (East), Verlag Die Wirtschaft.

Szajkowski, Bogdan (ed.) 1978. *Documents in Communist Affairs 1977*. Cardiff, University College Cardiff Press.

— (ed.) 1981. *Marxist Governments: A World Survey*. London, Macmillan.

— (ed.) 1982. *The Establishment of Marxist Regimes*. London, Butterworth Scientific.

Szelenyi, Ivan 1980. Whose Alternative? *New German Critique*, vol. 7, no. 20, pp. 117–34.

Szewczyk, Hans (ed.) 1982. *Der fehlentwickelte Jugendliche und seine Kriminalität*. Jena, Gustav Fischer Verlag.

Tate, Dennis 1984. *The East German Novel: Identity, Community, Continuity*. Bath, Bath University Press.

Territorialstruktur und umfassende Intensivierung 1985. Abhandlungen der Akademie der Wissenschaften der DDR, Veröffentlichungen der Wissenschaftlichen Räte, W4. Berlin (East), Akademie-Verlag.

Terry, Sarah Meikljohn (ed.) 1984. *Soviet Policy in Eastern Europe*. New Haven and London, Yale University Press.

Thalheim, Karl C. 1985. Das Wirtschaftssystem der DDR in der Fünfjahrplanperiode 1981 bis 1985: Kontinuität oder Wandel? *FS-Analysen*, vol. 12, no. 4, pp. 9–38.

The German Democratic Republic 1981. Berlin (East), Panorama.

The German Democratic Republic 1986. Berlin (East), Panorama.

United Nations Commission for Europe 1986. *Economic Survey of Europe in 1985–86*. New York.

United Nations Department of International Economic and Social Affairs, Statistical Office 1986. *Statistical Yearbook 1983/84*. New York.

Urban, Detlev 1986. Antisemitismus in der DDR. *Kirche im Sozialismus*, vol. 12, no. 2, pp. 54–5.

Voigt, Dieter 1975. *Soziologie in der DDR*. Cologne, Verlag Wissenschaft und Politik.

— (ed.) 1984. *Die Gesellschaft der DDR: Untersuchungen zu ausgewählten Bereichen*. Berlin (West), Duncker and Humblot.

Vortmann, Heinz 1985. *Geldeinkommen in der DDR von 1955 bis zu Beginn der achtziger Jahre*. Deutsches Institut für Wirtschaftsforschung, Beiträge Strukturforschung, no. 85, Berlin (West), Duncker & Humblot.

Vortmann, Heinz & Weißenburger, Ulrich 1986. Der Staatshaushalt der DDR 1980 bis 1985. *DIW Wochenbericht*, vol. 53, no. 42, pp. 525–34.

Voß, Peter (ed.) 1981. *Die Freizeit der Jugend*. Berlin (East), Dietz Verlag.

—— 1984. Das Verhältnis Jugendlicher zur Großstadt: einige Ergebnisse stadtsoziologischer Forschungen in Leipzig. *Informationen zur soziologischen Forschung in der Deutschen Demokratischen Republik*, vol. 20, no. 4, pp. 46–51.

Voßke, Heinz 1983. *Walter Ulbricht: Biographischer Abriß*. Berlin (East), Dietz Verlag.

Wallace, Ian (ed.) 1981. *The GDR under Honecker 1971-1981*. GDR Monitor Special Series, No. 1, Dundee, University of Dundee.

Weber, Hermann 1985. *Geschichte der DDR*. Munich, Deutscher Taschenbuch Verlag.

Wehling, Hans-Georg (ed.) 1983. *DDR*. Stuttgart, Berlin (West), Cologne, Mainz, Verlag W. Kohlhammer.

Weidenfeld, Werner (ed.) 1985. *Nachdenken über Deutschland*. Cologne, Verlag Wissenschaft und Politik.

Weidig, Rudi, Wittich, Dietmar & Taubert, Horst (eds) 1986. *Soziale Triebkräfte ökonomischen Wachstums: Materialien des 4. Kongresses der marxistisch-leninistischen Soziologie in der DDR 26. bis 28. März 1985*. Berlin (East), Dietz Verlag.

Wensierski, Peter 1983. Friedensbewegung in der DDR. *Aus Politik und Zeitgeschichte*, no. 17, pp. 3–15.

Wensierski, Peter & Büscher, Wolfgang (eds) 1981. *Beton ist Beton: Zivilisationskritik aus der DDR*. Hattingen, Scandica-Verlag.

Winters, Peter Jochen 1986. Die DDR und China. *Deutschland Archiv*, vol. 19, no. 5, pp. 511–19.

—— 1984. Personalentscheidungen und ihr politischer Hintergrund. *Deutschland Archiv*, vol. 17, no. 7, pp. 673–7.

Wittich, Dietmar & Taubert, Horst (eds) 1981. *Lebensweise und Sozialstruktur: Materialien des 3. Kongresses der marxistisch-leninistischen Soziologie in der DDR 25. bis 27. März 1980*. Berlin (East), Dietz Verlag.

Woit, Ernst 1986. Systemantagonismus und Weltfrieden. *Deutsche Zeitschrift für Philosophie*, vol. 34, no. 12, pp. 1078–87.

Woods, Roger 1986. *Opposition in the GDR under Honecker 1971-85*. Basingstoke and London, Macmillan.

Zentralkomitee der Sozialistischen Einheitspartei Deutschlands (ed.) 1954. *Dokumente der Sozialistischen Einheitspartei Deutschlands. Beschlüsse und Erklärungen des Zentralkomitees sowie seines Politbüros und seines Sekretariat*, vol. IV. Berlin (East), Dietz Verlag.

Zimmermann, Hartmut (ed.) 1985. *DDR Handbuch, 3rd edn*. Cologne, Verlag Wissenschaft und Politik.

Zur weiteren Vervollkommnung der wissenschaftlichen Arbeitsorganisation 1983. Abhandlungen der Akademie der Wissenschaften der DDR, Veröffentlichungen der Wissenschaftlichen Räte, W6. Berlin (East), Akademie-Verlag.

Periodicals, magazines, newspapers

DDR-heute. Frankfurt/Main, Internationale Gesellschaft für Menschenrechte, bi-monthly.
The Economist. London, The Economist Newspaper, weekly.
GDR Peace News. London, GDR Working Group of END, quarterly.
Junge Welt. Berlin (East), Verlag Junge Welt, daily.
Neues Deutschland. Berlin (East), Verlag Neues Deutschland, daily.
Der Spiegel. Hamburg, Spiegel Verlag, weekly.
Tribüne. Berlin (East), Tribüne Verlag. daily.

Index